The Patterns of Comics

Also available from Bloomsbury

Who Understands Comics? Neil Cohn
The Visual Narrative Reader, edited by Neil Cohn
The Visual Language of Comics, Neil Cohn

The Patterns of Comics

Visual Languages of Comics from Asia, Europe, and North America

NEIL COHN

BLOOMSBURY ACADEMIC
LONDON · NEW YORK · OXFORD · NEW DELHI · SYDNEY

BLOOMSBURY ACADEMIC
Bloomsbury Publishing Plc
50 Bedford Square, London, WC1B 3DP, UK
1385 Broadway, New York, NY 10018, USA
29 Earlsfort Terrace, Dublin 2, Ireland

BLOOMSBURY, BLOOMSBURY ACADEMIC, and the Diana logo are trademarks
of Bloomsbury Publishing Plc

First published in Great Britain 2024

Copyright © Neil Cohn, 2024

Neil Cohn has asserted his right under the Copyright, Designs and Patents
Act, 1988, to be identified as Author of this work.

Cover design: Elena Durey
Cover image © Shutterstock (hadaka zaru / David Grigg / R_lion_O)

All rights reserved. No part of this publication may be reproduced or transmitted
in any form or by any means, electronic or mechanical, including photocopying,
recording, or any information storage or retrieval system, without prior
permission in writing from the publishers.

Bloomsbury Publishing Plc does not have any control over, or responsibility for,
any third-party websites referred to or in this book. All internet addresses given
in this book were correct at the time of going to press. The author and publisher
regret any inconvenience caused if addresses have changed or sites have ceased
to exist, but can accept no responsibility for any such changes.

A catalogue record for this book is available from the British Library.

A catalog record for this book is available from the Library of Congress.

ISBN:	HB:	978-1-3503-8160-5
	PB:	978-1-3503-8164-3
	ePDF:	978-1-3503-8161-2
	eBook:	978-1-3503-8162-9

Typeset by RefineCatch Limited, Bungay, Suffolk
Printed and bound in Great Britain

To find out more about our authors and books visit www.bloomsbury.com
and sign up for our newsletters.

For Maaike

CONTENTS

List of Figures and Tables viii
Preface xii

1 Visual Language 1
2 Corpus-Driven Comics Research 31
3 Morphology 43
4 Page Layout 75
5 Situational Coherence 95
6 Framing Structure 115
7 Narrative Structure 145
8 Visual Languages Across Time 169
9 Cross-Cultural Visual Languages? 199
10 The Visual Language of *Calvin and Hobbes* 215
11 Towards a Visual Language Typology 233

Notes 247
Bibliography 251
Index 269

FIGURES AND TABLES

Figures

1.1	Parallel architecture for the structure of visual languages.	5
1.2	A page from *Far Arden* by Kevin Cannon.	6
1.3	Panels from *Far Arden* arranged in different ways.	9
1.4	A page from *Far Arden*.	11
1.5	A page from *Far Arden* that shows a multimodal interaction between text and image, the omission of the text, and the omission of the images.	16
1.6	Multimodal Parallel Architecture and its manifestations.	17
1.7	Multimodality of a page from *Far Arden*.	18
2.1	Example data of panels per page in comics across the VLRC.	39
3.1	Various visual affixes.	47
3.2	Examples of visual suppletion and reduplication.	49
3.3	Visual morphemes appearing in both Japanese and European comics.	51
3.4	Morphemes appearing across shonen and shojo manga.	55
3.5	Morphemes that were most frequently used in Dutch and Flemish comics.	58
3.6	Morphemes in Dutch and Flemish comics.	60
3.7	Three-part structure of carriers, tails, and roots.	61
3.8	Various types of carriers.	64
3.9	Various cues used to depict motion in graphic form.	66
3.10	Comparisons between the depictions of path structure in comics from satellite-framed and verb-framed languages.	70
3.11	Comparisons between satellite-framed and verb-framed languages.	72
4.1	Features of panel arrangements in page layouts.	78
4.2	Hierarchic structure for pages from *Boxers* by Gene Yang, and *Venom: Funeral Pyre #2* by Carl Potts and Tom Lyle.	80
4.3	Number of panels per page in comics from different countries, and across the first twenty pages of stories averaged across comics in the VLRC.	82
4.4	Frequency of different panel shapes in comics across Asia, Europe, and the United States.	84

FIGURES AND TABLES

4.5	Types of arrangements of panels in page layouts.	85
4.6	Directions between comic panels in page layouts.	88
4.7	Different gutter types in the VLRC.	89
4.8	Layout complexity values across countries and subtypes.	91
4.9	Layout constituents in comics from different countries and the number of panels per row.	93
5.1	Situational continuity in a page from *Far Arden* by Kevin Cannon.	97
5.2	Changes in meaning across panels in *The Amazing Spider-Man* #539 by J. Michael Straczynski and Ron Garney.	100
5.3	Summary of data related to situational changes in the VLRC.	102
5.4	Combinations of time, character, and spatial location changes between panels.	104
5.5	Findings related to the "runs" that maintain continuity of types of situational coherence across panels.	107
5.6	Relationships between situational changes across panels and aspects of layout.	111
6.1	Attentional Framing Matrix.	117
6.2	Attentional structure in all comics from the VLRC.	121
6.3	"Objective" and "subjective" storytelling techniques.	126
6.4	Frequency of runs using different types of framing.	128
6.5	Alignment of situational changes within attentional framing types.	129
6.6	Filmic shot scales illustrated for a human figure.	132
6.7	Paneling structure interacting with attentional framing types and across shifts in situational coherence.	135
6.8	Subjective viewpoint panels using attentional framing categories.	137
6.9	Subjective panels of different framing types.	141
7.1	An ambiguous narrative sequence with interpretations.	146
7.2	A narrative sequence with two narrative constituents.	149
7.3	Narrative schemas within Visual Narrative Grammar.	151
7.4	Varying correspondences between narrative conjunction with semantic information.	152
7.5	Narrative patterns created by the interaction between narrative schemas within Visual Narrative Grammar.	154
7.6	Frequency of sequences with different levels of narrative complexity in the VLRC.	157
7.7	Overall narrative complexity values.	159
7.8	Example sequence from *Vagabond* #195 by Inoue Takehiko and its narrative structure, along with the frequency of narrative constructions, and framing and narrative complexity values for *Vagabond* #322 in the VLRC.	160
7.9	Example sequence from *The Savage Dragon* #187 by Erik Larsen and its narrative structure.	163

FIGURES AND TABLES

7.10 Correlations between framing complexity and narrative complexity in comics, and framing-narrative complexity and word-syntax complexity for the corresponding spoken languages. 165

8.1 Changes in time for the numbers of panels per page over time in comics from Asia, Europe, and the United States. 171

8.2 The structure of layout constituents over time. 173

8.3 Shifts in situational coherence between panels from the 1940s to the 2010s in American and European comics. 175

8.4 Changes over time related to framing structure in American and European comics. 177

8.5 Changes over time related to narrative structure in American and European comics. 179

8.6 Multimodal sequences that have imbalanced semantic weight from *Lady Luck* by Klaus Nordling. 182

8.7 Balance of semantic weight in multimodal interactions in Mainstream American comics from the 1940s through to the 2010s. 183

8.8 Symmetry of the grammatical structure in multimodal interactions in Mainstream American comics from the 1940s through to the 2010s. 185

8.9 Average number of words in panels from the 1940s to the 2010s, and the relationship between this word count and semantic weight, and grammatical interactions within Mainstream American comics. 186

8.10 Dimensions of storytelling over time. 188

8.11 Carriers used for more than eighty years in comics from the United States and Europe. 190

8.12 Results of a cluster analysis of Mainstream American comics. 193

8.13 Sample pages from *Captain Marvel Adventures* #1 by Joe Simon and Jack Kirby, and *The Amazing Spider-Man* #328 by David Michelinie and drawn by Todd McFarlane. 195

9.1 Results of a clustering analysis across dimensions of panel units and storytelling. 201

9.2 Proportion of American comics per decade allocated to each cluster from the global cluster analysis. 203

9.3 Results of a clustering analysis of Japanese manga. 205

9.4 Results of a clustering analysis of comics from the United States. 207

9.5 Results of a clustering analysis of comics from Europe. 209

9.6 Diagram of processes related to comprehending a sequence with objective storytelling. 212

9.7 Diagram of processes related to comprehending a sequence with objective storytelling. 213

10.1 Frequency of Hobbes depicted in *Calvin and Hobbes*, and change of the average number of panels in *Calvin and Hobbes* strips across the Daily and Sunday strips.   217

10.2 Properties of layouts changing over time in *Calvin and Hobbes* Sunday strips.   219

10.3 Sample layouts from *Calvin and Hobbes* from its first and last Sunday strips, and the first Sunday strips of each year in between.   221

10.4 Changes in situational coherence over time in *Calvin and Hobbes*.   222

10.5 Change in *Calvin and Hobbes* strips over time.   224

10.6 Change in the multimodality of *Calvin and Hobbes* strips.   228

10.7 Number of words used in *Calvin and Hobbes* strips.   229

Table

2.1 Analyzed comics within the Visual Language Research Corpus.   36

PREFACE

I first began formulating my theories of visual language in college, after taking a semester with several linguistics classes. I had noticed that the theories about the structure of language were consistent with what I knew about the structure of drawing and comics. My actual major was on Japanese culture and religion, but, on the side, I began researching linguistics and cognition to build this theory. After my graduation, I sought to pursue this relationship further in graduate school, only to find that most graduate programs in linguistics and psychology didn't know what to do with me. I spoke with many scientists who studied language and heard a consistent message. They all thought the research I was doing was interesting, but that I was going about it the wrong way. Inevitably, the way they thought I should do it was however *the way they* studied language.

The funny thing was that I met with scientists studying language from many different perspectives, ranging from theorists and corpus linguists to experimental psychologists and cognitive neuroscientists. They used distinctive methods to study language, and often held contrasting theories about how language worked. At this nascent stage in my thinking, my ideas were largely theoretical, and although I was pushed to explore various theoretical frameworks, I was also encouraged to run experiments and gather data about the structure present in different comics—i.e., to conduct a corpus analysis.

These disparate opinions taught me a few things. First off, since people advocated for various methods, it told me that this *visual language* could be studied in all the ways that we study spoken or signed languages. If all their methods and theories applied to what I was doing, then surely I was on the right track. The second thing it did was to motivate me to learn these different perspectives on language research with an inclusive mindset, and to pursue *all* these methods. In fact, my first empirical analysis of comics was conducted in between my undergraduate and graduate studies all the way back in 2003 (published in 2011), on the advice of a corpus linguist who wanted me to do research "like them."

After several years of persistent (and often unsuccessful) applications to become a graduate student, I finally began my Ph.D. in a Psychology department, where my focus balanced the study of the brain with theoretical linguistics. But, I never stopped thinking about this full range of methods, particularly among them the study of cross-cultural diversity. My theories have always strived to account for the patterns present in all graphic representations, both to explain their consistencies and their diversity.

Throughout my career, I've largely balanced these primary poles of interest: building theories, carrying out experiments on cognition, and analyzing corpora. I believe that each method provides us with crucial insights that can inform the other. Ultimately, balancing the distinctive information gathered through these approaches is necessary for discovering an accurate view of what's going on in language (visual language or otherwise).

My books on visual language research have also all balanced these three interests, although each book seems to lean towards one primary focus. *The Visual Language of Comics* largely outlined the theoretical structure of visual languages, but also contained chapters on cognition and cross-cultural variation. *Who Understands Comics?* mostly focused on cognition, with chapters corresponding to subfields of psychology, but with opening chapters about theory and cross-cultural corpus analysis. So, the "corpus book" it seems was inevitable to be next, and that's what you now have in front of you.

This book provides an extended analysis of a corpus of roughly 350 comics analyzed by students of mine over several years, with a focus on comics from the United States, Europe, and Asia. The focus here is on what this data can tell us about how visual languages are built, both in general and in their cross-cultural manifestations. But, throughout, I've again attempted to show how this connects to aspects of theory and cognition.

Lots of this data has appeared in previous publications, including in one chapter of *Who Understands Comics?* and in many papers. I attempt throughout to go far beyond the analyses provided in those publications, and thus to offer a more expansive view of the data and what it tells us. Indeed, one benefit of writing a book is the ability to provide a more comprehensive and encompassing view than individual analyses in papers, and I've hoped to offer that here. As always though, there is much left to do, and other analyses could no doubt provide additional insights.

There are several people who I should thank for inspiring or directly assisting in this research. First, I owe formative inspiration to Scott McCloud for articulating a theory and then *using* it to analyze cross-cultural differences. Dan Slobin is thanked for nurturing and inspiring my interests in cross-cultural variation and typology while he served as a "foster advisor" for me for a year before I set out to graduate school, and to David Wilkins who urged on these interests with helpful advice during this time. The advice of my mentors Ray Jackendoff, Gina Kuperberg, Phil Holcomb, Marta Kutas, and Jeff Elman persists in my writing and reminds me to be mindful of the role of cognition throughout these analyses.

The data I analyze throughout constitutes the Visual Language Research Corpus (VLRC), and was gathered by student researchers at UC San Diego (Jessika Axnér, Justin Brookshier, Michaela Diercks, Sean Ehly, Ryan

Huffman, Kaitlin Pederson, Ryan Taylor, Vivian Wong, and Rebecca Yeh), and at Tilburg University (Mark Dierick, Lincy van Middelaar, Jeroen van Nierop, and Dieuwertje Schipper). Their passion and enthusiasm drove this work, and this book and its insights would not exist without their contributions.

The VLRC itself was made possible by generous donations of comics from numerous publishers, inluding Antarctic Press, Archie Comics, Dark Horse Comics, Drawn & Quarterly, Fantagraphics Books, First Second Books, Humanoids Inc., IDW Publishing, NBM Publishing, NetComics, Oni Press, Top Cow, Top Shelf, Udon Entertainment, Vertical Inc., and Viz Media. Their generosity helped provide the seeds for this work, and I am grateful for their support.

I also thank my graduate students, Bien Klomberg and Irmak Hacımusaoğlu, who dove into analyzing the VLRC with excitement and interest, and who have played a pivotal role in further development of Visual Language Theory (VLT) and our subsequent corpus projects. Joost Schilperoord has been my welcome partner in research for the past several years, and his contributions are often subtle and pervasive throughout. My other collaborators and members of my Visual Language Lab have provided innumerable insights to my work and companionship in carrying it out. They include Bruno Cardoso, Fernando Casanova, Emily Coderre, Tom Foulsham, Lenneke Lichtenberg, Morgan Patrick, and Aditya Upadhyayula.

Finally, I should thank the numerous colleagues and collaborators who contributed to this broader endeavor doing corpus research on comics, through conversations both in person and in the literature. They include John Bateman, Alexander Dunst, Charles Forceville, Jochen Laubrock, Oliver Moisich, Dušan Stamenković, Milos Tasic, and Janina Wildfeuer. Various other unnamed scholars should be thanked for their insights in providing feedback to my numerous presentations, papers, and/or in discussions on social media over the past years (hopefully you know who you are).

Finally, thanks go to Maaike, Perla, Sheikah, and Naya who help provide me inspiration outside of theories and datasets.

Neil Cohn
Tilburg, Netherlands
January 2023

CHAPTER ONE

Visual Language

When I was in my early teens, I read (and drew) a *lot* of comics. While growing up in Southern California in the early 1990s, most of my reading habits were of mainstream American comics, but translations of Japanese manga were on the rise. One day while over at my best friend's house, I noticed several small, yet thick, Japanese books in the back of his closet. His older brother was attending college in Japan and left behind these manga on his latest trip home. As untranslated manga, I'd never seen anything like them, and I was transfixed. My friend gave them to me, and with great curiosity, that night I devoured all five of my newly gathered volumes, each several hundred pages long. As I was mesmerized with these books, I made several observations . . .

First, I had to read them from right-to-left, which at first was difficult to grasp. I noticed my eyes fighting with my ingrained habits of reading from left-to-right. Second, I somehow was able to understand what was going on across the sequences of images, despite not being able to read any of the written Japanese text. I was *reading the images* alone. Third, many aspects of these manga were different from what I was used to in American comics. Most of the layouts were intuitive enough, but aspects of storytelling seemed different, as were many of the visual conventions, such as motion lines I hadn't seen before, or many markers of emotions or expressions that I just didn't grasp.

This experience planted enduring questions in my mind that only grew as I began seeking out more diverse comics from Europe, especially France, and other genres of American comics. Just how were these manga from Japan so different in structure from comics from the United States and Europe? How could we characterize these cross-cultural differences in a comprehensible way? Just how diverse were comics from around the world? Did these differences matter for how comics could be understood? What aspects across comics were universal? Does a comic creator's language affect the way they draw?

These questions are the topic of this book, and they have persisted throughout most of my research on the structure and cognition of drawing and visual narratives. In this book, I seek to address these questions in a scientific and quantitative way. Over several years, my students and I carefully analyzed the structure of more than 300 comics from Europe, Asia, and the United States, and throughout the subsequent chapters I'll report on the data that was found. But let's come back to that . . .

Before we can think about studying cross-cultural variation across different comics, we first must ask: just what is it we'll be comparing in the first place? These questions about cross-cultural diversity were foundational in the development of *Visual Language Theory* (VLT), my theoretical framework seeking to explain how visual narratives such as comics are built, and what our minds and brains do to understand them.

1.1 Visual Language Theory

A common view about drawing and pictures is that they reflect the way we see the world (Cohn 2014b). Under this view, a person's drawing style is a unique reflection of their own vision of the world, and people develop this style through their innate talent and/or explicit instruction. Because drawings often look like what they represent (i.e., a drawing of a person looks like a person), pictures are thought to be fairly transparent and easy to understand using only our visual perception.

The problem with this view is that it does not hold up to what we can easily see in drawings, and what research has told us about how graphics are structured, how we process them, or how we learn to draw. First, drawing styles are systematic, both for how individuals draw, and for styles shared across broader populations. We recognize that there is a "style" associated with American superhero comics in general, beyond the style of an individual person, and that this style looks different from the conventionalized style in manga or instruction manuals. This shows that we know there is regularity in the drawings that transcends each person's individualistic "vision of the world."

In addition, studies have shown that people learn to draw by imitating how other people draw (e.g., Wilson 1988, Cohn 2012), and that understanding a sequence of images requires proficiency gained through exposure and practice (Cohn 2020a). In essence, pictures and sequences of pictures are built of *patterns*. So, here's an alternative view to this "common sense" perspective . . .

Just as we speak using spoken languages, we draw using visual languages. This basic premise is fundamental to VLT, which proposes that graphics are structured using similar principles to all other languages because they share common *cognitive mechanisms* for organizing information. The phrase "visual language" is akin to saying, "spoken language" or "signed language." It is an abstraction, since languages actually manifest in specific cultural systems, whether spoken (English, Mandarin, Xhosa) or signed (American

Sign Language, Nihon Shuwa). Similarly, actual visual languages manifest in many different cultural systems, and substantiating this is a primary aim of this book.

At its heart, VLT recognizes graphics are built of *patterns*. In order to draw, we build up a vocabulary of graphic patterns in our minds, and we then combine those schemas in the creation of complex pictures. We also use systematic patterns to organize expressive sequences of images, both for their layout and their content. In addition, just as we need to acquire fluency in the regularities of a spoken language in order to speak it, we also need to acquire fluency in comprehending and especially producing graphics. When people say that they "can't draw" they are typically expressing that they "haven't learned the vocabulary of a visual language" (Cohn 2012).

Nevertheless, often people have an asymmetry in their fluency, with more people acquiring a capacity for comprehending pictures than producing them. This is because people more often are exposed to understanding pictures than they work to be able to produce them, and this asymmetry gives the illusion that pictures are transparent and require no learning to understand in contrast to the "talent" or "skill" of producing drawings. However, substantive research has shown that we don't get the understanding of individual or sequential images "for free" with being able to see, but rather this ability is conditioned by exposure to and practice with pictures and visual narratives (for review, see Cohn 2020a, Goldsmith 1984).

In the case of comics (and many other media), they are thus often created using two languages at once. They may combine both a written language of text and a visual language of drawings. It is worth emphasizing that *comics are not a visual language*. Collapsing these notions of comics and visual language into each other is inaccurate and misleading for what VLT claims. Comics are social constructs, defined through a variety of traits, including the genre(s) they convey, the communities that read and produce them, the distribution methods they use, the formatting they follow, and sometimes the visual languages they are drawn in. But, in the same way that we wouldn't say that "novels are a written language," we cannot say that "comics are a language"—this confuses a social object for the systems they are created with. Comics are just one of many social contexts that use visual languages, and indeed visual languages are used in many places that are *not* comics, since they are the systems used to create all graphic representations. The distinctive styles of instruction manuals, signage, historical artifacts, and other contexts all use different visual languages.

It should also be emphasized that the notion of visual language is not a metaphor, nor is the idea of a visual language based on surface level comparison with spoken languages. Such surface analogies might be like saying that pictures have "equivalents" of words or that there are visual versions of nouns or verbs. According to VLT, there are no "word units" in visual languages, nouns and verbs may not be the natural grammatical categories of visual sequencing (Cohn, Engelen, and Schilperoord 2019), and nor are "sentences" an appropriate designation for graphic sequences. Indeed, the focus on words and sentences as primary units of language arises because of the structure of writing systems, not speech (Chafe 1994), and is challenged by looking at a more diverse range of spoken and signed linguistic systems (Haspelmath 2018). VLT posits no such superficial comparisons between the surface constructs of different modalities, nor was VLT formulated by making such comparisons.

Rather, comparisons between spoken and visual languages are made at a more architectural, cognitive level for the way verbal and visual systems are built, and for how they are processed in the mind/brain. That is, spoken, signed, and visual languages use similar cognitive organizing principles, even though their specific manifestation as sounds, bodily motions, or graphics may differ. In fact, (neuro)cognitive research on visual narrative has substantiated this, showing repeatedly that similar brain responses are involved in processing a sequence of images as those used to process sentences (Cohn 2020b, a, Coderre and Cohn Under review, Coopmans and Cohn 2022). So, this notion of visual language is not merely a theoretical construct, but is supported by *empirical evidence*.

If there are common structures across spoken, signed, and visual languages, what might these structures be? At the coarsest level, languages are composed of three primary components: *modality*, *meaning*, and *grammar*. First, a *modality* is the sensory-cognitive channel by which expressions emerge. In spoken languages, the modality is the vocal-auditory system that is involved in the production and reception of speech. Sign languages use the visual-bodily modality to produce positions and movement of the hands, face, and body. Visual languages use the visual-graphic modality in the creation of configurations of marks. Second, *meaning* is the message that is being conveyed by an expression, which cognitively reflects our conceptual system, stored in semantic memory. Third, a *grammar* is the combinatorial system that organizes meaningful expressions. Complex grammars, such as those found in languages, assign roles to units (i.e., "parts of speech") and create hierarchic embedding structures that group those units together (Cohn and Schilperoord 2022b, Jackendoff and Wittenberg 2014).

These three primary components of languages—modality, meaning, and grammar—are distributed in a *parallel architecture* (Jackendoff 2002, Jackendoff and Audring 2020). This means that each structure contributes to the whole in an equal way, but they persist independently of each other with their own unique characteristics. These component structures can also be divided into subparts corresponding to **units** and **sequences**. This results in six primary structures, which for visual language are depicted in Figure 1.1.

VISUAL LANGUAGE

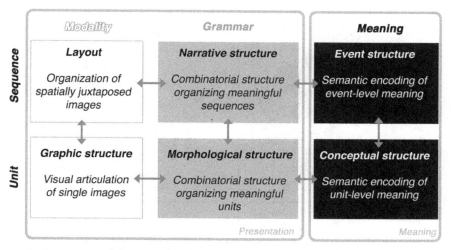

FIGURE 1.1 *Parallel architecture for the structure of visual languages.*

The modality is related to the graphic representation of drawings. This can be either the *graphology* of lines and shapes that compose individual units, or the graphic relationships between those units in a *layout*. The combinatorial structure of visual languages can either be involved in the *morphological* patterns of individual units, or the *narrative structure* that organizes those units into sequences. Finally, the meaning of visual languages is either expressed as the *conceptual structure* of units or the *event structure* expressed across sequences of units.

In the following sections I will elaborate on each of these substructures, within which I will describe those related to units and then sequences. I will then close our discussion of visual language by discussing how these structures interact with those of other modalities, such as the graphic expression of spoken language in writing, resulting in *multimodal* interactions. Indeed, there I will argue that this parallel architecture for visual languages is itself only a subpart of a larger multimodal architecture.

Rather than elaborate on these structures in the abstract, it's best to consider them in the context of an example. Consider Figure 1.2, which shows a page from the graphic novel *Far Arden* by Kevin Cannon. The page begins with the protagonist, Army Shanks, looking at a boat. In panel 2, he then leaps onto the boat as two silhouetted figures angrily run towards him on an opposite dock. In the next panel, he cuts the rope holding the boat as a young boy asks to join him. Panel 4 then shows Army asking who the boy is as the figures run towards the boat, and the boy replies that he's an orphan in the penultimate panel. Finally, Army reaches out to help the boy onto the boat in the final panel, as we see the shadows of the angry pursuers cast on the boat. Below, I'll break down this page across the dimensions of the parallel architecture.

FIGURE 1.2 *A page from* Far Arden *by Kevin Cannon (2009, p. 20, Top Shelf Productions). Far Arden © Kevin Cannon.*

1.1.1 Modality

Let's begin with the structure that we actually *experience* with our sensory perception. When we look at a comic page, we use our sense of vision to experience the **graphic modality**. Although we take in pictures through our vision, pictures are different from general perception, as they use lines, shapes, and/or colors on a surface to depict elements. Often, lines are used to show the contour of an object—it's outer edge—with the implication that it has a solid volume between the lines. Consider the boy in the final panel of Figure 1.2. He is composed almost entirely of lines, which are interpreted as representing the outer edge of his body parts, rather than being a wireframe. In contrast, the silhouettes in panel 2 show a whole filled in region, which we interpret as being the volume of bodies, unlike the exact same representation of Figures in panel 6 where we interpret them as being flat shadows cast on the boat. They use the same graphic representations, but imply different correspondences to volumes (which is part of our conceptual understanding of these graphics).

We experience graphics through the sensory phenomena of light using our sense of vision, but this experience corresponds to mental representations that organize this information. Just as speech sounds are organized using particular principles of *phonology*, the organization of graphic information involves a **graphology** or **graphic structure**. The basic components of visual expressions are marks that are made on a surface, but these correspond to cognitive primitives called *graphemes* for abstractions of graphics such as dots, lines, curves, spirals, and other elements of graphic representations. Graphemes combine to compose visual regions, which create well-formed expressions using line junctions (Willats 1997, Klomberg et al. Forthcoming). Contours often signal the boundaries of regions, and multiple regions might group together inside bigger regions in an embedded way. Panels are a coherent region that can contain multiple subregions of the elements within them.

Graphic representations can also maintain patterns for the systematic ways that different objects are represented. For example, in Figure 1.2, we see repeated graphic patterns appearing for the primary characters of Army Shanks, the boy, and the pursuing figures, as well as for the surrounding scene. These all use consistent graphic shapes, even though the particular manifestation of those graphics differs in each panel. By this I mean that, despite the physical lines being different for how Army Shanks is drawn in each panel, each instance uses similar shapes to depict his beanie (a curve over a shaded base), glasses (two circles), and hair (blob of lines). Other patterns may persist across characters, such as the regularized ways that hands are drawn on all characters. It's worth pointing out that when we learn to draw, we are building up our own library of these types of graphic patterns (Cohn 2012, Wilson 1988).

A higher level of organization for graphics comes when we arrange coherent units together, in their **layout**. This would be an **external compositional structure**, which is external to the panel as an organizing unit. Panels as units can be arranged in various ways depending on their alignment and proximity to each other. For example, the page in Figure 1.2 uses six panels organized into a 3 x 2 grid, where panels maintain a slight distance from each other to create a small gutter (the space between panels), as opposed to if they were right up against each other and no gutter is visible. We will discuss layouts in Chapter 4.

In this layout, the borders of all the panels align with each other. This creates a "+" shape in the junctions between panels, which signal what we have called a *pure grid* (Figure 1.3c). A similar alignment between borders of panels occurs if they are organized into a horizontal row (Figure 1.3a) or vertical column (Figure 1.3b). Other alignments are also possible. In Figure 1.3d, this same page has been reorganized to just have two rows. Because the panels are not identical sizes, their borders end up misaligned, creating a *horizontal stagger*. We can also stack panels on top of each other when set next to other panels, as in Figure 1.3e, an arrangement I call *blockage*.

Layouts can vary the physical arrangements of panels, but these arrangements do not necessarily determine the order that they are read. Indeed, the original layout in Figure 1.2 could be read in a left-to-right and down **Z-path** like written English (Cohn 2013b, c, 2020a), but it could also be read top-to-bottom in an N-path like written Japanese, or top-to-bottom-to-top in a U-path. These orders are guided by an ***assemblage structure***, which is an organizational structure of navigating layouts. Here, the overarching unit is a ***canvas***. As we read, we group panels together to form segments, and larger segments can form out of the groupings of segments. For example, a horizontal row (Figure 1.3a) and a vertical column (Figure 1.3b) are just simple groupings. Rows are then horizontal segments that are stacked on top of each other vertically (Figure 1.3c and 1.3d). We can also embed these relationships further, such as vertical columns embedded inside of horizontal rows, which are embedded inside a vertical column (Figure 1.3e).

It is important to note that these different arrangements do not change the overall meaning of the sequence of images. Layout is a property of the arrangements of elements within the visual modality, and while those units might convey meaning, the same principles of layout would apply if no content was in the panels at all. Certainly, some content may be more affected by their arrangement than others. However, this does not mean that layouts themselves are meaningful, but rather that we might have an alignment between how panels are organized in their layout and the meaning that panels convey. Part of the artistry of comics is creating these alignments in creative and evocative ways.

1.1.2 *Combinatorial structure*

In order to understand pictures, we make a correspondence between the lines and shapes in graphics and meanings. For example, a circle, dots, and a line alone are just shapes, but in a particular configuration we are able to make a correspondence of those shapes to understanding a face. We'll talk more about meanings below, but VLT argues that sometimes patterns can be

VISUAL LANGUAGE 9

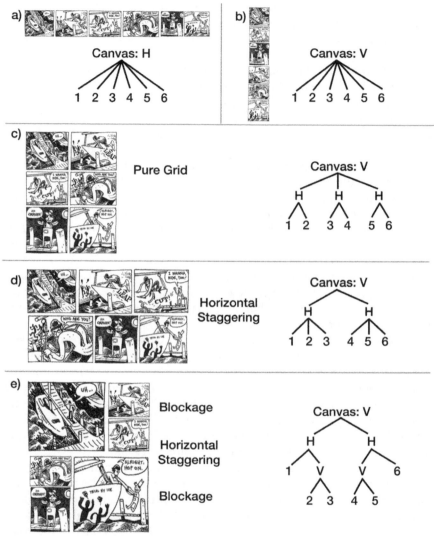

FIGURE 1.3 *Panels from* Far Arden *arranged in different ways as a) a row, b) a column, c) a 3 × 2 grid, d) a 2 × 3 grid, and e) two rows with embedded columns. Far Arden © Kevin Cannon.*

abstracted across these basic expressions, particularly for how elements combine together.

The combinatorial structure of individual images is what we can think of as its ***morphology***, which is about the construction of units. We will discuss morphology in Chapter 3. Morphology includes the small elements we use to construct drawings, such as patterns of hands, which attach to arms, which attach to bodies, etc. These objects and scenes constitute a fairly open-ended class of morphemes, since we can easily learn or invent new patterns for things we've never drawn before.

Other components of images are less open, and belong to a more "closed" class of morphemes. These are elements such as motion lines, speech balloons, and thought bubbles, or the various things that float above characters' heads, such as hearts, stars, or gears. We see a variety of these in Figure 1.2, including the dotted "scopic lines" that go from Army Shanks to the boat in panel 1, the motion lines indicating movement in panels 2 and 3, the squiggles above the characters' heads in panels 2 and 6 to show they are angry, and all the speech balloons and "sound effects" throughout.

Although these elements vary widely, they all share a common abstract structure. In all cases, they *attach* to the objects that they give meaning to. Speech balloons attach to a speaker, motion lines attach to a mover, and scopic lines attach to both the seer and the seen object. If we abstract across these elements, we can see that they are all *affixes* that attach to their *stems* (Cohn 2013c, 2018a). In linguistics, affixes are small morphemes that cannot stand alone, such as the prefix *un-* in *unhappy* or the suffix *-able* in *believable*. Affixes must attach to a stem, which is form that can stand alone, such as *happy* or *believe*. This same relationship holds in the visual form: a speaker can exist without a balloon, but the balloon cannot float around without a speaker.

Another layer of combinatorial structure occurs when we reach the level of a whole *panel*, which is a larger graphic unit than just stems and affixes. Panels provide a way to frame a scene, with the borders of a panel sometimes cropping out a selection of a wider storyworld. For example, in Figure 1.2, we understand that each panel only provides a "window" on what we see, and that the world extends beyond that frame. In panels 2, 3, and 6, we know that the boat extends beyond the edge of the panel, and in panel 4, we know Army Shanks has feet, despite them not being shown.

Because of this manner of windowing information, panels can vary for how much information they show at a time. For example, only the final panel of Figure 1.2 shows all the characters in the same panel (with some only being shown through their shadows). Other panels might only show Army Shanks (panel 1), the boy (panel 5), or various combinations of these characters. This selection of the scene is shown in Figure 1.4a. Here, each gray rectangle highlights the contents of each panel, but where lines pass through rectangles it implies characters are not shown, though we still maintain knowledge of them. Because of this, panels vary in the amount of information they convey. Some might show multiple interacting characters (like panels 2, 3, 4, and 6 in Figure 1.2), while others might show only a single character (like panels 1 and 5). Panels might also show portions of characters, like with an extreme close up, or just elements of the environment. We'll talk more about these aspects of framing in Chapter 6.

Sequences of images also can involve patterns. Even though we can associate meaningful information across panels (as discussed below), there

VISUAL LANGUAGE

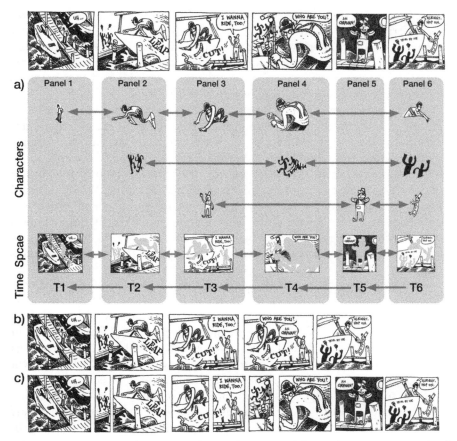

FIGURE 1.4 *A page from* Far Arden *a) diagrammed for its framing structure and continuity maintained for characters, spatial location, and time, along with altered narrative structure to have b) one penultimate panel, and c) only one character per panel until the end.* Far Arden © Kevin Cannon.

are various ways that images combine using systematic combinatorial structures. This aspect of sequential images can be called its ***grammar***, and is the system governing the way that meaningful expressions are organized into a sequence. Grammars have a range of complexity in the way that they organize information (Cohn and Schilperoord 2022b, Jackendoff and Wittenberg 2014), depending on how much the grammar itself contributes to the sequence.

Simple grammars do not contribute much additional structure to the organization of units, and are primarily guided by the meaning in each unit. The simplest sequences are pairs of images where we create an inference about the relationship between the images. For example, before-after patterns persist in advertisements, memes, and many other contexts, where usually a before-state shifts to an after-state through some inferred causation (Schilperoord and Cohn 2022), such as first seeing a dirty shirt (before), then a clean shirt (after), with the inference that some detergent caused the shirt to become clean. Other pairs of panels might show comparisons, or show yes/no contrasts (e.g., such as pictures showing that yes water is allowed in a room; no food is allowed).

Linear grammars are less constrained, where a sequence of images is guided only by meaningful relationships. Unordered linear grammars are essentially lists, such as visual sequences that are found on signage, instruction manuals, and many other contexts (e.g., images of things to do or not do in a park). These sequences are typically bound only by an overarching theme or meaningful associations (Saraceni 2016). Ordered linear grammars are sequences where the meaning of elements progresses only between each adjacent panel. This often occurs in instruction manuals, where each image shows a step-by-step progression, but the images are all equal in their status to each other, and don't necessarily create groupings of panels.

Compared to these simple grammars, which are based on meaning, complex grammars add structure in order to organize information. This either occurs through segmenting units to create groupings, or by assigning categorical roles to units to give them relative salience. For example, in spoken languages such as English, words may take categorical roles as nouns and verbs, which function in different ways in a sentence. Words will also group together to form phrases, which can create embeddings.

The sequences of images that appear in comics often use complex grammars. Here, the images also use categorical roles, but not nouns and verbs. Rather, they use a *narrative structure*, with units functioning in ways that set up, raise tension, climax, or release tension for a sequence. This type of narrative sequencing is another type of pattern, stored as a schema in our minds (Cohn 2013d, 2020b). Sequences of images can also form groupings, organizing several panels together into chunks. These groupings can embed within larger groupings as well, potentially even reaching recursive structures. Additional modifiers can further elaborate on the core narrative arc (Cohn 2015b), often leading to more complex patterns (Cohn 2019b). We will discuss narrative structure in more detail in Chapter 7.

This narrative structure is not the meaning of a sequence, but it provides a scaffolding to help organize the meaning. For example, in Figure 1.2, panel 4 shows Army Shanks holding a rope and panel 5 then shows the boy. These two parts could be presented in only a single panel, as in Figure 1.4b. Alternatively, all the characters could be given their own panels, as in Figure 1.4c, which would alter the framing in a way that also alters the pacing of the sequence. In all of these sequences, the same sequential meaning is conveyed, but these aspects of pacing are achieved by the narrative structure, for how that meaning is presented to the reader.

1.1.3 *Meaning*

These patterns of structure, whether morphological or narrative, provide packaging for how graphics convey meaning. Individual images convey substantial information on their own, often depicting characters and objects, their spatial locations, and the events that they are engaged with. In the *Far Arden* sequence in Figure 1.2, there are conceptual objects of people, a boat, docks, rope, and water, there is a spatial location of the docks, and there are events of seeing, running, leaping, cutting, speaking, and lifting. Characters' events are often encoded in their postures, along with additional morphological cues such as motion lines. For example, in the sequence from *Far Arden*, the first panel shows a man who sees a boat because he is standing across from it and scopic lines show the path of his vision. The second panel shows the man leap onto the boat through his posture, motion lines, and the text reading "leap." Each of these panels on their own conveys characters and events.

In order to understand a sequence of panels, we need to associate the contents of panels together. A first requirement is to link the identity of elements in one panel to those in other panels. For example, in all the panels except panel 5, we see various lines that all correspond to the same man, Army Shanks. In each panel, the physical lines are very different, and the exact configuration of lines is never repeated. But we still know each of these panels signals the same character. I call this recognition of co-reference the *continuity constraint* (Cohn 2020a, Klomberg et al. Forthcoming), and our brains appear to process these types of connections similarly to co-reference in spoken languages (Coopmans and Cohn 2022). In addition, if we saw the identical lines in each panel, we might not be able to tell that any meaning has changed across panels. So, the changes in lines are actually cues for changes in events, states, viewpoints, etc.—all of which give us the sense that these are not just a list of panels, but that they are a *sequence*. I call this recognition that changes across panels and provide cues for states the *activity constraint*.

If we did not maintain a continuity constraint across panels, then each panel would be viewed as having different characters. In other words, if you didn't recognize that each configuration of lines showed Army Shanks, then each panel would show a different man, with slightly similar appearances. Also, if you had no activity constraint, you would lose the sense of this being a progressive sequence. Instead, each panel would show its own independent scene, unconnected from the other panels.

The interpretation of a sequence of panels without continuity or activity may sound extreme or unlikely to seasoned comic readers. However, cross-cultural studies have revealed that people without experience with visual narratives often interpret panels as independent and with different characters, i.e., lacking the continuity and activity constraints. In addition, many children only seem to develop an awareness of these constraints between four and six years old, and this also depends on how much they engage in visual narratives, such as picture books and comics (Cohn 2020a). So, maintaining this type of continuity across panels requires exposure to and practice with visual narratives.

If a person has fluency, they will track multiple elements across panels at the same time. For our *Far Arden* sequence, the spatial location remains constant across the sequence, and time shifts between each panel, but not every character is shown in every panel. As diagrammed in Figure 1.4a, characters partially change in and out, sometimes requiring us to maintain them in working memory when they are not shown. As should be evident, this multiple changing situation is more complex than would be suggested by theories proposing that singular "transitions" occur between panels. We will discuss the shifting of meaning across panels in Chapter 5.

Although some integration of information across panels can progress fairly seamlessly, at other times key information might be left out of depictions. In these cases, we generate *inferences* to "fill in" what is not shown to us overtly. Imagine if we omitted the second panel of the *Far Arden* sequence. In this case, we would progress from a panel of Army Shanks looking at a boat to one with him on the boat. Because we would not see him leap onto it anymore, we would need to infer that action took place. Although inferences have been emphasized as a key aspect of sequential meaning-making, they do not occur "in between the panels" as is often claimed (Gavaler and Beavers 2018, McCloud 1993). Rather, inferences are often motivated by specific encoded narrative patterns, and they rely on integrating the *contents* of information that is shown to a reader (Cohn 2019a, Klomberg and Cohn 2022).

1.1.4 *Multimodality*

Although visual languages have their own structures, they often combine with written language within comics and other media, creating a ***multimodal*** interaction. Combinations of pictures and text can involve interactions at each of their levels of structure. That is, there are interactions of modalities, interactions of grammars, and interactions of meaning, and the sum of these sub-interactions are what results in the full interactions between pictures and text (Cohn and Schilperoord 2022b).

Modalities themselves combine in the ways that text and images interface with each other (Cohn 2013a). We see two of these interface types in the page from *Far Arden*. First, text such as the speech balloons and "sound" effects use affixes to connect with visual stems. However, these carriers of text are not part of the world of the images, and instead float above it unknown to the characters. In contrast, the name of the boat in the final panel ("Trial by Ice") is part of this visual world, since it is printed on the boat itself. Thus, modalities can vary in the ways that they connect with each other.

Combinatorial structures can also vary in their interactions. All of the panels in *Far Arden* use what we call *independent* relationships (Cohn and Schilperoord 2022b), where the grammar of the text does not interact with the grammar of the visuals. In addition, their combinatorial structures may vary in their complexity, creating different types of combinatorial **symmetry**. The full sentences in panels 3, 4, 5, and 6 all use complex syntactic structures, while the persisting narrative structure of the visual sequence is also complex. However, we also see simple grammars used by the individual utterances in panel 1 ("uh . . ."), panel 2 ("Leap"), and panel 3 ("Cut"!). These result in the sequence weaving in and out of different interactions between the grammars in the visual and verbal expressions.

Finally, interactions also exist between the meanings of the text and the images. In some cases, the text may directly connect with the contents of images (Tseng and Bateman 2018, Stainbrook 2016). In panel 2 we see Army Shanks leap onto a boat, along with the word "Leap," while in panel 3 the "I" in "I wanna ride, too"! connects with the boy who is speaking it. Other connections are left more implicit, such as when the boy saying "I wanna ride" carries the implication being that he wants to ride *the boat* that is depicted in the image.

Larger scale relations between meaning can also be identified, which is what we have called the overall **semantic weight** of the sequence (Cohn and Schilperoord 2022b). Essentially, which modality most governs the overall expression of meaning? We can test this by omitting modalities and seeing whether the overall gist is retained by the expression. For example, compared to the full multimodal interaction (Figure 1.5a), omitting the text of the *Far Arden* page leaves a sequence that is mostly understandable (Figure 1.5b), but omitting the visuals to only show the text renders the sequence much harder to comprehend (Figure 1.5c). Because more of the overall meaning could be retained when leaving only visuals compared to only text, it indicates that this sequence carries more of its semantic weight in the pictures rather than the words.

Given these multimodal interactions, we might then ask: What architecture in the mind supports the combination of pictures and text? The common answer to this question has been to treat each behavior as its own indivisible system, with pictures belonging to one system and words to another (e.g., Paivio 1986), leading to their combination being pictures *plus* writing. However, cognitive neuroscience research has largely converged on the conclusion that words and pictures do not involve independent encodings of meaning in the brain, and both tap into a common, integrated conceptual system (Kutas and Federmeier 2011, Lambon Ralph et al. 2016, Kuhnke et al. 2023). In line with this, VLT argues that consistent structures persist across visual languages, spoken languages, and signed languages, and research has supported that they indeed use similar cognitive mechanisms

FIGURE 1.5 *A page from* Far Arden *that shows a) a multimodal interaction between text and image, b) the omission of the text, and c) the omission of the images.* Far Arden © Kevin Cannon.

(Loschky et al. 2020, Cohn 2020b). All this suggests that writing and pictures are not independent, and ultimately belong to a broader, shared architecture.

Rather than pictures and writing being treated as independent systems, we have argued that they decompose into common parts of modalities, grammar, and meaning, and these parts are all shared within a holistic architecture (Cohn and Schilperoord 2022b, a). This ***multimodal parallel architecture*** thus consists of all three of our primary modalities (vocal, bodily, graphic), differentiation between simple and complex combinatorial structures, and a conceptual structure for the encoding of meaning. This architecture is depicted in Figure 1.6a. We will elaborate in detail on this model in future works, but I describe the basics here.

Because all modalities share a broader system, different behaviors, such as writing and drawing arise as emergent interactions from this holistic architecture. For example, spoken sentences arise as expressions of meaning using a complex grammar (syntax) in the vocal modality (Figure 1.6b). This is the interaction of components discussed (and debated) in most linguistic theories (e.g., Jackendoff 2002). Written sentences use this same interaction but with an additional correspondence between the vocal and graphic modalities (Figure 1.6f). This occurs because writing is the expression of speech sounds (vocal) in the visual-graphic modality.

Visual languages use a different, but similar, interaction. Visual narrative sequences involve the expression of meaning using a complex grammar (narrative structure) in the graphic modality (Figure 1.6d). This sub-selection for visual language reflects the same architecture that is depicted in Figure 1.1, only here it is seen in less detail and placed alongside other modalities in a broader architecture. Single images would simplify this to be the same interaction, only using a simple grammar (Figure 1.6e), just like single, written word expressions (such as *uh* ..., *leap*, or *cut!* from *Far Arden*) would also just use simple grammars (Figure 1.6c).

This multimodal parallel architecture allows a single model of communication to express multiple behaviors. In addition to unimodal expressions such as speech, writing, and drawings, multimodal interactions arise out of the co-activation of these components at the same time. The page from *Far Arden* would be reflected in the diagram in Figure 1.7. Here, we see the visual sequencing reflected in the interaction between the graphic

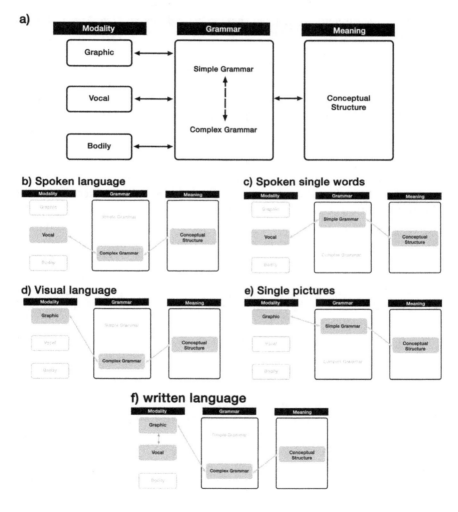

FIGURE 1.6 *a) The Multimodal Parallel Architecture and its manifestation into b) spoken languages, c) spoken single words, d) visual languages, e) single images, f) written language.*

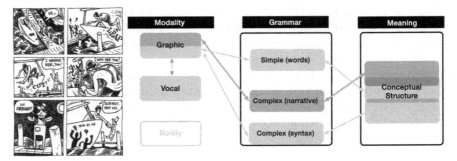

FIGURE 1.7 *The multimodality of a page from* Far Arden, *which combines a visual language sequence with written sentences and single words. Far Arden © Kevin Cannon.*

modality, a complex grammar, and meaning (in dark gray). The full sentences arise as correspondences between the graphic-vocal modality, complex grammar, and meaning, while individual words use the same correspondence with a simple grammar (both in light gray). This diagram characterizes the overall interactions of the whole page, but in actuality the expression weaves in and out of these interactions with each unit on the page. Regardless, the whole multimodal interaction is captured by a single architecture.

There are several important assumptions embedded in this proposed architecture that should be stated explicitly for the ways they contrast with traditional notions of language (Cohn and Schilperoord 2022a). Foremost, "language" is not "amodal" and it does not flow out of different modalities as expressive options. Rather, as depicted in Figure 1.6a, all modalities persist in parallel, and different expressions manifest as emergent states selected out of this broader architecture. Multimodality used in comics (or other media) is not "writing plus images" as the combination of independent systems, but rather spoken/written languages and visual languages both arise from a shared system in the first place.

In this regard, our graphic and bodily modalities are not peripheral expressive modalities, but are equal and complementary channels for communication that persist alongside our vocal (and written) expression. Because each modality uses different ways of organizing information with sensory signals (speech sounds, graphics, bodily movements), they each offer affordances that structure how they convey meaning. This may give the *appearance* of broad differences and independence between modalities, despite originating from a common architecture. Indeed, although we might think of modalities appearing independently and one at a time, most often we use multiple modalities to express ourselves, whether we combine gestures with speech or pictures with writing. Correspondingly, unimodal expression can manifest out of this architecture, but the broader organization of this model reflects that multimodality is our default predisposition for communication.

1.2 Hypotheses for structure across modalities

In the model of language and communication described in Figure 1.6a, all modalities belong to a broader shared architecture. This cognitive organization therefore leads to several consequences about the potential relationships between modalities' expressive systems and how they structure information. I here lay out four primary hypotheses that follow from this architecture, although similar questioning could persist in other models of the mind. Broadly, these hypotheses relate to cognitive consistency, cross-linguistic variation, universality, and the influence of modalities on each other.

1.2.1 Equivalence

The multimodal Parallel Architecture is guided by the idea that all modalities exist adjacent to each other within a shared system, and as such, all expressions arising from this architecture share common cognitive mechanisms. Overall, I have called this idea the *Principle of Equivalence* (Cohn 2013c), which posits that we should expect a degree of consistency across the structure of our different expressions:

> *Principle of Equivalence* – We should expect that the mind/brain structures different modalities in similar ways, given modality specific constraints.

This principle outlines that different modalities of expression should be structured and processed in similar ways, because they all stem from a common brain that uses the same types of cognition across expressions (segmentation, memory, attention, etc.). Indeed, several decades of research in cognitive neuroscience has provided support for this notion. We observe similar brain responses for the processing of meaning across modalities (Kutas and Federmeier 2011), and for the processing of the sequencing in language (Hagoort 2003), music (Koelsch and Siebel 2005, Patel 2003), and visual narratives (Cohn 2020b). Thus, the brain does seem to use similar mechanisms when processing information across different modalities.

Nevertheless, the ways in which those mechanisms manifest might be constrained by the characteristics of the modalities themselves. For example, the sound structures that guide speech naturally constrain information in ways that are different from graphics. Sound inherently unfurls across a linear duration in time, while graphics can appear all at once in an analog display (although graphics are produced across time as well). These variations in the sensory experience of an expression should naturally lead to differences in how these abstract mechanisms might arise in different modalities. That is, the organizational structure of each modality offers *affordances* for how structures may manifest.

This Principle of Equivalence describes the overarching way in which spoken and visual languages relate to each other in terms of their cognition. I have explored these broader cognitive relationships in previous work (Cohn 2020b, a). However, as we will see, these potential similarities might manifest in more specific ways that are relevant for the topic of this book, which is about the patterns that arise in visual languages and how those patterns might relate to those in other modalities.

1.2.2 *Cross-linguistic variation*

One way that systems in different modalities may uphold "equivalence" comes in the cross-cultural variation of structures within a given modality's expressions. VLT maintains a linguistic perspective on graphic representations, and the Parallel Architecture substantiates this by placing the graphic modality alongside all other modalities. If this is the case, then visual languages should manifest in ways that are parallel to languages in other modalities. Specifically, since we know that many diverse spoken and signed languages appear across cultures and contexts, many visual languages should also exist throughout the world. We might phrase this in a way that can reflect our multimodal architecture:

> *Cross-linguistic equivalence hypothesis* – Given that all modalities belong within a broader architecture, all modalities encode their specific constructions and patterns in varying ways.

The idea here is that we know that notions such as "spoken language" and "sign language" are abstractions, and that specific spoken and signed languages manifest with different structures across and within populations. The structures of French, Arabic, and Urdu differ from each other as spoken languages, and so do American Sign Language, Nihon Shuwa, and Nicaraguan Sign Language as sign languages. Thus, if all modalities belong to a common architecture, then we should expect similar variation across all modalities, including the graphic modality.

This expectation of cross-linguistic and/or cross-cultural diversity for graphics may seem somewhat trivial, but the widespread treatment of graphics has been that they are universal and transparently understood (e.g., McCloud 1993) or that visual information is not "coded" (e.g., Forceville 2020). Despite recognition of varying "styles," there has been little acknowledgement and study of cross-linguistic or cross-cultural graphic systems comparable to that of cross-culturally varying spoken or signed languages. Such studies would include specifying the distinctive properties of such systems and referring to them by name as different systems. In VLT, graphics are not universal, nor is there a notion of a single visual language. Rather, VLT posits many visual languages displaying varying patterns.

This idea of varying visual languages should be intuitive for people. It should be uncontroversial to say that the patterns stereotypically found in Japanese manga differ from those in American superhero comics. Surface differences are immediately apparent: they are drawn in different styles, American comics are read from left-to-right while Japanese manga are read from right-to-left, and various distinct visual morphology appear in each. The structures of these systems used in comics and manga also differ from visual languages used in other contexts, such as those recognizable in instruction manuals or in historical Japanese scrolls.

From a cognitive perspective, these different "styles" arise because authors encode various patterns in their minds related to the way they draw pictures, whether those patterns relate to individual images or images put into a sequence. Each person technically has their own unique patterns for drawing, just as they do for speaking, which aligns with what linguists would call a person's *idiolect*. To the degree that people might have the same cognitive patterns, we can say that they draw in a common visual language.

In these terms, we can then identify varying "styles" as recognizable visual languages that may arise from different contexts. Most manga are thus drawn in a Japanese Visual Language (JVL) that differs from the American Visual Language(s) (AVL) that characterize comics from the United States or from the visual language(s) found in comics from Europe. All of these visual languages differ still from other cross-culturally identifiable visual languages, whether those used in instruction manuals, sand drawings from Australian Aboriginals, or the myriad graphic systems from across human history that can be identified just by walking the halls of most art or history museums. To the extent we can recognize that graphics come from a different place, time, and/or context, we understand that they may use different visual languages.

Earlier, I described how "visual language" was separate from "comics": Although visual languages are the cognitive and structural systems we use to create graphics, comics are one sociocultural context that these systems appear. This separation can further be extended to specific visual languages, although they often play a role in how we categorize different works. For example, "JVL" is not a synonym for "manga" just as "visual language" is not a synonym for "comics" more broadly. Rather, JVL describes a graphic system that creators use to draw (whether by individuals within or outside of Japan), while "manga" is a sociocultural artifact that may or may not actually be written in JVL. This same relationship holds between written Japanese and manga: we would not say that "written Japanese is a synonym for manga" nor should we say that "JVL is a synonym for manga." Rather, manga are often *created in* written Japanese (the words) and JVL (the pictures). But JVL as a graphic system appears in many places that are not manga, such as advertisements, cartoons, doodles, and other contexts. However, because of their stereotypical association, JVL may be one of many of the defining criteria by which people identify manga (Kacsuk 2018), particularly compared to other types of visual narratives.

It is also worth noting that in everyday conversation, people often draw a distinction between a "language" versus a "dialect." Although these terms are often meant to describe a broader system (language) and its smaller variations (dialects), they often carry bias in implications of the relative value of the systems. In terms of cognition and structure, no linguistic system is privileged over another, and these biased distinctions come only from social and political considerations. To reduce the possibility of bias, I'll use the term "variety" when discussing the different range of recognized languages that share a larger association. For example, we might think of "English" as an abstracted notion of a language, but many varieties of English exist: British English, Indian English, Standard American English, African American Vernacular English, and many others. All of these are valid and complex varieties of a more abstract notion of "English" that in *idealization* reflects the shared patterns or range of patterns found across and within the minds of speakers of these varieties. Indeed, many of these varieties have quite widely different structures, but their family resemblance allows us to describe them as an idealized common system.

In previous works, I have already posited that different visual languages exist with varieties (Cohn 2013c, Cohn and Ehly 2016, Cohn 2010a). Since visual languages used in comics appear within print cultures, varieties may arise more from divisions, such as their particular audiences or genres rather than geographical boundaries. For example, I proposed that JVL might have varieties based on manga aimed at different demographics, such as a slight variation appearing between the varieties used in shonen (boy's), shojo (girl's), seinen (men's), or josei (women's) manga. Given the global reach of manga, there may also be varieties of JVL used outside Japan by different communities around the world (Brienza 2015). In AVL, I suggested we associate one variety with the representations common to mainstream superhero comics. I named this "Kirbyan AVL," in honor of the comic artist Jack Kirby who was an influential early creator of the style and characteristics of mainstream American comics. Thus, sometimes I might refer to the "style" of American mainstream comics as Kirbyan AVL, when discussing the properties of the visual language used in American mainstream comics.

Of course, an enduring question remains, to what degree can we find evidence of systems such as JVL, AVL, or Kirbyan AVL in the first place? Can we identify patterns that justify the identification of such languages, and how many varieties might those systems have? These questions are central to the aims of this book. Indeed, the orientations of VLT on these issues raise a variety of questions: Are comics around the world actually created using different visual languages? How many visual languages are there? How do different visual languages relate to each other? Have visual languages changed over time or influenced each other?

This book offers a first attempt at addressing these questions in an empirically driven way, by reporting the results of corpus analyses. Over several years, teams of students and I analyzed the properties of more than

350 comics by directly recording their properties. These analyses allow us to examine the properties of these comics in a data-driven way. This book will thus interpret the structure of the visual languages used in comics by reporting on all this data. Get ready for graphs, *lots* of graphs.

By basing interpretations on the data, this work will hopefully provide a distinctive and novel viewpoint on the structures used in comics. This empirical method contrasts with the many qualitative discussions of comics. So, why is it important to do this type of quantitative analysis rather than a qualitative, theoretical approach? First, many theories make generalizations about the structure of how comics work without any true analysis or data to validate claims. These theories then run the risk of having no grounding in actual phenomena, and thus may not hold up when faced with actual evidence.[1]

Other research uses case studies of specific comics or authors, sometimes to make cross-cultural comparisons, where specific comics are often held up as representative examples. In the cases when these works may use a corpus, they typically do no quantitative analysis. Although such works can provide many insights, such case studies often focus on exemplars. Often the "interesting" things that pop out are the exceptions, not the rules. Normative patterns are often harder to notice since they are less salient in the first place. But it is these normative patterns that I seek to characterize here, abstracting beyond individual authors to characterize the broader systems that are shared by creators: the generalized patterns used in the structures of *visual languages*. Although qualitative approaches can be insightful for answering certain questions, the methods here seek to justify generalizations by reporting the properties of analyzed comics directly and across a larger scale. How can you really know what's going on in different types of comics unless you actually look?

This corpus-driven approach comes from linguistics, where data has been used to compare languages for centuries, if not millennia. As in linguistics, I will use these analyses to inform several important themes throughout this book. These data analyses will provide evidence for the ideas that 1) patterns exist across comics that characterize them as sharing a *common* visual language, and 2) patterns exist between comics to substantiate their using *different* visual languages and/or varieties.

With regard to comics specifically, it's worth mentioning the importance of validating the systematic nature of such cross-linguistic and/or cross-cultural variation. Many scholars and creators of comics talk of a "comics medium" that somehow uniformly persists across all comics (e.g., Exner 2021), despite acknowledgment of differences in the "types of comics" and their "styles." A notion of visual language undermines this thinking of a uniform "comics medium." Rather, many visual languages with distinctive properties appear in the socio-cultural contexts of comics, and their patterns exist as a range of variation across abstract structural dimensions. Maintaining a view of a generic "comics medium" washes over this diversity.

1.2.3 Linguistic universals

Another dimension that is implicit to the multimodal Parallel Architecture is the degree to which languages share similarities. The idea here is that even though languages may have systematic patterns in the ways they vary, various patterns may transcend these cultural patterns in consistent ways. This orientation comes from studies of *linguistic typology*, which refers to these patterns as "linguistic universals" (Croft 2003, Greenberg 1966, Haspelmath et al. 2001), and several universals have been posited related to various aspects of the linguistic system, particularly for the spoken modality and often extended to the bodily modality.

One type of *typological universal* is a tendency for a particular structure to manifest in a particular way. For example, in classic work by the pioneering typologist Joseph Greenberg, his first proposed linguistic universal stated that grammatical subjects typically precede objects in languages (Greenberg 1966), and indeed more recent corpus research has suggested that this order persists in ~95 percent of languages' sentence structures (Hammarström 2016). Other universals might pertain to the relationships or tradeoffs between structures. One such argument is that languages generally use a tradeoff between the complexity of their units (morphology) and sequences (syntax). Thus, languages using more complex units (such as words) typically have less complex grammatical structures, while languages with simpler morphological units use more complex grammars (Ehret 2018, Koplenig et al. 2017, Bentz et al. 2022).

It is important to stress that in the linguistic sense, the term "universal" should not be mistaken for meaning that a pattern or relationship does not have exceptions, or that it appears in all languages. Typological universals are *tendencies* that operate across the structures of languages, even if they do not necessarily manifest in *all* languages. We might expect structures within visual languages to also have similar relationships, which would reflect the affordances of that graphic modality. That is, are there relationships between structures in visual languages that persist across cross-linguistic variation?

At the same time, the multimodal Parallel Architecture offers a slightly expanded view on linguistic universals, particularly related to the similarities of structures across modalities. In this case, we might think of how universals operate across modalities:

> *Modality universality hypothesis* – Given that all modalities belong within a broader architecture, "universal" organizing principles should apply to all modalities in consistent ways.

Again, with a single architecture that contains all modalities, we might posit that general cognitive principles constrain the systems manifesting in different modalities. These principles would transcend the *modality-specific universals*, and instead would suggest *modality-general universals*. Indeed, if universals reflect properties of cognition, then we might expect them to transcend the typological variation in individual modalities to be true across all modalities.

These types of cognitive universals would thus need to be general enough in their properties to persist across the differences between modalities. For example, Greenberg's observation that grammatical subjects typically precede objects may *not* be applicable, since visual languages have no forthright comparison for grammatical subjects or objects. Candidates for such cognitive universals might lie in more general "linguistic laws." These would include *Zipf's Law*, where there is often tradeoff in the length of units or sequences and their frequency (Zipf 1935), or the *Menzerath–Altmann Law* (Altmann 1980, Menzerath 1928), where the larger the whole of a construct, the smaller the size of its constituents. Such principles could apply abstractly across modalities, and would hint at aspects of cognition related to how the human brain structures and organizes information. These are the types of relations between visual languages and spoken and signed languages that guide the assumptions related to the Principle of Equivalence and VLT more broadly.

1.2.4 Conceptual permeability

The idea of cognitive universals relates to the way that consistent structures may persist across patterns instantiated in different modalities. An additional type of consistency may arise by how patterns in different modalities relate to each other. Indeed, a holistic architecture that includes multiple modalities raises the possibility of influence between the patterns manifesting in different modalities. I have called this idea *conceptual permeability* (Cohn 2016a):

> *Conceptual permeability hypothesis* – Given that all modalities belong within a broader architecture, the framing of a conceptualization in one modality may influence and/or be shared by the framing of that conceptualization in other modalities.

Within the Parallel Architecture, the patterns encoded in a modality and grammar provide the "presentation" for the meaning in conceptual structure. Because different modalities all tap into the same conceptual system in their own ways (Kutas and Federmeier 2011), we might posit that the particular patterns found in one modality might influence those in another modality. For example: might the structure of spoken English or Japanese influence the structures of the AVLs or JVLs, respectively?

Permeable effects might be posited to occur at various levels of structure. Surface permeability would manifest in shared lexical items. For example, various visual morphemes are direct depictions of verbal idioms, such as the stars shown in character's eyes to mean a desire for fame, which corresponds to the English idiom *stars in their eyes*. In French comics, characters may also be surrounded by candles when hit in the head, corresponding to the French idiom *voir trente-six chandelle* (*seeing thirty-six candles*) to mean being stunned by a hit. Permeability has also occurred from the JVL to Nihon Shuwa (Japanese Sign Language), which gesticulates a motion to draw lines across a forehead to show dread, just like the drawn lines on foreheads used by JVL in manga (Takeuchi 2012).

A more consequential, and likely more subtle, manifestation of conceptual permeability would come from cases where the typological patterns encoded in one modality influence those of another modality. For example, the spoken language of Aymara orients time so that the past is described as being forward and the future behind, in contrast to English, which maintains the past behind and future in front (*She put her past behind her, She looked forward to the future*). Correspondingly, speakers of Aymara also gesture in front of them when speaking about the past, and gesture behind them when speaking about the future (Núñez and Sweetser 2006). Similarly, Mandarin Chinese includes an orientation of the past to be upward and the future below, and speakers gesture upward when referencing the past (Gu et al. 2017). These would thus be permeable relationships between spoken language and gestures.

Some evidence also exists of a permeable relationship between the spoken and graphic modalities. The spoken languages of Central Australian Aboriginals maintain spatial orientations that also arise in both their gestures and visual languages (Green 2014, Wilkins 2016). In addition, as we will discuss in Chapter 3, the typological dimensions of motion events in spoken languages may also influence the depiction of motion events in visual languages (Hacımusaoğlu and Cohn 2022, Tversky and Chow 2017).

It is worth noting that many examples of conceptual permeability have been subsumed by, or taken as evidence for, the notion of **linguistic relativity** (Slobin 1996, Whorf 1956). This is the idea that the language a person speaks may influence other aspects of their cognition because linguistic constructions habituate the framing of concepts in a particular way. If behaviors such as gesture or drawing are indeed viewed as peripheral and outside the language system, it is easy to view these as relativistic effects, since linguistic structures would influence non-linguistic cognition. However, this view remains untenable with the organization of the multimodal Parallel Architecture, where modalities exist in parallel and equal status alongside the vocal modality. In this view, any influence of one modality (such as the spoken modality) on another (such as graphics) does not extend *outside* the linguistic system, but is structuring different modalities *within* the same architecture.

If our modalities are indeed all connected within a common cognitive system, we might *expect* permeability to manifest between our modalities.

However, I should warn that I do not necessarily expect such effects to be overly widespread, and many of them may be subtle if they arise at all. Evidence for permeability should thus be approached cautiously and with an aim to be replicated for further confirmation.

To summarize what we have covered throughout this section, the multimodal Parallel Architecture posits that our expressive modalities persist in parallel with each other, along with combinatorial structures (grammar) and conceptual structures. Because all modalities belong to a common architecture, it leads to a hypothesis of consistency across structures within systems manifesting in each modality (equivalence), including their manifestation in cross-linguistic varieties. In addition, patterns may arise across modalities motivated by the abstract cognitive structures that organize information (cognitive universals), and we may find influences between the patterns found in different modalities (conceptual permeability). These different hypotheses will be explored throughout this book using our data from comics.

1.3 Organization of the book

The subsequent chapters of this book aim to achieve several purposes. First, the chapters each lay out the structural principles of VLT, and they then explore how those constructs manifest within the properties of comics within our corpus. In this way, each chapter serves as a basic lesson in the structures of VLT. Second, the data analyses presented in each chapter provide evidence both for different visual languages and their varieties, but also for supporting the claims made by VLT in the first place. This relationship of data and evidence to VLT is worth emphasizing further.

VLT is a theoretical framework that is validated by, and has evolved from, empirical analyses. This includes both corpus analyses that are presented here, and the results of psychological experimentation examining people's behavior (using measures such as reading times, reaction times, or eye tracking), or direct measures of people's brains while they read comics (Cohn 2020a). The theory has shifted and changed over two decades based on this relationship with empirical evidence. Any theory of structure—including theories of structures used in comics—must be able to provide evidence for its claims through such empirical examination, including accounting for the existing evidence provided in research thus far.

In the next chapter, we further discuss this aspect of empirical analyses. Chapter 2 reviews various works that take a data-driven approach to the analysis of comics (or, in many cases, their visual languages). I then discuss the nature of the particular corpus that I will discuss throughout the rest of the book, the *Visual Language Research Corpus* (VLRC), a collection of 350+ annotated comics from Europe, Asia, and the United States, along with analysis of the complete run of *Calvin and Hobbes* comic strips.

Chapter 3 then begins the analyses of different structures from within the VLRC by starting with unit-level morphology, what are often referred to as the "symbology" of comics. We begin by comparing the morphology in shonen and shojo manga to ask whether we see evidence of a shared morphological system across a JVL, or whether those demographics might include recognizable varieties of JVL. Such questions are extended further in a comparison of morphology from Dutch and Flemish comics. I then turn to analyzing the "carriers" of text, such as speech balloons and thought bubbles across comics from several countries. Finally, I compare how various countries' comics structure their motion events. Specifically, I investigate how paths are depicted in those comics, how they arise in morphology like motion lines and characters' postures, and whether these structures have associations to the spoken languages of those authors.

In Chapter 4, we widen the analyses across more countries by examining the structure of page layouts. These analyses let us explore whether types of panel arrangements differ across panels, and how these arrangements might connect to different reading paths. We then use such cues to inform the differences in underlying assemblage structures of layouts.

Chapter 5 then turns to the ways that meaning flows between panels in a sequence. We will first discuss how meaningful changes in characters, spatial location, and time shift across adjacent panels, and then explore how continuity across these dimensions persists across longer sequential spans. The chapter closes by further asking about the interactions between shifts in meaning across panels and structures of page layout.

The framing structure of panels is then examined in Chapter 6, which looks at both how much information panels convey, as well as how their framing interacts with other surrounding panels. This analysis will further reveal a range of complexity to the framing structure of panels that manifests in distinctly varying ways across cultures. I will further explore how this framing structure interacts with types of filmic shot scales and the presentation of subjective viewpoints (i.e., "point-of-view" panels).

The insights from comparisons of situational coherence and framing are then brought together in Chapter 7, which examines patterns of narrative structure. This chapter will explore how narrative patterns range in their complexity and how this complexity manifests in different types of comics. Additional analyses will then explore how this complexity of sequencing might interact with the complexity of units, revealing tendencies into the ways that visual narratives distribute their meaningful information.

The final chapters attempt to tie together these structures into broader analyses with more focused topics. First, Chapter 8 asks whether comics have changed across time. This diachronic investigation primarily targets the structures used in mainstream comics from the United States—i.e., the development of Kirbyan AVL—with analyses of page layouts, storytelling, and multimodal interactions. It also looks at whether we can identify an influence of JVL within the structures of AVL, given the rising influx of manga into the United States since around the 1980s and 1990s.

The previous chapters largely take a "top-down" approach comparing data between countries and/or regions of the world. However, maybe using cultural classifications hides more nuanced comparisons or masks relationships that cut across cultures. Chapter 9 thus takes a "bottom-up" approach, using statistical clustering models that characterize groupings emerging out of the data itself to show the optimal ways they relate to each other. These analyses will thus incorporate the primary constructs of the previous chapters to provide evidence for different visual languages on the basis of the data itself. It then further describes the characteristics of these different visual languages.

Chapter 10 then deviates from investigating cross-linguistic diversity in longer visual narratives, with a case study of the structure of the comic strip *Calvin and Hobbes* by Bill Watterson. We analyzed every *Calvin and Hobbes* comic strip from the ten years it was in print, and thus are able to see how the work of a single author changed in structure over time. This chapter also gives an opportunity to compare the structures of a short-formatted comic strip from the United States with the structures found from longer comic books and graphic novels reported in the previous chapters.

Finally, Chapter 11 reflects on these analyses and their implications. For example, what does this cross-linguistic diversity tell us about the demands on readers when they comprehend these different types of comics? How do the general patterns that emerge across these analyses inform us how visual languages structure information in relation to spoken or signed languages? This work is thus situated as the start of a broader investigation of visual language typology, and poses questions for what might come next.

CHAPTER TWO

Corpus-Driven Comics Research

The past decades have seen a huge growth in research on comics. A substantial amount of this work has been theoretical, with authors positing about how people read and understand comics, or how comics use various structures in them. They may also theorize about how structures may differ between comics from different places. But, only rarely are these claims substantiated by evidence beyond choice exemplars used as examples. In contrast, VLT has sought verification of theoretical claims through empirical research, and has used that evidence to further shape the theory.

One form of evidence has been through psychological experimentation, such as measuring comprehenders' eye-movements or brain responses while they read comics (Cohn 2020b, a). An alternative method is to directly examine the properties of comics by tabulating how often certain things occur. With such data, you can then compare the quantitative patterns found in individual books against each other, or compare them to books across genres, countries, or time periods. This is the approach used throughout this book, which emphasizes using data to inform our characterizations and interpretations of the structural properties of comics. How else are we going to know what's *actually* going on unless we look?

This type of *corpus research* has a long tradition in linguistics and other fields, and has increased in frequency over the past decades in the analysis of comics. In this chapter, I will survey several of these data-driven analyses of the structural aspects of comics to contextualize this type of research. I will then describe the development of corpus analyses taken with VLT, leading to describing the corpus that will be analyzed throughout this book, the Visual Language Research Corpus (VLRC).

2.1 Data-driven analyses of comics

Many corpus studies have examined the written language found in comics, effectively using the multimodal context to enrich the analysis of text.

Although these are insightful, they do not focus on the structure of the visual languages, which is our concern here. The earliest corpus analysis of comics that I have found examined the structural aspects of comics in a dissertation by William Neff (1977). He compared several genres of comics: Adventure, Romance, Mystery, and Alien Beings or States. Specifically, he analyzed the shapes of panels (vertical, horizontal, square, circle), the angle of viewpoint taken (lateral, high, low), and shot scale (close, wide), along with various properties of the text. Although his sample size was fairly small, with only two comics in each genre, he took differences in structures to be indicative of the storytelling patterns of those genres.

More famously, comic artist and theorist Scott McCloud (1993) conducted a cross-cultural analysis of panel-to-panel changes in meaning, which he called "panel transitions." He presented the reader with various graphs characterizing the proportion of transitions in each of the books he analyzed, which included comics from the United States, Japan, and Europe, and spanned several genres. He specifically noted that comics from the United States and Europe used more shifts in actions than those of characters or scenes, while manga from Japan also introduced more shifts in "moments," in characters, and in views of the surrounding "aspects" of the environment. To explain these differences, McCloud appealed to cultural differences related to artistry.

Although these works formed precedents, the past several decades have seen the rise of several projects with data-driven analyses of comics (for review, see Laubrock and Dunst 2020). In the mid-2000s, media scholar Charles Forceville began analyzing the visual morphology of various comics, particularly related to their metaphoric qualities (Forceville 2016). He began with several case studies focusing on individual comics. These included an analysis of the metaphors underlying conventions conveying anger in *Asterix* (Forceville 2005), followed by examining the various morphology used in *Tintin and the Picaros* (Forceville 2011b), and specific metaphoric conventions in the manga *Azumanga Daioh* (Abbott and Forceville 2011). He also compared various representations of balloons across American and European comics (Forceville 2013, Forceville, Veale, and Feyaerts 2010b).

This targeted corpus approach has been taken by various papers that have looked at disparate aspects of structure across comics. For example, a wide range of visual morphology was examined across the Italian comic *Gea* by Luca Enoch (Tasić and Stamenković 2018), while visual morphology related to motion was examined in a corpus of comic covers (Juricevic 2017b, Juricevic and Horvath 2016), and a visual lexical item of asymmetrical close-ups of eyes was studied for its changes across time (Juricevic 2017a). Studies have also examined aspects of multimodal coherence in a corpus of American superhero comics (Gahman 2021) and in Chinese poetry comics by Cai Zhizhong (Chen and Zhong 2022). Other work has blended corpus analyses of close-ups in manga with focus groups of British manga readers (Tsai 2018).

Additional projects have strived to build more extensive corpora to carry out analyses. For example, John Bateman, Janina Wildfeuer, and colleagues formulated a taxonomy characterizing the layouts of whole comic pages (Bateman et al. 2016b). Along with McCloud's panel transitions, they then used their layout taxonomy to analyze the properties of 420 comics, from which they sampled only three pages from each book. By analyzing these works, they showed patterned styles from different eras of American comics (Bateman, Veloso, and Lau 2021), suggesting changes in the layout and storytelling across time. Similar analyses have also been carried out on the properties of thirty-seven comics produced as instructional posters (Wildfeuer et al. 2022).

Another extensive corpus project was undertaken by Alexander Dunst, Jochen Laubrock, and colleagues, who established the Graphic Novel Corpus[1] (Dunst, Hartel, and Laubrock 2017). This corpus consists of annotations of ~250 English-language graphic novels from North America since the 1970s (Dunst 2021). They designed analytical software tools to annotate basic dimensions, such as panels, characters, backgrounds, and balloons. Although this corpus has been used to inform about trends related to graphic novel publications (Dunst 2021), and for computer vision analyses (Laubrock and Dubray 2019), the annotations themselves have been combined with psychological experimentation. By merging annotated regions with measurements of comprehenders' eye-movements in reading these comic pages, insights were gained about the way that readers direct attention to elements within and across comic panels (Laubrock, Hohenstein, and Kümmerer 2018).

Some additional corpus projects have been undertaken with more of a societal or literary focus than a structural focus. The Claremont Run[2] is a corpus project led by J. Andrew Deman to analyze the properties of all the X-Men comics by writer Chris Claremont. The project tracks the number of appearances of main characters and their speech or narration, rates of passing the Bechdel Test for female character conversations not about male characters, and some additional analyses of non-X-men comics for comparison. Of a similar nature, the What Were Comics? Project[3] undertaken by Bart Beaty, Benjamin Woo, Rebecca Sullivan, and Nick Sousanis aimed to examine the properties of a random sample of 2 percent of the American comics from 1934 to 2019 (Beaty, Sousanis, and Woo 2018). Although the study aimed to look at some aspects of structure, such as page layout (Woo 2019) and word counts, it has also included analysis of elements such as advertisements and letter pages.

Finally, a substantive subfield analyzing comics has grown within computer science. This work has largely used openly available corpora of comics to train computational models to detect elements of comics and/or to simulate aspects of comprehension (Laubrock and Dunst 2020). However, they do not as much record the properties of the corpora themselves, as use them as an object of study. For example, a rich literature has grown around computers' abilities to detect elements such as panels, characters, and balloons (Augereau, Iwata, and Kise 2018, Nguyen et al. 2021, Rigaud and

Burie 2018). Some other computer science research has attempted analysis of more abstract properties, such as the ability of artificial intelligence to recognize inferences (Iyyer et al. 2017) or multimodal interactions (Chen and Jhala 2021).

2.2 Visual Language Research Corpus

This book continues this data-driven analysis of the properties of comics by reporting on the findings of the Visual Language Research Corpus (VLRC) Project. The VLRC contains comics analyzed using the constructs of VLT, but it was not the first corpus analysis to do so. Early corpus work investigating constructs from VLT first looked at how panels framed information in small samples (usually ten to fifteen books per group). This included annotation of framing types of how many characters appeared per panel, the angle of viewpoint, the filmic shot scale of a panel, and/or whether they depicted a subjective viewpoint on a scene (Cohn 2011, Cohn, Taylor-Weiner, and Grossman 2012). Following my early curiosity of the differences between comics from the United States and Japan, books from these countries were my primary comparison. These efforts were precursors to the VLRC Project, and largely preceded the rise of linguistic and computational analyses of comics. For example, the original annotation of comics in Cohn (2011) took place, and was posted online as a preprint, in 2003.

The VLRC grew from projects undertaken by students at the University of California, San Diego (2014 to 2016) and Tilburg University in the Netherlands (2017 to 2018). Students chose dedicated projects looking at particular structures (framing, layout, multimodality, etc.), either comparing the comics of several countries and/or seeing how structures changed over time. Other research was made for theses, such as comparisons of Dutch and Flemish comics over time (van Middelaar 2017, Dierick 2017), or analysis of how the *Calvin and Hobbes* comic strip changed over time (van Nierop 2018, Schipper 2018). Several of these efforts resulted in publications, such as examining how superhero comics from the United States changed across eighty years (Pederson and Cohn 2016; Cohn, Taylor, and Pederson 2017), in comparisons of visual morphology in manga (Cohn and Ehly 2016), and in cross-cultural comparisons of layouts (Cohn et al. 2019), paths (Cohn et al. 2017), and narrative patterns (Cohn 2019b). Throughout this book I will repeat and expand those reported observations, while also attempting to give a bigger picture viewpoint integrating their results.

A primary focus across these analyses were questions about cross-cultural diversity across comics of the world. This cross-cultural focus initially manifested in comparisons between books from the United States[4] and Japan, but grew to include comics from across Asia (Japan, Korea, China) and Northwestern Europe (France, Germany, Sweden, The Netherlands,

Flemish Belgium). In addition, we also asked about variation within a culture's comics. Thus, subtypes of comics from the United States and Japan were both analyzed. In American comics, we compared three primary groups. First, "mainstream" comics broadly consisting of superheroes and power fantasies. Second, independent or "indie" comics were works outside the mainstream and typically published as "graphic novels." Third, Original English Language (OEL) manga or "US manga" were works created by English speakers but were imitative of Japanese manga—in other words, they aimed to be drawn using JVL. Manga from Japan included four subtypes related to stereotypical readership demographics: shonen manga (boys), shojo manga (girls), seinen manga (men), and josei manga (women).

A second focus of the VLRC projects relates to questions about how comics may have changed over time, and if so, what influenced these changes? For example, as we will see in Chapter 8, mainstream American superhero comics have changed across numerous dimensions between the 1940s and the 2010s. Are these simply natural changes that occur in the development of Kirbyan AVL? Might these changes be related to alterations in formatting, such as altered physical sizes of comics or the shift from shorter to lengthier stories? Maybe there is an influence of manga given its growing presence in the United States since the 1980s?

Altogether, the VLRC consists of annotations of 361 stories from comic books and/or graphic novels from the United States, Asia, and Europe, amounting to analyses of 48,485 panels across 8,510 pages. In addition, it contains annotations of the complete run of the *Calvin and Hobbes* comic strip by Bill Watterson, totaling 14,712 panels across 3,151 strips. These totals are summarized in Table 2.1. Our data from the VLRC has been made openly available, and can be found online at visuallanguagelab.com/vlrc or via its DataverseNL repository (Cohn 2022).

Comics were incorporated in the VLRC through convenience sampling and/or chosen for study of specific comics (e.g., analysis of *Calvin and Hobbes*). Many comics came from generous donations from publishers, including Antarctic Press, Archie Comics, Dark Horse Comics, Drawn & Quarterly, Fantagraphics Books, First Second Books, Humanoids Inc, IDW Publishing, NBM Publishing, NetComics, Oni Press, Top Cow, Top Shelf, Udon Entertainment, Vertical Inc, and Viz Media. We asked for no specific works in donations, and attempted to select comics from these donations at random to reduce bias. We also relied on comics from public domain websites (www.comicbookplus.com) and/or purchased comics to fit specific sampling criteria, such as to have five comics per decade when analyzing comics across time in longitudinal analyses (of Mainstream American comics, and Dutch and Flemish comics). Comic books were analyzed in total if their page count fell within an approximate target length (twenty to thirty pages), but for works exceeding this length, researchers analyzed the first twenty-five pages or 120 panels (rounded to the nearest page), whichever came first.

TABLE 2.1 Analyzed comics within the Visual Language Research Corpus.

Country/Type	Years	# of stories	Total Pages	Total Panels	Panels/ Page
China	1946–2016	13	330	1,737	5.26
Japan (Josei)	2002–2015	10	224	1,089	4.85
Japan (Seinen)	1985–2014	10	202	1,019	5.03
Japan (Shojo)	1987–2010	22	749	3,717	4.96
Japan (Shonen)	2014–2014	41	1,897	9,819	5.17
Korea	2014–2014	15	316	1,325	4.19
Belgium/Flanders	2002–2013	40	633	6,097	9.63
France	1981–2014	25	543	3,809	7.02
Germany	1987–2007	19	285	1,525	5.35
Netherlands	1940–2016	41	819	5,876	7.17
Spain	2012	1	24	105	4.38
Sweden	1980–2011	23	249	1,532	6.15
USA (Indie)	2002–2014	12	407	1,611	3.96
USA (Mainstream)	1940–2014	72	1,440	7,384	5.13
USA (US Manga)	1991–2006	17	390	1,838	4.71
Total		**361**	**8,510**	**48,485**	**5.70**
Calvin and Hobbes					
Daily strips	1985–1995	2,702		10,339	3.83
Sunday strips	1985–1995	453		4,389	9.69
Total		**3,151**		**14,712**	**4.67**

As described above, the analysis of works in the VLRC originally came from disparate research projects and/or was supplemented by convenience sampling. As a result, a weakness of the VLRC is that there are inconsistent distributions of comics from different countries. We strove for having at least ten comics from each population or subtype. The lone exception to this was a single Spanish comic, which was the only one from this population available to us before data collection ceased. As this is only a single instance, I will exclude it from analyses throughout this book.

Annotations of comics were carried out by sixteen student researchers using spreadsheets, where each row represented a panel, and different columns represented our annotation fields. All students had previously passed courses on VLT (approximately thirty hours) and completed training and assessments of annotation methods before officially analyzing any of the books in the corpus. As 54 percent of the comics in the VLRC (199/362) were annotated independently by two researchers, I average across results from different annotators.

Finally, I'll note that throughout this book, I use several example comics to illustrate constructs and findings. Uncredited figures are all drawn by me. All other examples in figures come from comics directly analyzed within the VLRC (including *Far Arden*, from Chapter 1).

2.3 What can this tell us?

Before we progress to actual analyses of the data in the VLRC, it is important to address a few limitations in this data, and the interpretations that will be drawn from it. First, because the corpus was built from data in various subprojects, there are not always consistent annotations for all books. Not every comic has all the same structures analyzed, and varying numbers of books contribute to the different analyses. Because of this, I will try to point out the size and scope of the sample that I analyze in each analysis throughout the subsequent chapters.

Second, it is important to note that the views I offer here are limited by the scope of the corpus itself. The VLRC only analyzes comics from a handful of countries and the annotations across those comics are not uniform. Though I will often refer to comics from "Europe" or "Asia," I acknowledge outright that these designations here only include a small selection of countries from those regions, and a full accounting of characterizations of those regions (should it be possible) would need to include comics from far more places than is available here. Given this, although I do believe that the interpretations that I draw from this data are reliable, they should not be considered as exhaustive on the structures in comics from "around the world." The data can only tell us what the corpus has in it.

In this regard, further insight can only come from analyzing comics (and other media) from more places, and with even richer methods of analysis.

Such efforts are already underway in my own *TINTIN Project,*[5] which is progressing in its primary efforts from 2020 to 2025. We have designed software tools to facilitate annotations (Cardoso and Cohn 2022), and we are aiming to analyze a more diverse and inclusive corpus spanning the entire globe, rather than the dozen or so countries included in the VLRC. At the time of writing, we have accounted for comics from almost 100 countries in this TINTIN Corpus, and we are aiming for at least 1,000 annotated comics. Thus, the limitations that are present throughout the VLRC will hopefully be further addressed by this project and other future work, although the VLRC can lay a foundation for observations and analyses.

Finally, it is worth bearing in mind that the analyses here will largely be characterized in terms of the averages across numerous comics. This differs from the approach often taken in analysis of comics where scholars typically conduct qualitative analysis on the work of a single author, or make observations of exemplars. These examples are often chosen because they *deviate* from the recognized conventions and thus appear novel, creative, or innovative. However, by focusing on the exemplary or deviating cases, this leaves the character of these conventionalized norms to be taken for granted and without any grounding in analyses in their own right. The work here has the opposite aims, by seeking to establish these norms through quantitative analysis.

Given these different aims in research, some readers might balk at the idea of interpreting patterns at a larger scale, rather than exemplars. It is thus worth remembering that averages reflect the characteristics of the group, despite variation that might be found across the individual cases that comprise that data. For various analyses provided, readers may think of individual example cases that contrast this group characterization. This is inevitable since we would expect at least some variability across our sampled comics. However, by averaging across numerous books, we hope to separate the consistent patterns from the distinct outliers.

In most cases, I will present the data in figures that maintain a view of the different datapoints involved. This book will have a *lot* of figures of data, so now is a good time to illustrate this with an example. Figure 2.1a illustrates the rates of panels per page for each of the primary countries in the VLRC. Each background dot represents an individual comic, while the dark dot with crossbars represents the mean across those individual points. This mean is surrounded by error bars that represent the standard error, a measurement of the variability in the data surrounding that average. All graphs throughout this book will use error bars with standard error, unless specified otherwise.

As you can see, each country has comics with a range of average panels per page. Their variation is both visible in the size of the error bars, and in the spread of datapoints of comics: each dot represents a comic. Dutch (Netherlands) and Flemish (Belgium) comics both have a wide spread of variation, while Japanese manga have much less variation. Many countries

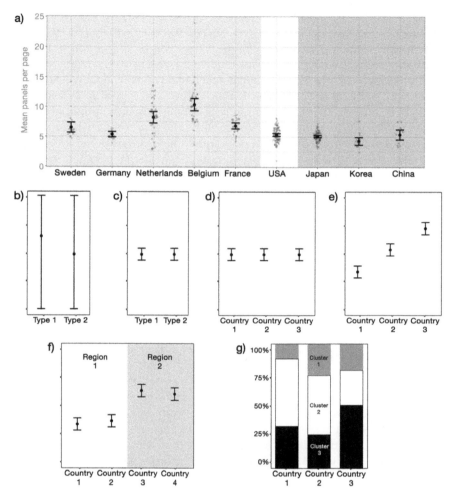

FIGURE 2.1 *Example data of a) panels per page in comics across the VLRC. Error bars represent standard error. Additional schematization is provided of different possible distributions of data, showing b) wide variability between works, c) consistency between works, d) no variation across countries, e) variation across countries, f) variation across regions containing countries, and g) clustering that cuts across countries.*

have visible outliers, with datapoints well above or below the cluster of datapoints surrounding the mean. Thus, averages do not imply uniformity or that individual cases may not deviate from the group. Rather, the average reflects the generalized character of this sample, despite variation from individual cases. Like in Figure 2.1a, I have intended the figures throughout this book to show this spread of variability.

Since most of this book will go through data analysis, we should first consider some general expectations related to what data might tell us. I schematize various possible outcomes in Figure 2.1b to g. First, if authors maintained their own individualistic tendencies with no overarching patterns or similarities to others, we might expect the range of data within each country to be fairly wide. This would look similar to Figure 2.1b, with long error bars and/or a big, scattered range of dots. In contrast, a tight grouping with little variation would show consistency and patterned structures, as in Figure 2.1c. This outcome would go against the idea that populations have no systematic tendencies, since various comics within that population would display similar properties.

We can extend this inference across countries. If we believed that there is a uniform "comics medium" that covers across all comics without differentiable stored structures, then we should expect similar patterns of data across countries. Such an outcome might be expected given the global and transnational reach of many comics. This is schematized in Figure 2.1d with narrow error bars, but a similar outcome could be predicted with longer error bars showing more variation across comics, as in Figure 2.1b.

Alternatively, if we believe that each country (and/or genre, or any population) has its own unique patterns, but which are not associated with others, then each group should have its own characteristic data distributions. In this case, each country would have distinct trends from each other. This is schematized in Figure 2.1e. However, if cross-linguistic patterns transcend individual countries as "visual languages," then we should expect similar patterns from distinguishable groups. For example, if the data between countries within a region (such as all European or all Asian comics) look similar despite boundaries of countries, but these regions differ from each other, then it may indicate broader cultural patterns. This is schematized in Figure 2.1f. Such patterns would reinforce the idea of visual languages being associated with broader cultures, since they would go beyond samples from a single location.

Another possibility is that classifications such as countries, continents, genres, and others might not be distinguishable in their trends, but consistent patterns do exist that cut across those designations. In this case, we might find that comics from different countries or regions all look similar in their basic patterns. Indeed, many comics creators work internationally across markets, and the distribution of many comics has a global reach. But, even if these "top-down" classifications might not reveal patterns, statistical techniques can reveal patterns from the "bottom-up" relationships in the data itself. Such patterns may cut across the cultural categories, such as countries, as in Figure 2.1g, or may tell us where authors from one country may in fact pattern more like those from another country. Such a finding would provide evidence for visual languages, but would inform us that they are not constrained to particular cultural boundaries.

Ultimately, all of these possibilities will be interrogated as we progress through our analyses of the data in the VLRC. To foreshadow a bit, most of these outcomes occur within the data in some form or another, and I will attempt to guide the reader through the implications of each analysis as best I can.

Along these lines, I will also note that I will largely refrain from reporting actual statistical tests for this data. This is done for a few reasons. First, I hope that the data I present here have distinguishable enough differences without needing inferential statistics to interpret the findings. I will thus only provide statistics in cases where they are necessary to support a proper interpretation. Second, many readers may not be familiar with what statistical analyses may tell them. Thus, including this technical information may hamper the reading experience or just seem like mathematical gibberish. So, when I do provide them, it's fine to just skip over them, as I'll explain what they indicate in the text as well. Lastly, statistics for at least some of these findings have been provided in previous publications, though I hope to go far beyond the analyses in those papers.

With this background in mind, let's now turn to the question at hand: What are the *patterns of comics*?

CHAPTER THREE

Morphology

We can examine differences between visual languages in aspects of their vocabularies. Certainly, the "styles" of comics might differ, such as the stereotypical way superhero comics from the United States are drawn compared to the stereotypical manga from Japan. These patterned aspects of drawing are part of the vocabularies of those visual languages. Even more apparent might be the distinctive visual signs that they use. For example, sleep or tiredness is depicted with a series of Zzzs in American comics, but manga use bubbles coming out of a nose. Without knowing these conventions, they might be difficult to construe in the intended way.

All of these graphic patterns—whether the elements of the graphic style or these visual signs—belong to the vocabulary of visual languages. To be specific, they are part of the *morphology* of visual languages. Morphology is the structure of these units, and no matter the modality, the term "morpheme" can be used to describe units of form-meaning pairs (Booij 2010, Jackendoff and Audring 2020). All languages, whether spoken, signed, or drawn, involve vocabularies of patterned units that encode a mapping of form to meaning. In speech, words are often considered a primary unit that specify a form (phonology) to meaning, while in visual languages these units are pictures and their components, which map a form (graphology) to meaning.

In older theories of structural linguistics in the early part of the twentieth century, much concern in morphology was placed on finding the "minimal" units that comprise a unit. This followed a general belief that linguistic structure could be reduced from larger to smaller levels: sentences are composed of words, which are composed of minimal units of morphemes, which themselves are made of minimal phonemes of sound. The idea was that if you found the minimal units, you could build up to understanding the larger structure. This focus on isolating "minimal" units was carried over to earlier structuralist accounts of graphic representations, including those of elements in comics (e.g. Gubern 1972, Hünig 1974, Koch 1971, Nöth 1990).

Nevertheless, contemporary views on morphology and the lexicon have largely rejected this focus on minimal units (Booij 2010, Jackendoff 2002,

Jackendoff and Audring 2016, Sadock 1991, Anderson 1992, Stump 2001), along with the idea that you can decompose all of language down to those minimal units. First off, structures of language are not decomposable to each other. The structure of sentences cannot be stripped down to the structures within words. Rather, different component structures of languages are independent and persist in parallel (Jackendoff 2002, Jackendoff and Audring 2020).

Instead of an importance placed on minimal units, there's an acknowledgement that language is built of stored patterns—i.e., lexical items—which are often networked in complex ways within a lexicon (Booij 2010, Jackendoff and Audring 2020). The lexicon includes elements at many levels of structure, whether morphemes smaller than words (*un-*, *-ness*), words (such as *cat* or *believable*), stock phrases (*mind your manners*), idioms (*spill the beans*, *bun in the oven*), constructions (<u>twist</u>*ing the* <u>night</u> *away*, <u>loung</u>*ing the* <u>day</u> *away*), or even just syntactic frames ($[_S$ NP-VP] = "a sentence consists of a noun phrase and a verb phrase"). In addition, languages across the world differ with the complexity of their "word" units, with some using only single morphemes per word, and others packing in as much information as might be in a sentence into single words (Haspelmath 2018).

In line with this, VLT also rejects this older focus on minimal units. Rather, it maintains the emphasis on the systematic patterns of form-meaning relationships in the graphic modality, regardless of size or internal complexity, as stored in the memory of drawers and comprehenders. Thus, I will use the term "morpheme" to describe units of meaningful visual representation (such as a heart shape), as well as more complex compositions of aggregate parts (such as whole faces, which themselves are built of eye, mouth, and nose morphemes), which may form perceptually salient meaningful units. These conventionalized morphemes can use various types of signification (Peirce 1931), be they iconic (faces), indexical (tails on word balloons), or symbolic (hearts).

Like spoken languages, the vocabularies of visual languages consist of two general classes (Cohn 2013c). ***Open-class items*** in a lexicon are productive, and new elements can easily be created. In visual languages, these representations are often iconic, i.e., they resemble their meaning (Peirce 1931), such as how the drawing of a face looks like a face. Iconic depictions are often open-class because an author can easily derive new patterns to draw things based on what they look like in perception. For example, open-class items often include the ways that authors draw characters' figures and body parts. Those elements are potentially variable in how they might appear, and new patterns can easily be created when necessary, such as when a character has an attribute for which the drawer has no established pattern.

Closed-class lexical items are harder to create, since they typically rely on conventionalized meanings that are unavailable without the knowledge of what they mean. In visual languages, these include elements such as motion lines to convey motion, hearts above the head or substituted for eyes to depict love or lust, or giant sweat-drops to mean anxiety. These morphemes require familiarity to be understood (Cohn and Foulsham 2022, Cohn and Maher 2015, Cohn, Murthy, and Foulsham 2016, Newton 1985, Nakazawa 1998, 2005a). Although we will discuss aspects of both types of morphology in this chapter, the primary focus is on closed-class items.[1]

3.1 Morphological structures

One similarity between visual and verbal morphology is the strategies they use to combine elements (Cohn 2013c, 2018a). A broad distinction holds between *free morphemes*, which can stand alone, and **bound morphemes**, which must connect to another "stem" morpheme. For example, the word *cat* is a free morpheme that can stand alone, but the plural -*s* must attach to a stem, as in the plural *cats*. In visual languages, most depictions of characters are free morphemes, since they stand alone just fine, but a speech balloon is a bound morpheme, since it has to connect to a speaker (the stem).

There are various ways that free and bound morphemes might connect. Morphemes may attach to each other (affixation), may replace other morphemes entirely or partially (suppletion), or might repeat morphemes (reduplication). These combinatorial strategies are *functionally similar* across modalities, even if the ways they manifest in spoken, signed, and graphic modalities might differ. For example, the comparison of affixation across modalities arises because they share a similar strategy of "attachment" in their combinatorial structure, whether or not those strategies share common cognitive mechanisms. Nevertheless, research has begun to show that visual morphology does indeed use comparable neurocognition as morphology in spoken or signed languages (Cohn and Foulsham 2022, Cohn and Maher 2015).

3.1.1 Affixation

Affixation may be the most prevalent way that visual morphemes combine, where one morpheme—the affix—*attaches* to another more dominant morpheme—the stem (Cohn 2013c, Engelhardt 2002). Consider the *carriers* that hold text, which are stereotypically thought of as speech balloons, thought bubbles, captions, and sound effects (Cohn 2013c, a, Forceville, Veale, and Feyaerts 2010a). In the case of a speech balloon, the balloon itself is an affix, which attaches to the stem of the speaker (Figure 3.1a). This affix cannot stand alone, and it would be unusual to have a speech balloon floating without a speaker (unless the speaker is inferred to exist off-panel).

However, the stem can exist without the affix: a person can be shown without speech balloons just fine.

Affixation in spoken languages is often recognizable for the position that affixes might take. *Pre*fixes appear before a stem (*un*usual), suffixes appear after a stem (shrink*able*), infixes appear inside a stem (abso-*frickin'*-lutely), and circumfixes appear around a stem (*en*light*en*). These positions are all constrained for words by their presentation in sound, which appears in a linear, temporal progression. Visual representations do not have this linear constraint, and so *visual* affixes can go in many different places relative to their stems.

Some visual affixes may remain fairly unconstrained, such as carriers like speech balloons, which can be placed in almost any position relative to their stems (speakers). Other affixes are more constrained. In JVL, a stylized vein has been used to show anger (in Figure 3.1c). Although it likely originated on characters' foreheads, it can now appear almost anywhere, including within speech balloons (Shinohara and Matsunaka 2009). Motion lines are a type of suffix, as they are the lines that trail a moving object to show its path (Figure 3.1a), and when moved in front of an object are rendered incongruous (Cohn and Maher 2015, Ito, Seno, and Yamanaka 2010). But, whether the motion line is to the left, right, top, or bottom of a moving object doesn't matter, only as long as the motion line remains on the opposite side of the object's direction of motion.

Many affixes appear relative to character's heads. A class of affixes go "up" above characters' heads (Cohn 2013c, Forceville 2011a) and thus have been named *upfixes*, including things such as hearts, gears, stars, or hamster wheels (Figure 3.1b). When these are moved to positions other than above a head, their meaning becomes harder to construe (Cohn, Murthy, and Foulsham 2016). Upfixes have been shown in experiments to be constrained by both their position and by the emotion of the face they combine with, and these constraints generalize to novel upfixes (Cohn and Foulsham 2022, Cohn, Murthy, and Foulsham 2016). This has supported that upfixes are not merely individual patterned instances, but constitute a broader class of affixes.

Affixes are associated with many other body parts, like those in Figure 3.1c. Affixes are placed on characters' foreheads, such as the JVL conventions for a single huge sweat-drop to depict anxiety, or vertical shadows on the head to show gloom. Noses are also prominent in JVL, where bloody noses depict lust, a bubble from the nose signals sleep, and steam may emit from a nose like a burst of smoke. Mouths use more iconic drool, a "breath mushroom" looking like a puff of smoke appears next to the mouth as a sign of relief, and fire might emerge from the mouth to show anger. It is unclear whether these affixes are constrained to individual cases that happen to maintain similar placement, or whether they might create other classes of affixes related to different body parts (Foreheadfixes? Nosefixes?). Many other affixes are described in Cohn and Ehly (2016).

MORPHOLOGY

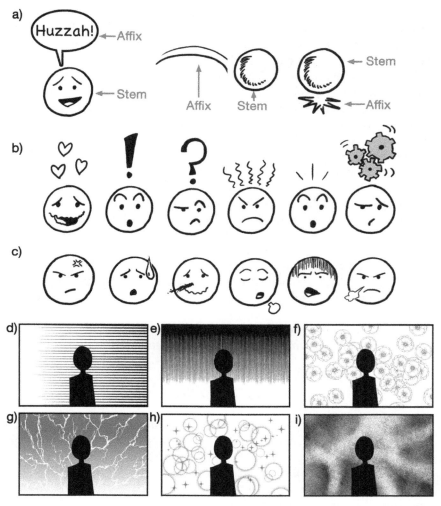

FIGURE 3.1 *Various visual affixes a) highlighting their stems and affixes, b) upfixes that float above character's heads, c) various affixes from the JVL used in manga, and example backfixes showing both d) motion and e) to i) emotion.*

3.1.2 Backfixes

An additional type of affix makes use of the properties of a visual scene, rather than just attaching elements to an individual character or object. In this case, whole backgrounds of a scene might change to show an emotion. We have begun referring to these as ***backfixes***. Many backfixes are used in manga in patterned ways to convey characters' emotional states (Shinohara and Matsunaka 2009, Sakurai et al. 2011, Brenner 2007), but backfixes showing only lines might indicate motion, as in Figure 3.1d (Ito, Seno, and Yamanaka 2010). Like many visual morphemes, several backfixes require experience with the visual language used in manga in order to be understood (Nakazawa 2005b, Kikuchi, Yoshida, and Yagi 2005, Murata 1994).

Various backfixes convey emotion. Simple backfixes might color the background entirely black, make the entire representation (including the characters) shaded in gray, or leave only the primary character shaded gray, with often a white or omitted background. Other backfixes extend morphemes, which could also apply to character's bodies, such as hearts to convey love or vertical lines to convey gloom or anxiety (Figure 3.1e). Other emotional backfixes depict fuzzy circles, sparkles, or wavy lines (Figure 3.1h).

Another class of backfixes show aspects of nature or weather, such as flower petals to represent joy or love (Figure 3.1f), and fire, lightning, or fog (Figure 3.1g) to represent anger (Shinohara and Matsunaka 2009). These backgrounds do not depict nature or weather in an iconic way where the weather actually exists. In this case, flowers do not actually appear in the scene (Figure 3.1f), nor might there be an actual storm (Figure 3.1g). Rather, these backgrounds invoke a metaphorical frame connecting emotions to metaphors that surround a person (Shinohara and Matsunaka 2009). A backfix of a "storm" is thus interpreted as "stormy" or "turbulent" emotions, not as a physical phenomenon in the world of the image.

3.1.3 *Suppletion*

Another common morphological strategy is that of *suppletion*, which is where one morpheme replaces another. In full suppletion, whole units might be replaced (ex. *go* becomes *went* in past tense, replacing the whole word), while in *partial suppletion* only parts of units might be replaced (ex. *teach* becomes *taught* in past tense, retaining the onset "t"). A form of internal replacement occurs through *umlaut* (ex. *sing* becomes *sang* in past tense, changing only the internal vowel).

Conventionalized suppletions include things such as fight clouds (Figure 3.2a), which replace characters fighting for a cloud with their limbs and other elements sticking out. The lines of characters might also be replaced, such as for dashed lines to show invisibility (Figure 3.2b), or wavey lines to show fear or worry.

A fairly large suppletion is recognizable in JVL of "superdeformation," where a character suddenly converts to a chibi style (*chibi* often is used to mean "short/small person/child")—an extremely cartoony and cute style indicating a state of overwhelming emotion (Figure 3.2c). Superdeformation can occur to whole bodies or just to parts of bodies, such as the face. Less common is where a character will turn into paper and flutter away at times of embarrassment or deflating emotion. Similarly, a character might melt from embarrassment. Another suppletion from JVL is when characters may take the shape and representation of Edvard Munch's famous painting *The Scream* when they are surprised (Figure 3.2d).

A class of suppletions seems to substitute various morphemes for the eyes of characters, which I have called **eye-umlauts** because they are an internal replacement for eyes (Cohn 2013c). As in Figure 3.2e, eye-umlauts include the replacement of eyes for hearts, stars, swirls, dollar signs, or other items to convey additional meaning beyond iconic eyes. However, various iconic "eye schemas" might also provide specific variations to convey meaning, whether they are considered as suppletions or not. These include wide eyes, narrow eyes, etc. along with drawn circles, black dots, bubble eyes, glowing eyes (surrounded by shading the upper head), and replacement of eyes for the shape: ><. Eyes can also be left empty, erased, or "pop" out of the head, or pupils can be shrunken or omitted from an iris.

We might also consider enlargements or shrinkage of body parts as a type of suppletion. For example, mouths might grow to enormous sizes when showing a character is shocked, or ears might grow larger to show someone is listening to something far away. In JVL, the "giant yelling head" enlarges a head to an enormous size when angry—with or without a smaller body—to yell at a person (sometimes with a megaphone). By increasing in size so much, this manipulation invokes the metaphor that anger becomes so

FIGURE 3.2 *Examples of visual suppletion (a–e) and reduplication (f–g). These include a) a fight cloud, b) invisibility lines, c) chibi deformation, d) Munch's* Scream *suppletion, e) eye-umlauts, f) polymorphism, and g) offset reduplication.*

pressurized that it expands the "container" of the head (Lakoff 1993), a frequently used metaphor in visual morphology across cultures' comics (Forceville 2005, Shinohara and Matsunaka 2009). Enlargements only can somewhat be considered suppletions, since they are not "replacements," so much as manipulations of morphemes to create *hyperbole*. This may be analogous to manipulating the internal sound structure of words to convey meaning, such as extending the vowel in *loooooong* to emphasize length (Clark 1996).

3.1.4 Reduplication

An additional type of morphological strategy repeats morphemes. This is called reduplication, and occurs when repeating words to create contrast, such as saying *salad-salad* to mean a leafy green meal instead of potato salad or fruit salad (Jackendoff 2010). In the visual form, both whole objects can be repeated or just their parts. When characters move, we might see several figures in different postures repeated in a single panel, which we've called *polymorphism* (i.e., "multiple forms"). A partial polymorphism occurs when body parts alone are repeated, such as a body with multiple arms to show that it is waving (not that it actually has multiple arms), as in Figure 3.2f. Figures can also be repeated, and often with overlapping offset lines, to show shaking (Figure 3.2g). This same representation might be used to show a character's double vision, such as if they were drunk.

3.2 Morphology within and across cultures

Visual morphology is perhaps the clearest case where we would expect to find cross-cultural variation. Many scholars readily acknowledge that visual morphology provides a good comparison to language, though they might deny that linguistic structures persist in more subtle ways across the whole system (Davies 2019, Forceville 2020). Recognition of this variability is in line with spoken languages, as morphology is the most "language-specific" and "least generalizable" (Baerman and Corbett 2007) structure of language, making variation between systems easier to see than in their grammars or semantics.

In the VLRC, we analyzed visual morphology in just two studies, each of which targeted specific cultural comparisons. The first study analyzed twenty Japanese manga to compare differences in the morphology used by shonen (boys') and shojo (girls') manga, with ten books coming from each demographic (Cohn and Ehly 2016). This analysis looked at seventy-three different visual morphemes.[2] A subsequent study then compared the morphology in fifty Dutch and forty Flemish comics spanning the 1940s to 2010s, expanding the previous list to 155 visual morphemes (van Middelaar

2017). In these analyses, panels were annotated for how many of the analyzed morphemes they contained. Here I report means calculated as the total number of a given morpheme per book, divided out of the total number of morphemes per book.

Let's first compare the seventy-three morphemes from manga that were investigated in both of these studies. Of these morphemes, only 22 percent (sixteen out of seventy-three) appeared in both Japanese and either Dutch or Flemish comics. Since only this small number of morphemes overlapped across these cultures' comics, this is a first indication that their visual languages use fairly distinctive morphology. In many cases, only one instance of a morpheme appeared across all the Dutch and Flemish comics. If we exclude these single-instance cases, we get the nine morphemes in Figure 3.3.

In almost all cases, these morphemes appeared more prevalently in Japanese manga than in Dutch or Flemish comics. Only polymorphism for shaking was more prevalent in both types of European comics, while spike upfixes and impact stars were more prevalent in Flemish books than Japanese or Dutch books. The overall greater frequency of these morphemes in manga might not be surprising, given that these fields were originally developed for analysis of Japanese manga. However, most of these overlapping morphemes are fairly well-described in generalized discussions of the lexical items of comics (Forceville 2005, 2011b, Walker 1980, Cohn 2013c). More than half of this list are upfixes (heat lines, spikes, !, ?, and hearts), along with impact stars, zoom lines, shading of people, and reduplication to show shaking. The inference is that, of those we have studied, these morphemes are the ones that have achieved the most saturation across cultures to the point that these are often pulled out as general exemplars of visual morphology (often along with speech balloons, thought bubbles, and motion lines, which are all discussed in their own subsequent sections).

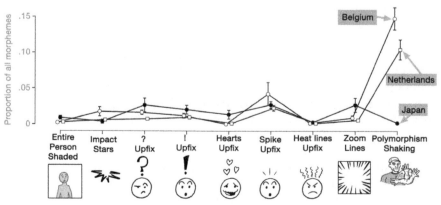

FIGURE 3.3 *Visual morphemes appearing in both Japanese and European comics.*

Our next sections will compare groups within our populations of Japanese and Dutch/Flemish comics. These analyses attempt to address questions related to visual language varieties. Specifically, can we find evidence of consistency or variation across sub-groups? In the case of Japanese manga, this relates to whether shonen or shojo manga demarcate varieties within a larger JVL. The inverse relationship is asked about Dutch and Flemish comics. Given the similarities between the spoken languages from two neighboring countries—Flemish spoken in Belgium is only slightly different from Dutch spoken in the Netherlands—might their visual morphology be similar or different?

3.2.1 Shonen versus Shojo

Our first corpus study of visual morphology asked about potential variation between manga aimed at different demographics, specifically shonen (boys) and shojo (girls) manga. We asked, might different types of manga from Japan sponsor contexts for distinct varieties of a broader JVL? In previous work, I had hypothesized that a generalized JVL persisted across authors of manga, but which had varieties ("dialects") based on these types of demographics (Cohn 2010a, 2013c). This idea came because visual languages used in comics are often print cultures unrestricted by geographical boundaries that would separate populations of "speakers." Without such physical borders, varieties may instead be demarcated by genres, since they may divide groups of people who interact with these different works. Although I report on a comparison of shonen and shojo manga here, I will provide analyses of these and other demographics of manga in later chapters.

Although genre intersects with it, distinctions between manga are often defined by the demographics of a so-called intended audience. Primary demographics include shonen, shojo, seinen, and josei, which are ostensibly marketed to boys, girls, young men, and women, respectively. Despite this categorization of intended audiences, shonen remains the predominant genre read by everyone, and is the stereotypical and best-selling genre of manga both within and outside of Japan (Allen and Ingulsrud 2005). In contrast, shojo manga have a more select readership. In general, shonen are thought to have themes around adventures, fantasy and sci-fi worlds, sports, samurai/ninja, and others involving physical conflict, while shojo manga have themes of romance, daily life, and school, but also possibly adventures, but primarily relating to characters' emotional psychological states (Brenner 2007, Gravett 2004, Schodt 1983, Drummond-Mathews 2010, Prough 2010).

The stereotypical shonen manga style is often attributed to the "God of manga," Osamu Tezuka. Although he is frequently credited with starting the shojo genre as well (Schodt 1983, 1996), this style has origins in other authors from the 1950s, such as Makoto Takahashi, and to earlier magazine

MORPHOLOGY

illustrators, such as Jun'ichi Nakahara from the 1930s (Takahashi 2008). The influence of these artists contributed to the stereotypical shojo style of more rounded shapes and soft lines, as well as "oversized" eyes—particularly with stars/sparkles—along with floral backgrounds to reinforce the emotions of a scene (Takahashi 2008, Prough 2010). These stereotypical shojo elements contrast with the more angular shonen manga, which have been claimed to use morphology to reinforce action, such as motion lines and zoom lines (Brenner 2007, Schodt 1983, Takahashi 2008).

It is also worth mentioning that, despite these trends in readership and style, rigid borders do not separate shojo and shonen manga. Many authors of shonen manga have also created shojo manga (such as Osamu Tezuka), and various manga tread the line between demographics. In these cases, authors may either maintain their same idiolects regardless of the genres, or they might alter their styles to adapt to the expectations of a given genre's structure. In addition, not all authors of manga draw using JVL, such as if an author drew more in the Kirbyan AVL characteristic of American superhero comics, but was published in Japan. Thus, it is worth remembering that "JVL" is not the same as "manga," and if varieties of JVL may be associated with genres of manga, they may not be exclusive to them.

In line with this, the subsequent analyses are not necessarily attempting to describe the characteristics of shonen or shojo *manga*—i.e., the actual publishing categories—but rather to describe the system(s) used in works that are bound by those common labels. This analysis and those throughout this book are also not a deterministic attempt at claiming uniformity across all creators and readers of manga. Rather, it is an exploration of the features of their shared visual languages, directly analogous to descriptions of linguistic systems. No analysis of spoken Japanese or English (or their varieties) would encapsulate all the unique patterns found in the idiolects of *every speaker*, but it could help characterize the patterns across a population, including their patterned diversity (i.e., in "varieties").

Given these differences between shonen and shojo manga, we predicted that a comparison of their structures might provide evidence for differences in varieties of an overarching JVL. Before jumping into the analysis, it's again worth revisiting what I mean by a language "variety," which has become a replacement for the term "dialect." I use *varieties* to refer to systems that share an overarching similar structure (such as part of a generalized, but abstract, JVL), while retaining distinctive distinguishing patterns. This would be analogous to how Kanto Japanese (spoken in areas surrounding Tokyo) and Kansai Japanese (spoken in areas surrounding Osaka) are varieties of the generalized "Japanese spoken language." These varieties maintain many similar dimensions of structure in ways that are mutually intelligible for speakers, though differences persist across many structures (pronunciation, vocabulary, syntax, etc.).

It should be stressed that varieties are no different in their cognitive status from "languages," and all reflect the same degree of patterned structures in the minds of their speakers. Despite this, socio-cultural status may be assigned differently to various varieties. For example, Kanto Japanese is typically thought of as more reflecting "standard" Japanese than other varieties, although all varieties are equal in their cognitive status as linguistic systems. A recognition of one variety as the "standard" is a socio-political designation, not a linguistic one.

These notions would thus carry over to visual languages. Here, we may find that a "Shonen JVL" differs across certain dimensions of structure from a "Shojo JVL," while both share in a broader, generalized JVL. Such varieties would maintain the same status as cognitive phenomena, although they may carry different socio-cultural status. For example, given its breadth in distribution and readership, the JVL used in shonen manga may be perceived as more stereotypical of a JVL as a whole, thus being marked as "standard" in a similar fashion to certain spoken varieties. Like in spoken languages, such a designation as standard would be more socio-political than linguistic.

Our primary question for this section then is to what degree morphology annotated in shonen and shojo manga might be similar (belonging to part of a shared JVL), and to what degree might they be different (signaling their own distinctive varieties). Although we only analyze morphology in this chapter, these same questions will persist across further chapters analyzing other subtypes of Japanese manga. The combination of these analyses can hopefully better inform these questions about varieties than each individual analysis alone.

Because JVL as a visual language should extend across varieties, similar visual morphology should appear in both shonen and shojo manga. However, certain morphemes may differ in proportions between genres or be unique to one genre or another. These cases would support distinct varieties, analogous to how vocabulary might vary between varieties of spoken and signed languages, despite their overarching similarities.

Across all the manga that we analyzed, 63 percent of panels contained visual morphemes (3,191 of 5,007 panels), with an overall average rate of 1.49 morphemes per panel. This rate did not differ between shonen (mean: 1.48, standard deviation: .19) and shojo manga (mean: 1.46, standard deviation: .19).

Although we analyzed the possibility of seventy-three different JVL morphemes, only sixty-one of them appeared in the books in the sample. Across books, 84 percent of morphemes (fifty-one out of sixty-one) appeared in both shonen and shojo manga. Only ten morphemes were found in a single genre, and several of these were only found in a single book. These findings overall tell us that, although visual lexicons might be large, lexical items might not all appear at frequent rates. Second, these genres of manga mostly share the same morphemes, suggesting an overall shared visual lexicon.

The most frequent morphemes across all books are depicted in Figure 3.4a. These included superdeformation to a chibi style, zoom lines, and exclamation mark upfixes, which averaged around a rate of 10 percent of

MORPHOLOGY

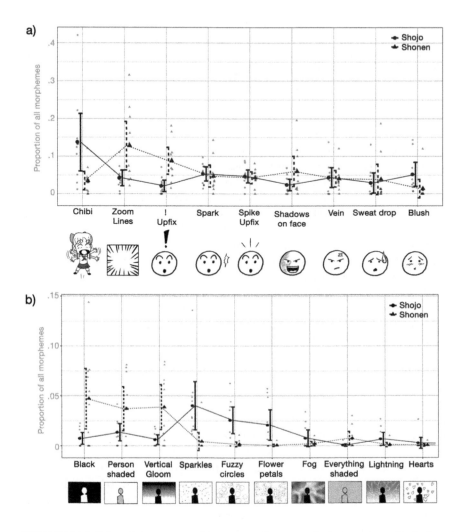

FIGURE 3.4 *Morphemes appearing across shonen and shojo manga, both for a) the most frequently used and b) for backfixes.*

total morphemes in a comic. After this, other morphemes fell around 5 percent, including spiked upfixes, scopic sparks floating next to character's eyes, shadows on character's faces, veins, gigantic sweat drops, and blush on the cheeks. In most cases, the proportion of these morphemes remained equal in both shojo and shonen manga, and indeed many of these morphemes are characteristic of the visual lexicon of JVL as a whole. However, certain morphemes are distinctly more common in shojo manga (chibi superdeformation, blush) or shonen manga (zoom lines, exclamation mark upfixes).

Shonen and shojo manga also differed in their expressive backgrounds—their backfixes. As in Figure 3.4b, shojo manga use more sparkles, fuzzy circles, flower petals, and to a lesser degree, lightning. Aside from lightning, which expresses anger, these all express fairly positive emotional states (Shinohara and Matsunaka 2009). In contrast, shonen manga use backgrounds that are all black, have vertical lines indicating gloom, or shade everything, including the entire person. These primarily suggest shock or some sort of ominous emotion.

These differences across morphemes further suggest that shonen and shojo manga have characteristic morphemes that they use in greater frequency. Indeed, these distinctive morphemes often define the stereotypes of those genres. The emotional backfixes of flowers, sparkles, or fuzzy circles are all associated with the shojo manga aesthetic (Takahashi 2008, Prough 2010), as are the superdeformed chibi style and blush/flush on characters' cheeks. These morphemes conveyed meanings of embarrassment (blush), overwhelming emotion (chibi), and joy (sparkles, flower petals). In contrast, the morphemes from shonen manga were related to emotions of moodiness (gloom lines, shadow on face, black backgrounds), anger (pointed teeth, giant yelling head), and action (zoom lines). Thus, the differences in morphemes in these books also express the stereotyped emotional themes of those genres.

Indeed, to further confirm whether these genres differed from each other, I used a statistical technique called a k-means (neighborhood-based) clustering analysis. This analysis examines the data without consideration of their origins, and then creates "clusters" out of similarities within the data. So, if there is only a single JVL, we might expect it to create just one cluster, or for books from shonen and shojo manga to be distributed in an inconsistent way across clusters. However, if these genres form distinctive groups, clusters should uniformly divide between shojo and shonen manga.

This latter option is what occurred. I put all of the data for the sixty-one morphemes across twenty books that we analyzed into the clustering analysis, and it indicated that there were two optimal clusters that could be derived from this data. The first cluster contained eleven comics, which included all of the shojo manga plus one shonen manga (specifically, *Rosario+Vampire II*). The second cluster contained nine comics, all of which were shonen manga. Statistical analysis showed that these clusters differed from each other between genres, suggesting that they were indeed distinctive groupings ($\chi^2 = 16.3$, p < .001).

Overall, these comparisons of specific morphemes, along with this clustering analysis, imply that the differing proportions of morphemes across genres index distinct varieties. Nevertheless, it is noteworthy that both genres used substantial proportions of nearly all of these morphemes. This suggests that, although shonen and shojo manga have distinguishing properties, their differences are less about specific *types* of morphemes, and more about the proportional use of different morphemes within a broader abstract JVL.

3.2.2 *Dutch versus Flemish Morphology*

The previous study about Japanese manga contrasted structures used in manga with different target demographics to explore the degree to which these systems may belong to a larger visual language and/or constitute distinctive varieties. In a follow-up study, students of mine then sought to explore an inverse question: might there be similarities or differences in comics created in different countries, but which largely share a common spoken language? Do those different countries share a single visual language, maintain separate visual languages, or might the countries create boundaries of varieties within a shared system? This was explored in a thesis by Lincy van Middelaar (2017), along with annotations by Mark Dierick, which compared the morphology used in Dutch and Flemish comics.

The spoken languages of Dutch and Flemish are largely considered varieties of a common language, with each sometimes referred to as Netherlandic Dutch and Flemish Dutch (Brems 2018, Meesters 2012), as they are spoken in adjacent countries of the Netherlands and northern Belgium respectively (also known as Flanders). Their relationship could be comparable to the differences between British English and American English, as varieties that share a wider structure. This is the same sort of relationship argued for varieties of JVL in manga described above, and given this relationship, it creates questions about the degree to which Dutch and Flemish comics may share or deviate in their structures.

Comics in the Netherlands and Flemish Belgium both have traditions dating back more than a century, although their contemporary comics industries blossomed after the Second World War. Belgium is a multilingual country, resulting in comics created in both Flemish (mostly in the north) and French (mostly in the south). Earlier Flemish comics creators often catered to Flemish readership, as opposed to the French Belgian authors who directed their works to the French market (Lefèvre 2012). Despite this, Belgian comics of both types were often exported to other European countries, including the Netherlands (Vries 2012). Indeed, comics from the Netherlands began as a strong national industry, but grew to have a much higher prevalence of imported comics (Vries 2012). In the case of Flemish comics, despite the similarities in the spoken languages, comics were often translated between Flemish and Dutch (Brems 2018, Meesters 2012). This shared history might lead us to believe that Dutch and Flemish comics largely use common structures, which could constitute a uniform visual language.

This analysis compared the morphemes in forty Flemish comics and fifty Dutch comics. These works were published across a span of eighty years, with at least five chosen to represent each decade, which allowed for analyses of whether the use of certain morphemes changed over time.

We identified 155 morphemes to be investigated, which included the seventy-three from the study of Japanese manga. However, from this broader inventory, only sixty-three morphemes were found in at least one book that we analyzed. Out of these, 78 percent (forty-nine out of sixty-three) appeared in both Dutch and Flemish comics, leaving only fourteen morphemes that were found in comics of only one country. However, eleven morphemes appeared only in a single comic each. If we exclude these, the rate of overlap between Dutch and Flemish comics rises to 94 percent (forty-nine out of fifty-two). Thus, overall, we again see a broad sharing of morphemes between these populations.

The most frequent morphemes across all comics are shown in Figure 3.5. The most frequent morphemes overall had to do with the depiction of motion, with either straight motion lines or circumfixing motion lines, which all had a proportion of near or more than 10 percent of all total morphemes. Other prevalent, but less frequent motion-related morphemes, were swirling motion lines, and clouds left behind to show movement. We

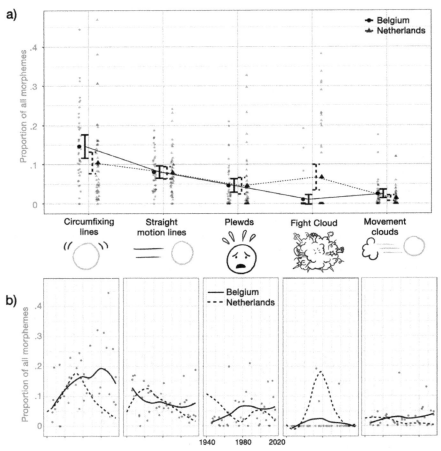

FIGURE 3.5 *Morphemes that were a) most frequently used in Dutch and Flemish comics and b) how these morphemes shift in usage over time.*

will return to discussing motion events later in this chapter. The next most frequent were leaping sweat drops, also called plewds (Walker 1980), and fight clouds, which each constituted near 5 percent of morphemes. Out of these morphemes, circumfixing lines appeared only slightly more in Flemish comics than Dutch comics, while fight clouds were much more prevalent in Dutch than Flemish comics. All other morphemes appeared at the same rates.

Because we recorded this data for comics that spanned from the 1940s through to the 2010s, we can also look at how these morphemes have changed in their frequency over time. Figure 3.5b graphs these morphemes across the publication dates of their comics. Here, we can see, for example, circumfixing lines, fight clouds, and straight motion lines all peaked in their usage in Dutch comics near or before the 1980s. In contrast, many of the morphemes appear to have increased slightly over time in Flemish comics.

If we look across all sixty-three morphemes that appeared across books, only eight differed statistically between Dutch and Flemish comics, and other than circumfixing lines and fight clouds (as in Figure 3.5a), most of these appeared near or less than 1 percent of morphemes (Figure 3.6a). In other words, although they differed from each other, they remain fairly infrequent. These morphemes that differed across countries include radial lines and stars showing pain, impact stars, and upfixes with exclamation marks, skull and crossbones, and swirls and stars.

On the whole, more of these morphemes appeared in Flemish comics than Dutch comics. However, analysis of these morphemes over time adds some nuance. As depicted in Figure 3.6b, many of these morphemes only differed in older comics, where Flemish comics used them in greater prevalence than Dutch comics. In later years, these differences declined and the populations look more similar.

Finally, I carried out the same clustering analysis on Dutch and Flemish comics as I did with the Japanese manga. This analysis again revealed two primary clusters, but with much more overlap between groups. The first cluster consisted of seventeen comics (seven Dutch, ten Flemish), while the second cluster consisted of seventy-three comics (forty-three Dutch, thirty Flemish). This intermixing of countries suggests that fewer distinct groupings were formed by comics of these countries, and indeed this distribution of clusters and countries did not differ statistically (χ^2 = 1.7, p = .185). Altogether, these results suggest that Dutch and Flemish comics largely share an overarching visual lexicon without distinct varieties demarcated by national borders.

3.3 Carriers

In the previous analyses, we compared books from within cultures to explore how visual languages may or may not display varieties. Let's now compare

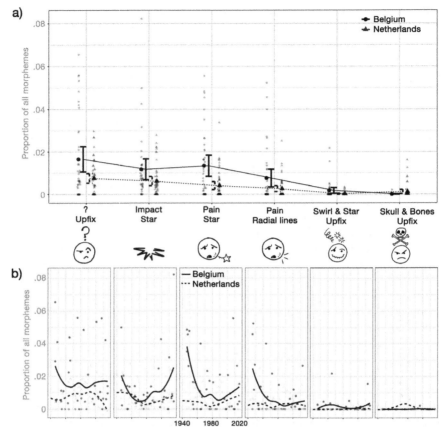

FIGURE 3.6 *Morphemes in Dutch and Flemish comics that a) significantly differed from each other, and b) changed over time.*

morphology across comics from different regions by focusing on some of the most recognizable aspects of visual morphology: the elements which carry text. These are stereotypically described as speech balloons, thought bubbles, sound effects, and captions. However, across all of these we can abstract a generalized structure where there is some *carrier* of text (the content) that connects to a *root* through a *tail*. As depicted in Figure 3.7a, in the case of a speech balloon, the balloon is the carrier, the speaker is the root, and the line or pointy part coming off the balloon is the tail. All carriers are thus affixes to their roots.

This three-part structure of carrier-tail-root persists even when some parts are not depicted overtly. For example, as depicted in Figure 3.7c, it is possible to omit the carrier or omit the tail, and yet this three-part structure is still understood. A root could even be omitted, such as when a panel is all black and the characters are in the dark, or when a speech balloon tail points off-panel to indicate that someone out of view is speaking. In these cases, we understand that a root is still there, it is just left unseen. Thus, the structural properties of this affixation persists even when some parts of it may not be depicted overtly.

Within the VLRC, our data about carriers is a little inconsistent across cultures. However, we have basic carrier data from eight countries within our corpus, although there were varying amounts of books analyzed from each country (266 comics analyzed in total, ten to forty from each country). Figure 3.7b depicts the total number of carriers per panel, no matter which type of carrier they used (discussed below).

Comics from the United States used more carriers than any other country, with an average of roughly 1.8 carriers per panel. This sample of comics

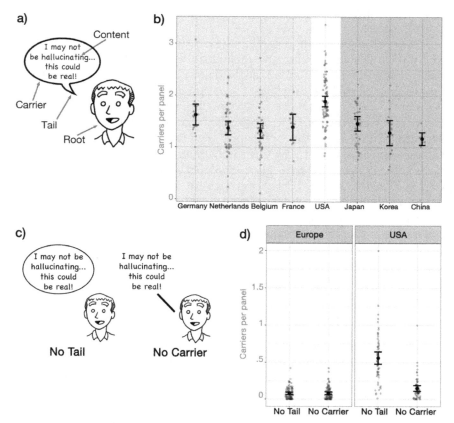

FIGURE 3.7 *a) The three-part structure of carriers, tails, and roots. b) The average amount of carriers per panel appearing in different comics. c) Modulation of the carrier-tail-root structure to lack showing either a tail or carrier, and d) the proportion of these modifications in comics from Europe and the United States.*

from the United States actually spanned across eighty years, from the 1940s to the 2010s, as did comics from the Netherlands and Flanders. Here we generalize across these different dates, but we will discuss the change over time for carriers in these American and European comics in Chapter 8. German comics used the next most carriers, around 1.6 per panel. Other countries all hovered at, or just below, 1.5 carriers per panel, including comics from France, the Netherlands, Flanders, and Korea. Finally, Chinese manhua used the least, around 1.1 carriers per panel.

Just to offer some detail, the book with the most carriers in our corpus was *Wonder Woman* #289 by Roy Thomas and Gene Colan (DC Comics, 1982), with a rate of 3.3 carriers per panel. In contrast, the American book with the least was in a US Manga, *Twilight X* #2 by Joseph Wight (Antarctic Press, originally published in 1991), with a rate of only 0.83 carriers per panel. However, the least carriers in any comic in the corpus actually came from a Flemish book (Belgium), the comic *Otto* #2 by Frodo De Decker (Het Syndikaat, 2013), with only .11 carriers per panel—practically a "silent" comic.

It is worth pointing out here that no general trend of global region seems to persist in this data. Although Korean manhwa and Chinese manhua used the least carriers, Japanese used the third most of all countries, suggesting no uniformity across Asia. Similarly, European comics used carriers from 1.6 per panel (Germany) to the fairly low 1.3 per panel (Netherlands and Flanders). Nevertheless, it is noticeable that most all the averages fell between 1 and 2 carriers per panel, reinforcing the prevalence of text throughout comics, which are ultimately multimodal documents.

In some comics, we have also annotated whether tails or carriers are overtly depicted. Figure 3.7d shows the rate that carriers and tails are not drawn in comics from the United States and Europe, specifically from the Netherlands and Flanders. In these European comics, the lack of drawing carriers and tails occurs infrequently, at a rate of only .1 per panel. American comics use omitted carriers at only slightly higher rates, but they more often show an omitted tail, at a rate of .5 per panel. This suggests that it is more common for tails to be omitted than carriers, where the indexical connection to roots would need to be inferred more.

As described above, carriers are stereotypically thought of as speech balloons, thought bubbles, sound effects, and captions. These constructs are often based on their physical features (a round circle, a cloud-shaped carrier, a box shape, etc.) or what they presumably mean (speech, thought, sounds, exposition). However, these surface features are sometimes not helpful for determining the meaning of carriers.

For example, stereotypical speech balloons (which use rounded circles with pointy tails) do not always show speech, and also appear to depict characters' thoughts or emotions when they solely contain exclamation marks (!) or question marks (?). These are effectively upfixes, just with an extra carrier that contributes little meaning of its own. Upfixes can also use thought bubbles in this same way. Speech can also be shown with a variety of representations that only slightly modify this core meaning—jagged lines for loudness, dashed lines for whispering, etc.—but all are recognized in an abstracted way as speech (Forceville, Veale, and Feyaerts 2010b). Conversely, the boxes that are often used for narration or labels might also be used to depict a character's thoughts, instead of using the cloud-shaped thought bubbles. Finally, the depiction of words used as sound effects are not always onomatopoetic sounds (such as *Pow!*)—sometimes a similar depiction and context might occur for descriptive labels (such as *Leap!,* as in the *Far Arden* example from Figure 1.1), and in manga a range of words for other states appear in these contexts (Pratha, Avunjian, and Cohn 2016). All of these phenomena suggest that the surface visual features of carriers are not necessarily motivating their meaning in transparent ways.

VLT classifies types of carriers based on two semantic features, rather than surface meanings such as "speech" or "thoughts" (Cohn 2013a). These semantic features revolve around which characters in the scene have access to the contents of carriers, a property we call "awareness." If the root of a carrier has access to the contents of the carrier, it is called **Root Awareness**, while if other non-root "adjacent" entities in a scene know what is in the carrier, it is called **Adjacent Awareness**. With these two dimensions, we can derive four types of carriers depending on whether roots or adjacent entities have awareness of the contents of the carriers, as outlined in Figure 3.8a.

First, consider a carrier where the root knows the content, but so does everyone else in the scene. This is a **Public** carrier, as everyone is aware of its contents. This is the typical status of a speech balloon, but these semantic features motivate carriers whether they are shown as a rounded balloon, a jagged carrier indicating loudness, or other modifications on the meaning (Forceville, Veale, and Feyaerts 2010b). A carrier where only the root has awareness, but adjacent entities do not, would thus have content only accessible to the root. This is a **Private** carrier, most typically a carrier that conveys the thoughts of a root (or their memories, dreams, imagination, etc.). Private carriers appear both as cloud-shaped thought bubbles, but also when "narrative caption boxes" convey a character's direct thoughts.

When only adjacent entities know the contents of a carrier, but the root itself does not, it is a **Non-Sentient** carrier. These are stereotypically sound effects, where an object (a fist to a face, a gun, a drop of water, etc.) itself might not be aware it is creating the sound, but the surrounding entities are aware of that content. Finally, some carriers are not accessible by the roots or the adjacent entities. **Satellite** carriers have content that is not accessed by any entities in a scene, and thereby exist entirely outside the plane of the narrative world. These are most stereotypically labels, which retain a tail connected to a root in the scene, or they can be "narrative captions" that remain disconnected to the content and have no tails to begin with. Some satellites may look like sound effects, such as descriptions (*Punch! Hit!*) of

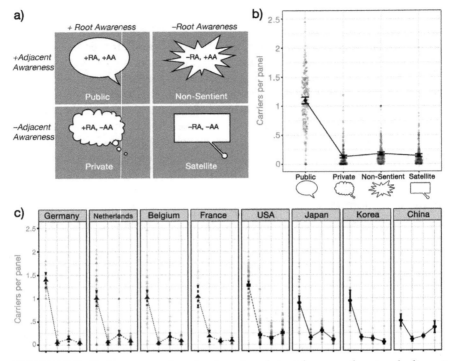

FIGURE 3.8 *Various types of carriers based on their a) features of root and adjacent awareness, and b) the overall distribution of these carrier types, and c) their distribution in countries in the VLRC.*

actions that are not actually sounds, but are more like labels (Pratha, Avunjian, and Cohn 2016).

Overall, these carrier types abstract across the surface features of their physical appearance and/or their meanings. We used these categories in analyses of carriers in the VLRC, providing more nuance to the carrier analyses depicted in Figure 3.7b. The summary in Figure 3.8b depicts the carriers per panel for all carrier types. Public carriers are clearly the most frequently used, at a rate of 1.1 public carriers per panel, while all others remain far lower in frequency. The next highest is Non-Sentient carriers (.18 per panel), then Satellites (.15), and Private carriers (.13).

When looking across countries, as in Figure 3.8c, we see Public carriers consistently maintained as the most frequent type, while other carriers vary widely. For example, in comics from the United States, after Public carriers, Satellites seem most frequent, followed by Private and then Non-Sentient carriers. In Japanese manga however, Non-Sentient carriers are more frequent than either Private or Satellite carriers, implying they use less exposition and thinking, and more depictions of the storyworld, a pattern also appearing in Dutch, Flemish, and German comics. Chinese comics had the most varied pattern, as they used the least amount of Public carriers (only .5 per panel), followed by the highest frequency of Satellites, and then Non-Sentient, and then Private carriers.

Overall, these frequencies suggest that comics primarily emphasize the speech of characters, although they may vary in the extent to which they use text in other ways. It is also noteworthy that all countries analyzed used all of these types of visual morphology. Although they vary in their frequencies, no country lacked a particular type entirely, suggesting that these conventions on the whole have spread across the world's comics. Nevertheless, some surface variation remains in how these forms manifest across cultures, which has yet only received limited investigation (Forceville, Veale, and Feyaerts 2010b). For example, how often do Private carriers appear as thought bubbles versus boxes, or how often do Public carriers actually appear as speech balloons? As these graphic conventions are only annotated in a limited way in the VLRC (only for Dutch and Flemish comics), studying the range of their depiction remains an interesting future study.

3.4 Motion events

For our final look at visual language morphology, we will again compare different countries, but where underlying patterns in the spoken languages also might vary in systematic ways. Here our question will be whether structures within the spoken languages might influence or modulate the structures displayed in the visual languages. Our particular domain of interest here is that of *motion events* and the depiction of paths.

The depiction of motion in graphics remains a challenge, since motion involves dynamic action that unfurls across space in time, while drawn graphics inherently remain static. As a result, multiple cues are used to signal such dynamic change. A first cue is simply the postures of characters, which signal the types of actions and events characters are engaged in. For example, the posture of the character in Figure 3.9a tells us that this character is running because of the position of their arms and legs. Research has shown that static depictions of postures activate motor areas of the brain (Kourtzi and Kanwisher 2000, Senior et al. 2000) similar to what occurs when people view actual dynamic movements (Dupont et al. 1994). In studies with comics, preparatory actions such as reaching back an arm to throw an object or to punch have been shown to sponsor predictions about those upcoming actions (Cohn and Paczynski 2013) and their absence renders the subsequent events as harder to process (Cohn, Paczynski, and Kutas 2017).

Nevertheless, postures alone provide only a static snapshot of a character's action, while the dynamic nature of the event remains implicit. Additional cues have thus arisen to signal this sense of movement and dynamism. One such cue is the repetition of characters' postures, showing a figure or their

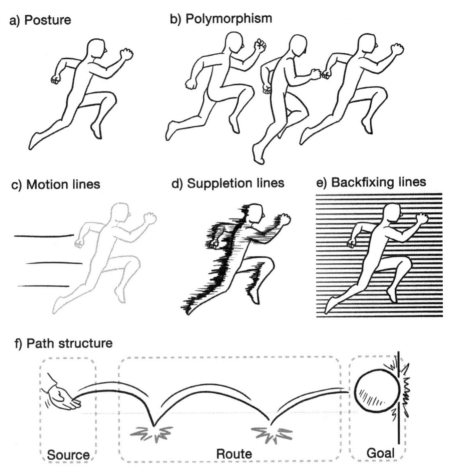

FIGURE 3.9 *Various cues used to depict motion in graphic form including a) postures, b) polymorphism of repeated Figures, c) motion lines, d) suppletion lines, and e) backfixing lines, along with f) the structure of paths.*

parts repeatedly in multiple stages of an action in a single panel, which I've called *polymorphism* (Cohn 2013c). As depicted in Figure 3.9b, we see multiple figures in different postures of running: we understand this is one person in multiple positions over time, rather than multiple people (although this is also a possible interpretation). Polymorphism can also apply to parts of figures, such as the arms in Figure 3.2f. Even young, pre-school-aged children recognize that multiple postures indicate dynamic motion (Friedman and Stevenson 1975).

More subtle dynamism arises from the use of ***motion lines***, also sometimes called speed or action lines. These are affixes that extend behind a moving object to show the path that this mover has traversed, as depicted in Figure 3.9c. Some work has speculated that motion lines reflect an iconic depiction of the way our eyes perceive motion (Burr 2000), while other work has speculated that they are metaphoric depictions (Juricevic 2017b) that derive from extensions of real-life paths, such as trails like those left by animals or vehicles (Forceville 2011b, Kennedy 1982).

But, a simpler view is that motion lines provide a conventionalized representation of a conceptual path. Motion lines collapse across both the starting point of a path (at the start of the line) and its endpoint (the location of the object) to imply the overall trajectory of a path. Indeed, paths are a basic semantic primitive in most theories of how we understand the world (Jackendoff 1990, Talmy 2000, Johnson 1987), and paths have been posited as part of our innate conceptual machinery (Mandler 2010). As such, we do not need a metaphor to understand motion lines (also, what are they a metaphor *of?*), because these lines can directly map to the understanding of paths themselves.

Indeed, research has indicated that children learn the meaning of motion lines over time (Friedman and Stevenson 1975, Brooks 1977), and children undergo a shift from understanding them as iconic interpretations (such as "wind blowing") to symbolic representations of motion (Gross et al. 1991). Both the size and quantity of motion lines impacts their understanding, with longer and more lines both indicating faster movement (Hayashi et al. 2013). In addition, the presence of motion lines facilitates the understanding of actions more than the absence of lines or even incongruous reversed lines (Cohn and Maher 2015, Ito, Seno, and Yamanaka 2010), and this processing is modulated by expertise in reading comics (Cohn and Maher 2015).

In addition, although motion lines attach lines to moving objects, other lines might replace lines on the object itself. These *suppletion lines* apply lines directly onto the moving object to give it a sense of motion without traversing across a trajectory (Cohn 2013c). Lines can also be set behind a moving object to give the sense that a viewer is moving at the same pace as the object, and the background itself might be blurred (McCloud 1993), as in Figure 3.9e. Like motion lines, these *backfixing lines* have been conventionalized to the point that they may no longer depict a perceptual blurring sensation, and facilitate the motion comprehension even when backfixing lines converge in a manner that belies natural perceivable motion (Ito, Seno, and Yamanaka 2010).

These morphological cues all provide ways that motion may be understood, and they can appear in combination with each other. As hinted above, this understanding of motion involves the conceptualization that a moving object traverses a path, which is most exemplified by motion lines. Paths themselves break down into subparts, as depicted in Figure 3.9f. The start of a path is its *source*, where an object begins its motion. It then travels across a *route* that is the trajectory of the path itself, before reaching its *goal* or endpoint. Paths might also have distinguishable characteristics of their *manner* of motion. A default path might be straight, but depending on the object, its manner might be bouncing, spinning, twirling, or other types of motions. Graphically, manner of motion might be encoded in the shape of the motion line, in the layering of polymorphic figures, and/or in aspects of the posture.

Spoken languages also use various strategies to convey motion across a path, where a similar challenge persists in conveying motion events through verbal expressions. Languages have been argued to have conventionalized grammatical constructions for how they allocate path information. The most well-known typology divides languages into two broad types, although subsequent work has found that there may be more nuance than this binary classification (Talmy 1985, Zlatev et al. 2021). In *satellite-framed languages* such as English, an event might be expressed like *She ran out of the house*, where the primary verb (*ran*) encodes both the motion and manner information, and the path information appears in a "satellite" (*out*). In verb-framed languages such as Spanish, the event would be expressed as *Ella salió de la casa corriendo* (*She exited from the house running*), where the primary verb (*salió/exited*) expresses the motion and path, while the manner is encoded in a secondary verb (*corriendo*). This binary typology cuts across cultures, as satellite-framed languages include English, German, Dutch, Russian, Mandarin, and others, while verb-framed languages include Spanish, French, Turkish, Hebrew, Japanese, and others.

Because of this difference in the way paths are encoded, various works have argued that they can influence how speakers of these languages think about and describe events. The argument here is that, because satellite-framed languages encode both motion and manner into the main verb, it increases the salience of paths in the motion events (Slobin 2000). Indeed, this difference in the salience in paths has been shown in several studies, including in descriptions of the events depicted in visual narratives (Slobin 2000, Naidu et al. 2018). In corpus studies of translated comics, Molés-Cases (2020b, a) and Alonso (2022) found that manner information was often omitted or altered when translating between satellite-framed and verb-framed languages. However, this manner information was often present in the accompanying visuals, which compensated for its omission in the verbal expressions. An additional study found that participants rated comic panels from satellite-framed languages (American, Chinese) as conveying more action than those from verb-framed languages (Japanese, Italian), further supporting the idea that the verbal encoding might affect the graphic depictions (Tversky and Chow 2017).

These studies all suggested that the ways spoken languages divide up motion event information might have an influence on understanding and creating graphic depictions of motion as well. I have referred to such a phenomena as *conceptual permeability* (Cohn 2016a), which is the idea that the structuring of conceptual information in one modality might influence the structuring of similar conceptual information in another modality. In this case, the patterns used to convey motions in the spoken language might affect how they are structured in the visual language.

Although these studies have shown evidence for the interpretation or effect of the structure of the spoken language on interpreting graphic motion events, they have not directly looked at path information in the panels of comics. To investigate this possibility, Irmak Hacımusaoğlu and I looked at path information directly within a subsection of the VLRC (Hacımusaoğlu and Cohn 2022). This sample consisted of eighty-five comics from six countries, which were annotated for both path segments (source, route, goal) and the morphological cues signaling motion (postures, motion lines, polymorphism, suppletion lines, backfixing lines).

We hypothesized that satellite-framed languages should have more depictions of paths, and especially their routes, given the increased salience of motion and manner in their main verbs (Slobin 2000). This path salience would also lead satellite-framed languages to use more motion lines that directly encode the manner of the path, reflecting how these languages encode both manner and motion information into a main verb. Meanwhile, verb-framed languages may use cues such as suppletion lines or backfixes that highlight the mover in the middle of the path, with less of an emphasis on the manner. This would be akin to the encoding of motion and path into the main verb, with manner appearing in a secondary verb.

Let's first consider our findings for path segments. Overall, routes were depicted more often than goals, which were more frequent than sources, as in Figure 3.10a. This indicates that the primary part of the path (the route) is depicted more than its start or end. In addition, the greater prevalence of goals than routes aligns with observations that endpoints are more salient than starting points in events (Lakusta and Landau 2005, Regier 1996, 1997). However, the distinctions of linguistic typology of motion events did interact with this pattern. Routes depicted in comics from satellite-framed languages were more frequent than those that came from verb-framed languages. This aligns with our predictions that path information in satellite-framed languages should be more salient, and thus more frequent.

Cross-cultural differences in path segments can be seen in Figure 3.10b, which plots the frequencies of routes alone across our selection of countries. As can be seen, the countries with satellite-framed languages (solid line) primarily use more routes than those from verb-framed languages (dashed line), although routes in comics from France (verb-framed) and the United States (satellite-framed) were roughly the same, falling in the middle of the others. Such results suggest that, although the structure of motion events in languages appears to influence their depiction of graphic paths, they may fall on a more continuous distribution. It is also worth noting that these findings are more consistent with the linguistic typology of motion events than distinctions of culture, such as between Western (Germany, France, USA) and Asian countries (China, Korea, Japan), which was found in previous work (Tversky and Chow 2017).

Although we see that comics from satellite-framed languages use more paths overall, we also hypothesized about the segmentation of these paths into panels. Since verb-framed languages isolate manner information into a secondary verb, might the depiction of routes (which contain the manner) be isolated to their own panels in comics from these languages? As depicted in Figure 3.10c, in fact all path segments isolated to their own panels out of all paths were more frequent in comics from verb-framed languages than satellite-framed languages. This result was also partitioned across language

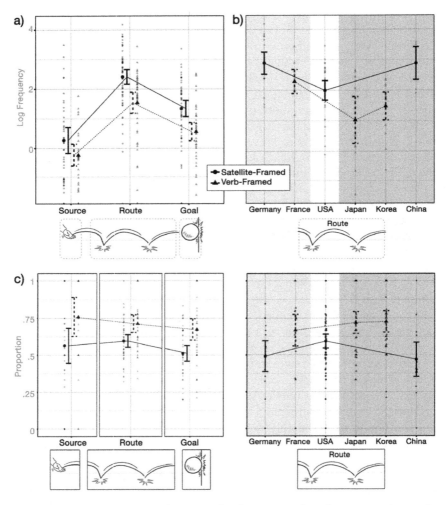

FIGURE 3.10 *Comparisons between the depictions of path structure in comics from satellite-framed and verb-framed languages for a) path segments overall (plotted with a logarithmic transformation), b) for routes specifically across countries, c) path segments isolated to their own panels, d) isolated routes across countries.*

types. As shown in Figure 3.10d, routes depicted in their own panels were all more frequent in comics from verb-framed languages compared to those in satellite-framed languages. Thus, in line with our expectations that the segmentation of manner into its own auxiliary verb in verb-framed languages, panels in comics from verb-framed languages divide path segments into their own independent panels more often than satellite-framed languages.

The non-uniformity of cross-cultural differences is also interesting when considering our findings about morphological cues for motion. First, postures occurred more frequently than any other motion cues, at a rate of .15 per panel, followed by motion lines at .12 per panel, and all other cues occurred less than .03 per panel. To better have a sense of the intensity of these morphemes, we can instead look at which morphemes are greater in proportion when compared against each other, particularly in relationship to our typological distinctions.

As in Figure 3.11a, postures were consistently the most frequent cue in panels from both satellite-framed and verb-framed languages. However, motion lines were used slightly less in those from verb-framed languages than satellite-framed languages, aligning with our prediction that path salience would be heightened in satellite-framed languages with a greater presence of motion lines. Also interestingly, suppletion lines and backfixing lines were more prevalent in panels from comics from verb-framed languages, implying that instead of motion lines, they use other types of motion cues. These cues indeed show a mover in the middle of their path with less hints of their manner, as predicted by the main verbs of verb-framed languages.

Nevertheless, although this typological distinction appears to be supported, once again, breaking apart this data into different countries provides a more complicated view. First, at least semi-distinct regional profiles appear for the comics from Europe and Asia. European comics (France, Germany), and to a lesser degree American comics, used only motion lines and postures, with little use of other cues. But, between these European books, French books (verb-framed) used far more postures than motion lines, while German books (satellite-framed) used motion lines comparably to postures. Similarly, Asian comics all used more suppletion lines and backfixing lines, although again the typological distinctions emerge for Japanese manga (verb-framed) using far more postures than motion lines, while Chinese manhua (satellite-framed) used postures even less than motion lines. The exceptions here are Korean manhwa (verb-framed), which balanced postures and motion lines more like the other satellite-framed books, and the reverse occurring in the American comics (English: satellite-framed), which used postures far more than motion lines.

Altogether, these results suggest that the typological differences for motion events encoded in spoken languages may influence the structure of

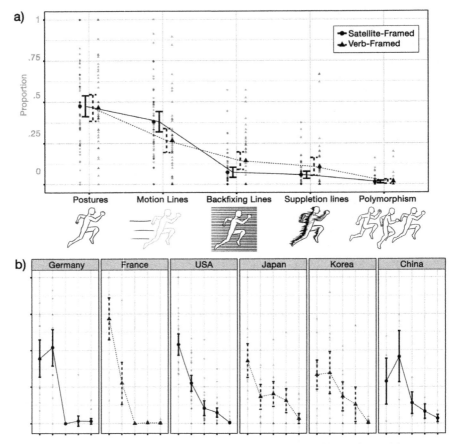

FIGURE 3.11 *Comparisons between satellite-framed and verb-framed languages for a) morphological cues related to motion events overall and b) for those cues across countries.*

motion events in visual languages. Comics from satellite-framed languages consistently used more routes overall, but comics from verb-framed languages more often isolate path segments into their own panels. This finding upholds the expectations of typological path saliency, and as path segments relate the most to the abstract aspects of the motion events, this finding provides the strongest evidence for permeability in these results. Indeed, these patterns of path structure cut across cultural dimensions such as American, European, or Asian comics. This typological dimension only somewhat arose in the morphological cues signaling motion events. Here, any influence of verbal typology appears to intersect with culturally recognizable patterns for their respective visual vocabularies.

3.5 Conclusions

This chapter began our exploration of the structure of visual languages by looking at several case studies in morphology. Overall, these comparisons create a multifaceted view of the complexity of morphology and visual languages. In our comparison of Japanese manga, morphological variation suggests the presence of an overarching JVL, but with varieties aligning with genres of shonen and shojo manga. By comparison, Dutch and Flemish comics seem to use a common morphology suggesting one overarching visual language. In addition, some differences arise in the morphology between cultures, such as between Dutch/Flemish comics and Japanese manga, or in the morphology related to motion events. But, in other cases we see patterns that transcend specific cultural varieties, such as the treatment of carriers of text that were largely consistent across cultures. Some consistent patterns may also cut across cultural dimensions, as in the depictions of paths of motion events. Here, we saw that patterns of depicting paths followed a possible influence from spoken languages, rather than aligning with global distinctions of cultures or regions. Altogether, these findings suggest that visual morphology arises within and across visual languages in complex ways.

CHAPTER FOUR

Page Layout

Page layout is one of the most salient characteristics of comics, and it often influences what people see as unique about comics compared to other visual narratives. Layouts reflect the physical composition of panels across a page, involving their arrangement, alignment, or proximity to each other and to the canvas as a whole. A reader uses these physical relationships to navigate through this canvas, assembling panels into a reading order.

Many approaches to layout have emphasized the associations between layout and a sequence's meaning (Barber 2002, Caldwell 2012, Postema 2013, Gavaler 2018). This focus on meaning has persisted in theories emphasizing dynamic relations in the tension between linear panel-to-panel relations and spatial page compositions (Bateman and Wildfeuer 2014b, Fresnault-Deruelle 1976, Groensteen 2007, Molotiu 2012). Other work has emphasized taxonomies of layout expressiveness, contrasting layouts that use conventional or regular features without meaningful qualities, with those layouts that convey meaning (Groensteen 2007, Peeters 1998 [1991]). These approaches all emphasize the functional uses of layout in relation to its semantic structure.

Although a reader must access the content of a sequence via its visual composition, ultimately layout and meaning are different from each other. As long as a reader orders panels in a consistent way, many panels can be (re)arranged into various layouts without altering the sequential meaning. Imagine a simple six-panel comic strip with equal-sized panels. It might be presented in a horizontal row, a vertical column, a 2 × 3 grid, or a 3 × 2 grid, all likely without changing the sequential meaning. Consistent with this, studies examining participants' eye movements show that altering page layouts does not necessarily change where people look within panels, nor does it change their comprehension of the sequence (Foulsham, Wybrow, and Cohn 2016, Omori, Ishii, and Kurata 2004). Other experiments have shown that participants choose to order comic panels in consistent ways through page layouts, even without any content in the panels (Cohn 2013b, Cohn and Campbell 2015). These findings all support that properties of page layout exist independently of the meaningful content within the panels.

Nevertheless, although layout and meaning are separate, they might still interact. For example, meaning can be coordinated across layout to heighten the inference of motion that might take place within the frames. A person shown to be falling might be better conveyed through a vertical stack of panels than a horizontal one, since the verticality of the panel arrangement would align with the verticality of the character's motion (Cohn 2014a). This is a case where the layout interfaces with the meaning, not that they are inseparable, since you can use a column of panels without the inference of vertical motion (and vice versa). I will discuss more about relationships between layout and meaning in the next chapter.

VLT clarifies the organization of layout into two parts. The *external compositional structure* (ECS) relates to the physical arrangement of panels on a page, while the *assemblage structure* refers to the cognitive organization of those panels in a way that allows a reader to navigate through them. Put another way, ECS is the spatial composition of a layout, and assemblage structure is the principles that allow for navigation of that composition. This relationship between two parts is often reflected in scholars' observations of a tension between the "tabular" spatial surface of a page and the linear succession of panels (Witek 2009, Molotiu 2012, Fresnault-Deruelle 1976). As we will see, although the navigation of a page might produce a seemingly linear order, it is motivated by a more complex organizational structure. We next turn to detailing each of these structures.

4.1 The structure of layouts

The spatial arrangement of graphic elements on a canvas can all be thought of as their composition. Since panels provide units on a canvas, we can distinguish types of composition relative to those panel units. An *internal compositional structure* of panels would thus describe the composition of elements within each panel. In contrast, the ECS is the organizational structure "external" to panels, reflecting their composition relative to each other (Cohn 2013b, c).

These spatial properties of ECS can be detailed for the ways that panels are arranged with each other, without reference to panel content. For example, Bateman et al. (2016b) provide a classification scheme that characterizes the properties of whole layouts in contrast to each other. A similar approach has been taken by Gavaler (2017), who provides a broad inventory of layouts. These approaches can all be considered as using a "top-down" approach by characterizing whole arrangements. VLT instead takes a "bottom-up" approach, by characterizing the specific spatial relationships between panels (detailed below). Ultimately, these approaches should be complementary, since top-down classifications of whole pages can be broken down into their bottom-up parts, while detailing these parts could eventually add up to page-level categories.

First, an overarching unit of layout is the *canvas*, which in the context of printed comics is usually a page. However, a canvas could also be a web page, a wall, an individual strip, a page full of strips, or other surfaces that contain a spatial arrangement of elements. Some work has argued that the page itself operates as a segmental unit, a meta-panel (Eisner 1985) or multiframe (Groensteen 2007). The idea of this canvas-level unit also acting as a storytelling unit will be explored further in the next chapter.

The most basic properties described by theories of layout are the spatial arrangements of panels. The default layout is most often considered to be the grid, which arranges panels into horizontal rows and vertical columns. In its most stereotypical arrangement, grids place primary importance on the rows, which are vertically arranged on the canvas. The typical navigation of grids uses a *Z-path* similar to the canonical order of words in the alphabetic writing system (Cohn 2013c): left-to-right and down for American and European comics, but the reverse (*S-path*) for many Asian comics.

Panel arrangements can be modulated by a feature of *alignment* between the borders of panels: how much do the borders of panels line up with each other? We use the term *pure grid* to describe relations when contiguous borders persist between all adjacent panels, as in Figure 4.1a. Here, both the internal and external borders of panels are all aligned, to create what some have called a "waffle iron" grid. Misaligning the borders of adjacent panels can then create *staggered* panels. When horizontal borders of panels are maintained to form rows, but the vertical borders of panels are discontinuous, it uses *horizontal staggering* (i.e., it is staggering that maintains horizontal contiguity), as in Figure 4.1c. Misalignment of the horizontal borders of panels while maintaining the integrity of the vertical columns would result in *vertical staggering*, as in Figure 4.1b.

Sometimes, panels stacked vertically may persist next to a whole panel. In these cases, we call them *blockage*, as in Figure 4.1d. However, the shift between vertical staggering and blockage may be gradual. As demonstrated in psychological experiments, the greater the misalignment between panel's horizontal borders, the more likely an arrangement will be interpreted as blockage rather than just vertical staggering (Cohn and Campbell 2015). Finally, some arrangements place panels inside of other panels. An *inset* panel (Figure 4.1f) is a panel that is fully enclosed inside another, *dominant* panel.

Panel relationships can also be related to each other through *proximity*. The space between panels is called the *gutter*, which can vary in its width. A "normal" size gutter typically uses just a small width, but this might be determined by the particular patterns of each artist. Having *no gutter* would mean that panels have no gap between them, and are separated only by a shared border (such as a single line). Varying from this, a *separation*

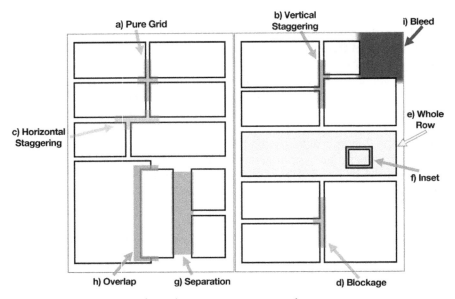

FIGURE 4.1 *Features of panel arrangements in page layouts.*

features a non-normative gap between panels (Figure 4.1g). In the reverse direction, an *overlap* occurs when panels are layered on top of each other (Figure 4.1h).

Beyond their relationships, panels themselves also have distinct features. They can vary in shape (square, rectangular, quadrilateral, circular, irregular, etc.), and in the properties of their borders. A standard line is the normative type of border, but these can vary in thickness, texture (scratchy, solid color, etc.), implied meaning (such as thought bubbles as panels, etc.), or the absence of a border altogether. When they are *borderless*, panels have no defined frame at all, and *bleeds* occur when panels extend past the edge of the printed page (Figure 4.1i).

The external compositional structure of a page relates to the physical, graphic aspects of panels' relations to each other. But, what governs how these panels are ordered when navigating a page layout? Consider a grid arranged with two panels in each row. This could be ordered with the canonical Z-path of alphabetic text. However, it could also be read in columns, with an "N-path" of top-to-bottom, and then right-to-left, typical of some Asian scripts. It could also be read in a "C" shape (top-right, top-left, bottom-left, bottom-right), a "U" shape (top-left, bottom-left, bottom-right, top-right), and several other orders. So, what pushes a reader to order these panels in one way or another?

Although readers may use simple rules such as following the Z-path, navigation of layouts actually uses more nuanced and complicated principles

(Cohn 2020a). Guiding this process is an aim to construct an ***assemblage structure***, which is a cognitive organization we seek to build by grouping panels together into chunks within a broader structure (Cohn 2013b, c, 2020a). Consider first the layout in Figure 4.2a, from Gene Yang's *Boxers*. This page has three rows, with the top pair of rows using a horizontal stagger, and the bottom rows related through a pure grid. These rows are diagrammed in the tree structure as three "horizontal" constituents. They are stacked on top of each other, which means that these three rows are organized vertically. This vertical arrangement reflects the placement of the rows within a larger vertical constituent. This is also the maximal level of the layout, the ***canvas***. Notice also that the final two panels in the last row form a column (blockage). This vertical constituent is thus embedded within the horizontal grouping of the row.

For another example, consider Figure 4.2b, from the comic *Venom: Funeral Pyre* by Carl Potts and Tom Lyle. This page uses more varied aspects of the external compositional structure, with long, vertical staggered panels, and overlapping of a large, borderless panel. But, despite this compositional variation, this ultimately uses a fairly simple assemblage structure. At the top level it has a horizontal constituent, with a row formed between the leftmost panel and the column of panels to the right. This column then consists of a horizontal row of three panels. Although these panels are staggered and overlay a borderless panel with the kneeling figure of Venom, it is ultimately still just a row. These three panels then are vertically arranged with the final panel 5.[1]

As in these examples, assemblage structure primarily uses a hierarchic organization of columns and rows embedding inside each other. Additional embeddings occur for the relationship of inset panels within dominant panels, which is reflected in their physical relationship as well. Hierarchic structures like these have been implicated for page layouts both through psychological experimentation (Cohn 2013b, Cohn and Campbell 2015), and through automatic parsing of comics pages using computational methods (Cao, Chan, and Lau 2012, Tanaka et al. 2007).

If we return to the example of a 2 × 2 grid, a reading with the Z-path would involve two rows, embedded within a vertical column, starting with the upper-leftmost panel, similar to the *Boxers* example. However, if we were to read those four panels using an N-path, it would involve two vertical columns embedded within a horizontal row, starting with the upper-right panel. In other words, the same ECS can be parsed in different assemblage structures that reflect the reading order of the panels.

So, what determines these orders? One influence is the reading paths from the orientations of text in writing systems. This should be noticeable when comparing comics from the United States or Europe, which are read with a left-to-right Z-path, while those from Japan use a right-to-left S-path (or a "reverse Z-path"). It is worth noting that this S-path differs from the top-to-bottom and right-to-left N-path of traditional Japanese script. Manga's use

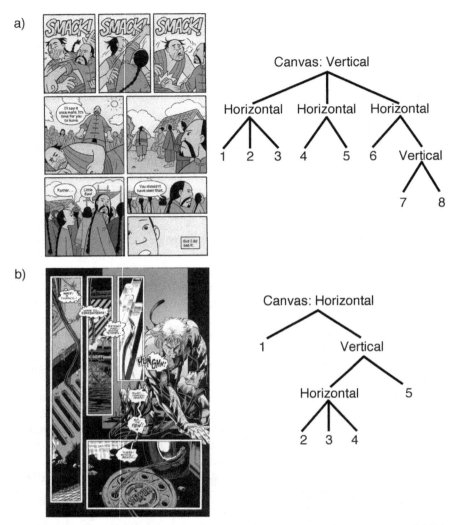

FIGURE 4.2 *Hierarchic structure for pages from a)* Boxers *by Gene Yang (2013), and b)* Venom: Funeral Pyre #2 *by Carl Potts and Tom Lyle (1992).* Boxers © *Gene Yang,* Venom © *Marvel Comics.*

of an S-path may derive from the formative influence of American comic strips in the early-twentieth century, and Japanese strips which followed, which in fact maintained the left-to-right Z-path (Exner 2021).

The Z-path persists as a primary influence on the navigation of page layouts (Cohn 2013b, Cohn and Campbell 2015, Kirtley et al. 2022), and indeed page layouts with grids are read with similar eye-movements to text (Foulsham, Wybrow, and Cohn 2016). However, other cues from the ECS might push a reader to take different routes. Greater misalignment of panel borders and/or greater separation or overlap of panels can push readers in different directions from the horizontal Z-path (Cohn 2013b, Cohn and Campbell 2015, Kirtley et al. 2022). For example, participants show a strong preference for a vertical ordering of the panels in a column stacked next to a single panel (i.e., blockage), flouting the horizontal expectation of the Z-path. In many of these cases, readers are using the cues from layouts to maintain the hierarchic organization of the assemblage structure, rather than following surface-level paths through a layout (Cohn 2013b, 2020a, Tanaka et al. 2007, Bateman et al. 2016a, Kirtley et al. 2022).

4.2 Panels per page

Let's now turn to analysis of layout within the VLRC. We can begin with a simple dimension: How many panels are there per page? Collapsing across all comics in the VLRC, comic pages used an average of 6.4 panels per page, with a standard deviation of 2.6. The minimum number of panels per page in a book was one (i.e., all splash pages), which was in the American comic *Set to Sea* by Drew Weing (2010). The most panels per page on average was twenty-four in the Flemish comic *Het Grote Kabouter Wesley Boek* by Jonas Geirnaert (2010), where every page used 4 × 6 grids.

We already previewed the cross-cultural data for panels-per-page back in Chapter 2, but I repeat it in Figure 4.3a. As should be evident, comics from Europe used more panels per page than those from the United States or Asia. These panel counts remain constant across the pages of a book as well. Figure 4.3b shows the number of panels used across the first twenty pages of comics in the VLRC. Again, it should be visible that European books use more panels per page than those from Asia or the United States. The average number of panels per page largely maintains across the course of the books. However, European comics gradually use fewer panels per page as comics progress, and American and Asian books tend to begin with just slightly fewer panels in the opening pages of the books.

This larger proportion of panels-per-page is especially prominent in comics from Belgium, the Netherlands, and France. These greater proportions of panels per page likely come from the European album formats, which have larger page sizes. However, also note the wide range of panels per page in comics from Belgium and the Netherlands especially, which might arise from varying formatting sizes (Lefèvre 2000, 2013).

In contrast, panels from Asian and American comics had fewer panels per page, and often have a fairly tight range. This may reflect slightly smaller page sizes than the European albums. Note also, German comics used the second fewest panels per page, and our sample had relatively few album-sized German comics, and several that were even smaller than American-sized comic books.

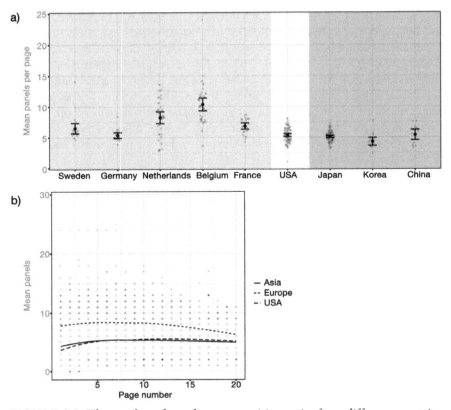

FIGURE 4.3 *The number of panels per page a) in comics from different countries, and b) across the first twenty pages of stories averaged across comics in the VLRC.*

Page sizes might be one explanation for the number of panels per page, but it is worth noting that this assumes that there is an optimal physical panel size. Larger pages only mean more panels if panels maintain a target size across formatting, and it is certainly feasible to just print a larger panel in a larger formatted page size. Whether there actually is an optimal relative size for panels on a page would be a fruitful question for future research. Regardless, if larger page sizes lead to more panels per page, it would invoke the classic linguistic principle of Menzereth's Law, or the Menzerath–Altmann Law (Altmann 1980, Menzerath 1928), which states that the larger the whole of a construct, the smaller the size of its constituents, and vice versa. In this case: the larger the page, the more panels that fit within it.

Of course, other possibilities exist for why panels per page might differ. There may be aspects of storytelling that would necessitate larger or fewer panels per page (such as using all splash pages in *Set to Sea* by Drew Weing), or certain types of arrangement (such as grids versus non-grids). It could also relate to practical reasons: authors in Europe may be afforded more time to draw but with stricter page limits, and then need to fill limited space with more content, but have the time to be able to do so. In contrast, other authors adhering to a monthly (or faster) schedule may need to produce the pages faster, and thus reduce the overall panels they have to draw. All of these factors could potentially influence these amounts of panels per page that could influence their cross-cultural variability.

4.3 Panel properties

Now let's look at more specific aspects of layout. For all subsequent layout analyses, I excluded the older American comics before the 1980s, so that all comparisons are made within relatively consistent dates. This older data will be incorporated into analyses of how page layouts from comics from the United States have changed over time from the 1940s through to the 2010s in Chapter 8.

Before turning to the relationships between panels, let's first look at some of the qualities of panels themselves. A first question relates to the shape of the panel. Figure 4.4a shows the proportion of panels using different shapes across European, American, and Asian comics. All comics primarily used rectangular panels, followed by a small proportion of square panels. Other shapes appeared infrequently. European and American panels by and large did not differ, but Asian panels used fewer rectangles and greater quadrilaterals (i.e., four sided panels of irregular shapes).

In addition to panel shape, we also examined panel borders. Here I emphasize the distinction between panels that have an explicit border and those without borders. We again see cross-cultural variation between the European and American panels compared to Asian panels. European and American panels consistently had borders more often than those without borders, while Asian panels maintained near equal frequency of those with or without borders. In combination with panel shape, the greater lack of borders in Asian panels implies more variety in the units of the layout.

4.4 External compositional structure

Let's now look at the structure of the external compositional structure—the physical makeup of the layouts of comic pages. In this analysis I looked at 105 comics from France, Sweden, Japan, China, and the United States. To keep to more contemporary comics, I again excluded all books with publication dates before 1980, which we will analyze in Chapter 8.

We begin with examining the structure of the arrangements of panels. Figure 4.5a shows the panel arrangements used across all analyzed comics. Pure grid patterns are clearly used more than all other types, although with

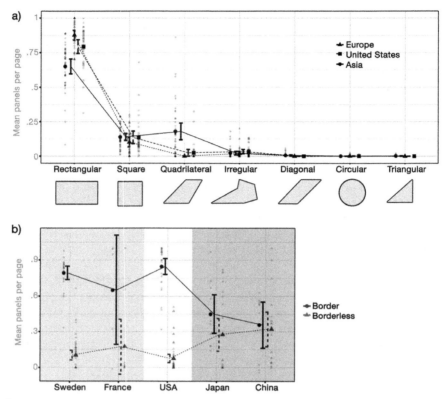

FIGURE 4.4 *a) Frequency of different panel shapes in comics across Asia, Europe, and the United States, and b) contrasts between bordered and borderless panels in different countries.*

wide variance in the patterns of individual books (visible by the large spread of dots, each representing a comic). Row-based structures in fact constituted all of the major arrangements, starting with pure grids, then horizontal staggering, and then whole rows (i.e., a single panel constituting a row). Comparatively, blockage layouts that use embedded columns constitute a small proportion of the arrangements. These findings reinforce that the row-based Z-path is the predominant type of external compositional structure in the layouts of comic pages.

Nevertheless, differences do arise when we look at the arrangements used by comics from different countries. As in Figure 4.5b, the pure grid is most prominent in comics from the United States and both Japanese and Chinese comics. Although they are also frequent in Swedish comics, these and French comics both use large proportions of horizontal staggers, which further reinforce the row-based structure of layouts. American comics also used some horizontal staggering, but it was almost entirely absent from Asian

PAGE LAYOUT

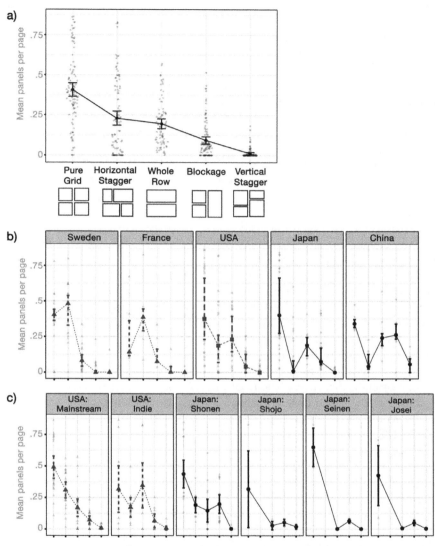

FIGURE 4.5 *Types of arrangements of panels in page layouts, both a) across all analyzed comics and b) across cultures, and c) across subtypes of American and Japanese comics.*

layouts, suggesting less reliance on row-based structures. The prevalence of such row-based structure in comics from Europe might also motivate why European theories of page layout emphasize the "strip"—i.e., the row—as a structuring construct in compositional structure (Peeters 1998 [1991], Groensteen 2007, Chavanne 2010). In this light, such emphasis may simply arise from a culturally-specific pattern in the comics most engaged by those scholars.

In contrast to these row-based arrangements, both American comics and those from Asia use more whole rows—single panels that span the length of a page. When placed in succession, whole rows can create a vertical column that has been called a "widescreen" layout. A column structure is also evident in Asian comics specifically. A greater proportion of blockage appears in Chinese manhua and Japanese manga than any of the other layouts in our analysis. I will return to these points below.

Further nuance comes from looking at subtypes of American and Japanese books (Figure 4.5c). Both mainstream and indie comics from the United States maintain row-based structures, but with different emphases. American mainstream comics use more grids, then horizontal staggers, and then whole rows, while indie comics use grids and whole rows in equal amounts, with lower amounts of horizontal staggering. Japanese subtypes all used grids and blockage, but shonen manga also used a fair amount of horizontal staggering and whole rows. However, this contrast between shonen manga with shojo, seinen, and josei manga should be treated cautiously, as the non-shonen manga may be skewed by slightly fewer datapoints.

Some additional clarity to the character of these layouts can be found by looking at the directions between each panel in the reading path of a layout. To assess panel-to-panel directions, we approximated the centerpoint of a panel in relation to the centerpoint of the preceding panel in the flow of the narrative. We then recorded the spatial vector between these points in terms of one of eight directions (*right, left, up, down,* and in-between). So, as an example, a 2 × 2 grid ordered using a Z-path using a left-to-right and down order would result in directions of right, down-left, right. Because books in the VLRC might differ in their basic directional preferences (left-to-right for Western books, right-to-left for some Asian books), I collapse across surface directions to create "normalized" directions of *lateral* (left, right), ***down-angle*** (down-left, down-right), and ***up-angle*** (up-left, up-right) in addition to ***down*** and ***up***.

Figure 4.6a depicts the overall directionality used across all the books. Here, the directions typical of the Z-path indeed dominate, with lateral directions used the most (~35 percent), suggesting shifts within rows, and then those at a down angle (~38 percent) indicating the shift between rows. Directions straight down were then the next most (~11 percent), indicating shifts between panels in a column, and then only a small amount (~3 percent) of upward angles suggesting shifts between columns. As there were hardly any upward directions, (<1 percent), I leave them out of the figures.

These directions varied across cultures in ways that reinforce the arrangements mentioned above. The European comics (France, Sweden) were dominated by lateral and down-angle directions, suggesting a strong emphasis on a row-based structure. These layouts used almost no upward-angles and very few downward directions. It is worth pointing out that the ratio between frequencies of lateral and down-angle directions should imply differences in the number of panels per rows. Since French books have a greater lateral-to-down-angle proportion than Swedish comics, it implies that French books use more panels per row than Swedish comics. I will further discuss length of rows below.

Comics from the United States had just a slightly lower proportion of lateral and down-angle directions, but which were still clearly the predominant directions of the layouts. However, American comics had a higher proportion of downward directions than European comics. These reflect the higher proportion of whole rows discussed above, where "widescreen" layouts use several panels spanning the width of a page in a single, vertical column.

Comics from China and Japan clearly differed from these trends. These books used near equal amounts of lateral and down-angles, suggesting that rows have fewer panels in them than in European or American comics, which used far more laterals than down-angles. In addition, Asian comics used far greater amounts of downward directions (~20 percent) and upward-angles (~10 percent). The presence of upward angles in addition to the downward directions suggests more embedded columns, rather than the widescreen columns vertically used in American comics. The widescreen format maintains a row-based structure, only with single panels as rows. Embedded columns reinforce more actual vertical segments. These same vertical segments seem to be maintained across all subtypes of Japanese manga (Figure 4.6c)—shonen, seinen, shojo, and josei manga—indicating that the layout types are consistent within Japanese manga as well as with those from the Chinese manhua in our corpus.

One reason for the greater proportions of vertical segments in Asian layouts might be the influence of vertical writings systems. Traditionally, Chinese and Japanese scripts were written with a top-to-bottom and rightward N-path that contrasts with the left-to-right and down Z-path of Western alphabetic writing. The orientation of a writing system—left-to-right versus right-to-left—has been shown to be a strong influence on various aspects of perception, including biases for depicting temporal relationships (Chan and Bergen 2005, Tversky, Kugelmass, and Winter 1991), for assigning semantic agency to objects (Dobel, Diesendruck, and Bölte 2007, Maass and Russo 2003), and for perceptually scanning arrays (Padakannaya et al. 2002). Thus, writing systems could naturally extend to influence comics' layouts as well.

Nevertheless, writing systems might not be the only influence on Asian layouts, especially when bearing in mind their history. Comics in Japan originated from influence by Z-path structured comics imported from the United States in the early-twentieth century (Exner 2021). Readers were tasked with adapting to this left-to-right Z-path despite their traditional reading directions, and indeed the Z-path is still retained as the dominant directionality in these layouts, as evidenced by the greater amounts of grids and lateral directions. However, the increased prevalence of vertical segments

88   THE PATTERNS OF COMICS

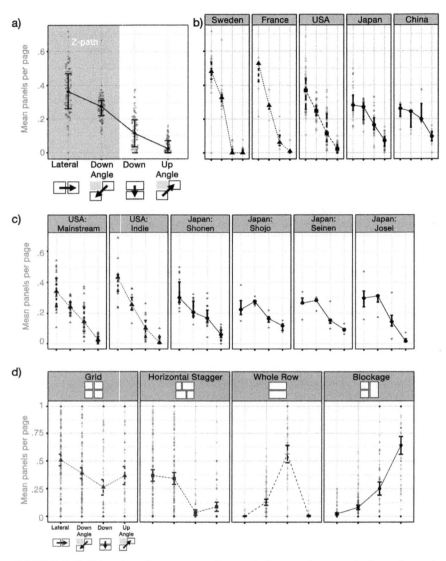

FIGURE 4.6 *Directions between comic panels in page layouts a) throughout the whole corpus, b) across countries, c) across subtypes of comics from the United States and Japan, and d) directions used by the different panel arrangement types in page layouts.*

in Asian layouts compared to European and American layouts—despite the maintained predominance of the Z-path—may show the influence of the verticality of the traditional scripts. This historical influence of US comics in Japan may be why both vertical segments and blockage are greater in Chinese manhua than Japanese manga.

An additional confirmation of the relationship of directions between panels and arrangements of panels can be seen when showing their relationships, as shown in Figure 4.6d. Here we can see the directions of panels involved in different panel arrangements. Grid arrangements are associated with almost all directions, although lateral directions remain most prevalent (within rows) followed by downward angles (between rows). The presence of up-angle and down directions with pure grids likely indicates their interactions with other types of arrangements, such as blockage appearing alongside pure grids or panels within blockage using a pure grid. Row-based structures are clearer in horizontal staggers, which are solely dominated by lateral and downward angles. On the other hand, whole rows are almost solely related to downward directions (down-angles are likely also prevalent because of entering or exiting whole rows). Blockage meanwhile is associated with downward directions (within the column) and upward-angles (exiting the column). These findings further support the relationships between arrangements and directions interpreted above.

The directionality and arrangement of panels largely relates to their alignments. However, we can also consider the *proximity* between panels. The space between panels—the gutter—reflects the distance between each panel as a compositional unit. A ***normal gutter*** width was one with a normative distance between panels, as determined by the standard width used within a given comic (these occupied most of the gutters in the corpus). Those with ***no gutter*** placed panels up against each other and were separated only by a line. A ***separation*** extended the distance between panels beyond the normative width, while ***overlap*** placed one panel on top of another.

Gutter types across all the books in the VLRC are shown in Figure 4.7a. Overall, normal gutters were clearly used more than all other proximities, at a frequency near 75 percent. This was followed by substantially smaller proportions of no gutters, then overlapping, and separations.

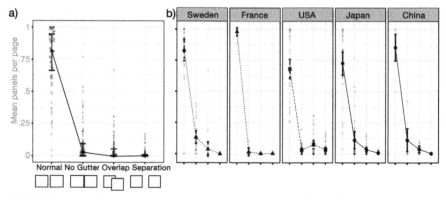

FIGURE 4.7 *Different gutter types in the VLRC for a) all books in the corpus, and b) across countries.*

Slightly more nuances arise when looking across countries (Figure 4.7b). Again, normal gutters persist as the most frequent proximity between panels. This frequency is most prevalent in the layouts from French bande dessinée, which used few other types of gutters. Across both the Japanese, Chinese, and Swedish comics, the second most frequent width was having no gutter at all—i.e., panels placed right up against each other. This contrasted with comics from the United States, where overlaps were the second frequent non-normal gutter. These results suggest that a "normal" gutter is indeed the normative width for separating panels, but that the proximity of panels creates another source of variation across comics from different places.

4.5 Layout complexity

In the previous sections I presented several dimensions of external compositional structure. Various theories have posited categories of layouts based on the functionality of their features, such as conventional compared to decorative layouts, or those where the narrative invokes qualities of meaning compared to those that do not (Groensteen 2007, Peeters 1998 [1991], Caldwell 2012). Although these approaches often inappropriately conflate aspects of layout with those of narrative/meaning, they all contain the insights that layouts range from having more normative to more variable properties. For example, they often describe that basic layouts maintain similarly shaped panels with grids, then progressing towards layouts that vary in panel shapes, and then to those with more varied and decorative properties.

It would be possible to combine our annotated layout properties to create such categories, but these classifications often serve better as descriptive theoretical categories than as the basis for empirical analysis (Woo 2019). Rather than compare discrete categories, I instead aggregated the various annotations of layout into a gradual singular metric, which I will refer to as *layout complexity*. Low layout complexity would characterize more normative or conventional layouts, while high complexity would reflect those with more varied properties. To calculate this scale, I first gave values to each of the dimensions of layout annotated in the VLRC: panel shape, arrangements, directionality, and proximity.

Within the dimension of panel shape, I had three levels. Square panels were given a value of 1, rectangular panels were 2, and all other panels shapes were given a 3. For directions of panels, I considered Z-path directions (lateral, down-angle) to be more basic than those that flouted the Z-path (down, up-angle). Within this, I considered lateral directions as the most basic (1), followed by down-angle directions (2), which signaled the shift between rows. Downward directions also maintained the coherence of a column (3) instead of upward-angles shifting between columns (4). Arrangements were similarly less complex if they maintained a row-based structure, including pure grids, horizontal staggering, or whole rows (1),

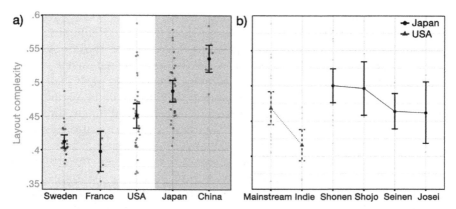

FIGURE 4.8 Layout complexity values across a) countries and b) subtypes, incorporating dimensions of panel shape, arrangement, directionality, and panel proximity.

followed by slightly more complex row-based arrangements, such as vertical staggering and whole columns (2), while inset panels and blockage flouted the Z-path the most (3). Finally, I also considered the proximity of panels to each other—i.e., the width of the gutters. Normal gutters were given the lowest value (1), then those with no gutters or separation (2), and then those with overlapping panels (3).

I added together values from each of these dimensions, and divided them by the total possible (thirteen across all dimensions). This division created a value with a mean from zero to one, which reflects the full complexity of a layout. The resulting complexity values for each country in our analysis are depicted in Figure 4.8a.

First, most comics here displayed a mid to low range of complexity overall, with values between .4 and .55. With this aggregate measure, layouts in Asian comics (Japan, China) displayed the most complexity (a value of ~.47), followed by layouts in American comics (.45), and finally those in European comics (Sweden, France) with the lowest complexity (~.42). When broken down by subtypes (Figure 4.8b), layouts from all Japanese manga demographics maintained their high complexity, but a distinct difference appeared between genres of comics from the United States. Mainstream American comics maintained a complexity close to that of the seinen and josei manga, while indie comics had a distinctly lower complexity, more comparable to that of European comics.

4.6 Assemblage structure

From these analyses of ECS we can also derive clues about the assemblage structures of the comic pages. As described above, layouts consist of several segmental boundaries. Foremost, the page serves to segment canvases from each other, while groupings of panels such as rows and columns create segments within a page. We can thus identify three types of transitions across these segments: shifts between pages, shifts within-constituents (within rows/columns), and shifts between-constituents. In the VLRC, all shifts between pages were explicitly annotated. However, shifts within- and between-constituents of layouts were not. We thus used our directions between panels as a proxy for finding these shifts. Transitions within-constituents were identified through downward or lateral directions, while transitions between-constituents were identified through downward-angles (shifting between rows) or upward angles (shifting between columns).

The expectations here are straightforward. Imagine a page that uses a 3 × 3 panel grid of nine panels. This page would have a single change between pages, two shifts within each row to total six within-constituent shifts, and only two between-constituent shifts between the rows. This logical decrease in the number of shifts in layout segmentation is exactly what is shown in the VLRC data in Figure 4.9a, where we see more shifts between panels involved within constituents (rows, columns) than between constituents, and even more than between pages. This relationship holds across all countries in the corpus and with similar proportions, appearing as a basic universal structuring principle of layouts.

Next, let's examine within these constituents a little more carefully. Overall, pages used an average of 2.8 layout constituents per page (i.e., rows and columns). As depicted in Figure 4.9b, Japanese manga used more constituents than other books in our corpus (around 3.5 per page), while those from the United States used the least (~2.25 per page). Pages from France, Sweden, and China all had intermediate amounts around 2.5 to 3 constituents per page.

Within this, rows were more prevalent as constituents than columns. Rows also varied in length, with the average length being fairly short, at only 2.3 panels long. As depicted in Figure 4.9c, the shortest rows (two panels long) appeared the most often, and rows of longer and longer length became progressively less frequent. The relationship here between frequency and length for the number of panels in rows maintains a well-attested "law" of linguistic regularity. *Zipf's Law* established that there is a negative relationship between frequency and length (Zipf 1935), and originally described the properties of words: shorter words are more frequent in languages than longer words. Specifically, Zipfian distributions have a "decaying" trend where each progressively longer length is about half as frequent as the next shortest one. Here we see this relationship arise for rows, where smaller numbers of panels in rows occur more frequently than larger numbers of panels. This same relationship persists across all the cultures in our analysis, suggesting it is a more "universal" principle of information structuring. We will see this same relationship persisting repeatedly for other structures in later chapters.

PAGE LAYOUT

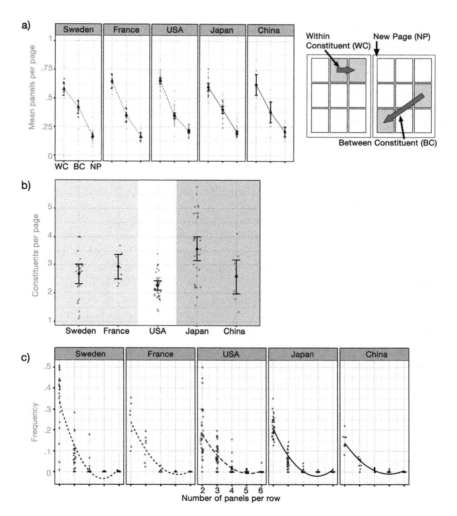

FIGURE 4.9 *a) Shifts between panels in layout constituents, b) Constituents in page layouts of comics from different countries, and c) relationship between number of panels per row and their frequency in comics from different countries.*

4.7 Conclusion

This chapter began our analysis of the sequential structure used in comics in the VLRC by investigating their physical relationships within page layouts. Distinct layout structures were used by different cultures' comics. European comic pages were characterized by a row-based structure using a Z-path, supported with either pure grids or horizontal staggering. They also tended to use rectangular or square panels with defined borders, with more panels per page than layouts from other cultures. Indie comics from the United States also used more horizontal staggering, but mainstream comics used more pure grids, along with an increase in whole rows. Because of these "widescreen" panels, American layouts also used more verticality than European layouts, yet while maintaining a row-based structure with rectangular and square panels with clearly defined borders. Finally, Japanese manga and Chinese manhua primarily used an overarching row-based structure, but with an increased amount of embedded vertical columns. These Asian layouts favored pure grids alongside the columnar arrangements, such as blockage, but also had more variation in their panel shapes, using rectangular, square, and quadrilateral panels, along with near equal amounts of panels with and without borders.

In addition to these cross-cultural patterns, we also found tendencies that persisted in similar ways across cultures. Comics from all regions maintained the expected proportions of shifts within constituents, between constituents, and across pages. In addition, we found a clear tradeoff between the frequency of rows and their length in terms of the number of panels. This relationship between frequency and length was consistent across cultures and with findings in the structure of language. These results align with the general tendencies in linguistic typology for finding a balance between diversity and universality that will persist as a theme throughout subsequent chapters.

CHAPTER FIVE

Situational Coherence

How do we make meaning out of a sequence of images? This question has been the focus of many theories and research into the study of visual narratives, such as comics. Indeed, this is not a trivial question. Although it might feel effortless for many people to understand a sequence of images, this ability comes with substantial development over childhood (and sometimes adulthood), and people not exposed to visual narratives might have difficulty construing a sequence of images as being sequential. Also, children do not seem to gain this ability to understand an image sequence until somewhere between four and six years old (Cohn 2020a). So, just what is it that we learn to do in order to comprehend an image sequence?

In order to understand a sequence of images, connections need to be made between the meaning in a panel and its preceding panels. Many approaches to sequential image understanding have proposed inventories for different types of "transitions" or "relations" between panels. The most well-known of these taxonomies came from comic creator and theorist Scott McCloud (1993), who posited six types of "panel transitions" characterizing whether panels shifted in moments, actions, subjects (i.e., characters), aspects (i.e., glimpses of the surrounding environment), or scenes (i.e., spatial locations), along with "non-sequitur" transitions characterizing panels that may have "no logical relationship" to previous panels. McCloud posited that as a reader progressed through a comic, these transitions reflected different types of inferences that suture the understanding between each panel.

Not only did McCloud propose an inventory of panel relationships, but he used this taxonomy to then analyze different comics—i.e., he did a corpus analysis! As we discussed in Chapter 2, McCloud characterized the distribution of transitions in comics from the United States, Europe, and Japan, largely showing similarities between the American and European comics in contrast to the Japanese manga. Specifically, American and European comics primarily shifted between actions, with some additional changes in characters and spatial locations. In contrast, Japanese manga shifted more between characters across panels, but also introduced more changes between moments and aspects of the environment.

As a prominent early work of research on comics, McCloud's use of this method is important for several reasons. First, it showed that a theory could be used in an active way to analyze comics. This suggested an empirical method where a theory can be used to generate data to offer insights into how comics may differ from each other. Second, it indeed showed that there were differences! This implied that comics from different places may have patterns, and if so, it further suggested that people's minds might need to do different things when comprehending these varying patterns. As should be evident, these themes will be present throughout this chapter, and indeed throughout this book.

Since McCloud first posited his transitions, many other researchers have proposed expansions or revisions to his taxonomy (Cohn 2003, Dean 2000, Saraceni 2016, Stainbrook 2016, Gavaler and Beavers 2018), while the notion of transitions has also received substantial criticism (Davies 2022, Cohn 2003, 2010b, 2020b). Other work has proposed alternative models where meaningful relationships build hierarchic groupings (Cohn 2003, Bateman and Wildfeuer 2014b). Nevertheless, all of these approaches have significant limitations in their ability to capture the ways that visual sequences convey meaning across panels.

One limitation is that most of these approaches posit *exclusive* "transitions" or "relations" between panels. That is, they typically describe the changes between panels in terms of a single characterized shift between panels. However, in many cases multiple dimensions of meaning may change at once: characters, spatial location, or events all may or may not change simultaneously (Loschky et al. 2020, Cohn 2020b, Tseng and Bateman 2018). What then privileges the characterization of a "transition" for one dimension changing over other dimensions? If you only highlight one dimension, the classification then glosses over all the other changes that may simultaneously occur.

Related to this, transitions are often described as being *binary* changes: a transition is either on or off. For example, there either is a change in characters or not, or there is a change in spatial location, or not. But, both full and partial changes between panels can occur (Tseng and Bateman 2018). Consider again the page from *Far Arden* featured in Chapter 1, depicted again in Figure 5.1. Panel 2 shows Army Shanks on the boat and two other people running from behind, while the next panel shows Army and the boy. So, one character stays the same across the two panels, but across panels characters change. Would this be a character transition or not? A binary transition has difficulty characterizing this relationship.

Over the past decade, growing research on sequential image understanding has used psychological experimentation to explore what happens in the mind/brain while comprehending a visual narrative. This research has measured how fast people read comics or what their eyes do when viewing

SITUATIONAL COHERENCE

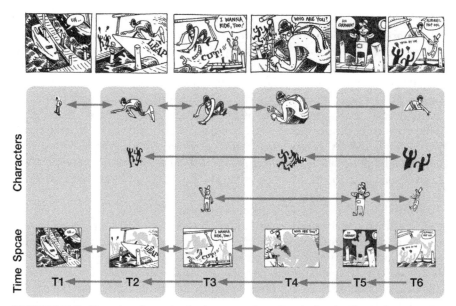

FIGURE 5.1 *Situational continuity in a page from* Far Arden *by Kevin Cannon.* Far Arden © Kevin Cannon.

visual narrative sequences, and many studies have directly measured the electrical activity of participants' brains while they comprehended a sequence of images (see Cohn 2020a for review). By directly analyzing people's behavior and neurocognition, this research has been able to construct cognitive models of how we understand sequences of images beyond the theories of previous approaches (Cohn 2020b, Loschky et al. 2020). Below, I will give a sketch of how these models describe the process that unfurls in comprehending a visual sequence.

A good starting point is an important distinction made by Loschky et al. (2020) between the "front-end" processes involved with sequential images and the "back-end" processes. The front-end processes are related to a comprehender's direct engagement with the graphic material, specifically characterized by the ways their eyes move across the visual surface of the image, and the processes that they carry out to extract information from that display. The back-end processes characterize more what happens in the mind/brain once that information is extracted. Although front-end processes must precede back-end processes, simply because you have to see something before you process it, it's important to note that these stages ultimately inform each other: what you see leads to how your brain might comprehend that visual information, but that comprehension may in turn influence what you see.

Front-end processes break down into a few stages. First, a comprehender needs to survey an image in order to assess the relevant aspects of panels.

This involves a process of *visual search*, where they move their eyes throughout the visual surface, and *attentional selection* where their focus rests on different parts of that display. While looking at parts of an image, *information extraction* takes place where content progresses through the visual system to be passed to subsequent comprehension processes. Although panels in a comic might be fairly complex, only certain information is actually relevant for understanding a sequence (Foulsham and Cohn 2021). This constrained information is what people typically look at in a comic panel, while the rest of the visuals of a panel are left unattended and/or are captured by peripheral vision (Laubrock, Hohenstein, and Kümmerer 2018, Hutson, Magliano, and Loschky 2018, Foulsham, Wybrow, and Cohn 2016).

From here, the back-end processes occur. The extracted information cascades through the brain eventually *accessing* meaningful representations in semantic memory, which is the encoding of meaningful information across modalities (Lambon Ralph et al. 2016, Kutas and Federmeier 2011, Baggio 2018). For example, the second panel of Figure 5.1 shows Army Shanks, a boat, and two figures running in the distance. These graphic representations thus activate a range of associated concepts. Although we might recognize Army Shanks as a specific person, it will more subtly activate information about male humans, sailors, and other related concepts. Similarly, the image of the boat will activate concepts not only about what boats look like, but also how they operate, what they do, etc.

The difficulty of accessing information in semantic memory depends on what information has already been activated. In Figure 5.1, Army Shanks and a boat repeat across panels, which will make it easier to comprehend them each time they are seen, because that information would have already been activated in earlier panels. Since the ease of processing the incoming information depends on the overlap with the previous information, unexpected or incongruous information will be harder to process. This also means that at the start of a sequence, where nothing has yet been activated, this process remains fairly demanding as you "lay a foundation" for the subsequent sequence (Cohn 2020a, Gernsbacher 1990, Loschky et al. 2020).

Although this activated information constitutes the "stuff of meaning," it also serves as the raw materials to be fed into a *situation model*, which is a constructed conception of the information of the scene (Cohn 2020b, Loschky et al. 2020, van Dijk and Kintsch 1983, Zwaan and Radvansky 1998). This is the "model" of the "situation" the comprehender is reading about. As they progress through a sequence, this situation model is *updated* with new information from all the changes that occur across panels. These changes could be related to which characters are shown, the events they are doing, the goals they have, or the spatial locations that scenes take place in. Comprehenders keep track of all this information and monitor for when changes occur across any of these situational dimensions. Greater changes between panels thus incur greater updates to this situation model, and substantial changes may trigger a complete revision of the structure to start a new situation model.

Thus, to summarize this process again ... a reader moves their eyes across the words and pictures that constitute a comic panel, searching for the visual elements that are relevant for comprehension. Upon finding these elements, they extract this information, which makes connections with representations of meaning in the brain ("these lines correspond to a person"!). This information becomes incorporated into a situation model that constructs an understanding of the ongoing scene, and as this process repeats over and over, the situation model becomes updated to reflect the changes that occur across a sequence.

5.1 Situational changes

Our approach to analyzing meaning across panels in the VLRC largely followed from these psychological conceptions of incremental sequential image comprehension. Instead of characterizing meaningful relations in terms of "transitions" or "relations," we recognized that multiple aspects of meaning might change at once. Thus, we annotated for whether characters, spatial location, or time changed between adjacent panels.

In addition, we didn't view these changes as binary, since shifts in meaning are not always "on or off," and incremental changes also occur. For example, across some panels there might be a full change of characters, where all the characters in one panel are different from those in the previous panel. In other cases, some characters might stay constant across panels, while others are added or omitted. This would be a partial change. These nuances are not characterizable by theories of "transitions" or "relations" between panels (e.g., Bateman and Wildfeuer 2014b, Gavaler and Beavers 2018, McCloud 1993).

Our analyses thus looked at whether changes occurred between panels in terms of the depictions of characters, spatial location, or time. Changes between characters were marked with a "0" if there was no change (all the same characters across panels), a ".5" if there was a partial change (some characters added or omitted across panels, while some remained the same), or a "1" if all the characters changed across panels. For example, Figure 5.2 shows a short series of four panels from *The Amazing Spider-Man* #539 where he leaves an injured Aunt May at a hospital. The first panel shows only Spider-Man and Aunt May, and the second shows people in the hospital, and since all characters change, this would be a full change. In the next panel, some medical staff run into a room, but these are only some of the people from the previous panel, making it a partial character change. Finally, the last panel shows only Aunt May, making it again a full change.

Our analysis of spatial location across panels also allowed for incremental change. Again, if the same location was shown across panels, there was no

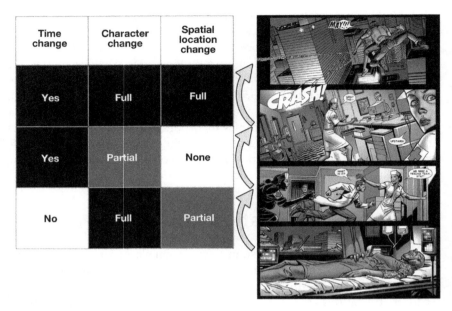

FIGURE 5.2 *Changes in meaning across panels in* The Amazing Spider-Man #539 *by J. Michael Straczynski and Ron Garney. Spider-Man © Marvel Comics.*

change and we gave it a "0." A partial change shifted locations within a space, such as moving from one room to another in the same building, and thus was given a ".5." A full change completely shifted locations, and was given a value of "1." Figure 5.2 begins with a full spatial change, as the depiction in the first panels shows the exterior of the hospital, and then the second panel shows inside the hospital. No change in the spatial location occurs in the third panel, as it continues depicting the hallway of the hospital. A partial spatial change then occurs for the final panel, where it shows a different room in the hospital than the previous hallway.

Finally, unlike character and spatial location changes, time changes were considered as binary: we assigned a "1" if there was a clear time change, or a "0" if time was ambiguous or did not change. Note that we maintained no overarching assumption that time always changes between panels. Time changes were only recorded if they had explicit cues indicating such change. For example, although time apparently changes across the first three panels of Figure 5.2, it is unclear whether the fourth panel occurs at the same moment as the preceding panel, or at a different moment. This change would be considered ambiguous, and not recorded as a time change.

Although we did not presuppose time changes as occurring between panels, we did consider that the progression of time across panels is considered as normative in comics. That is, a comprehender might expect that time will pass between panels as an aspect of maintaining *continuity* across panels. In contrast, changes in characters or spatial location across panels were considered as types of *discontinuity*. This conception of continuity and discontinuity are again in line with our psychological viewpoint. Changes in time between panels are thought to not evoke updating costs as much as panels that maintain a similar time, while changes in characters or spatial location will incur updating costs, unlike showing the same characters or space across panels. To assess all of this together, we therefore also computed the overall *situational discontinuity*, which was the average of instances where character and spatial location changed across panels along with time discontinuity (i.e., no time changes).

In addition, we posited a hierarchic relationship between these dimensions of meaning (Cohn 2010b, Zwaan 2004). Characters belong within a spatial location, and this broader spatial understanding would then shift across temporal event states. Thus, we might posit that time changes will occur more often than discontinuity in characters (i.e., character changes) or spatial location (i.e., spatial change).

In the VLRC, we first looked at changes that occur between adjacently juxtaposed panels, i.e., what are the changes that occur between one panel and its previous panel? On average the sum of semantic changes between panels was 1.49 (out of three possible from time, characters, and spatial location). This suggests that, on average, adjacent panels have a shift in at least one dimension plus an additional partial change (for example, a time change plus a partial character change, or a full spatial location change plus a partial character change). This gets clearer when we look at the types of shifts.

Figure 5.3a depicts the rates of situational coherence when collapsing across all comics, averaging across the values for full, partial, and no changes. For all types of situational coherence, the value here reflects a range, where closer to one means more change. Time changes are at .8, which means they change at very high rates. Since character changes are at .47, this means that on average some characters are changing while others are staying the same across panels. Spatial location changes meanwhile average at .21, suggesting that across panels spatial location is more likely to stay in one place than change, even with only partial changes.

In addition, the overall situational discontinuity was .29. As a reminder, this score reflected whether characters or spatial locations shifted across panels, and/or whether time did not shift across panels. This average suggests that discontinuous shifts between panels occur to a fairly low degree overall (again, on a zero to one scale).

We can also characterize change in meaning that is more exclusive or binary, like in the theories of "transitions." Figure 5.3c shows when only one dimension changes at a time with a full change (no partial changes). Time changes again remain the highest, still at .8 (since they had no partial changes anyhow). Character changes reduce substantially though, falling to only

.27 (from .47) and spatial location changes fall to .15 (from .21). Overall, this indicates that many partial changes take place between characters, since the overall rate of character changes was much higher when partial changes were included than when only shifts between full characters occurred.

Overall, we see the persistence of our expected hierarchic relationship between situational dimensions. Time changes occurred the most, and then characters changed more often than spatial locations. However, these differences become a bit more nuanced when we look at situational changes across comics from different countries. As depicted in Figure 5.3b, comics from Europe used time changes most prevalently, used fairly low amounts of character changes, and used few spatial location changes. A similar trend also appears for comics in the United States. However, Asian comics showed a different pattern. They displayed a reduced rate of time changes, which were only slightly more prevalent than character changes.

These preferences become even more distinct when removing partial changes from the analysis and only focusing on full situational shifts. As depicted in Figure 5.3d, all types of comics display a prevalence for time

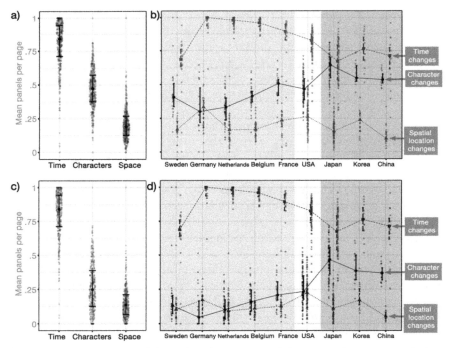

FIGURE 5.3 *Summary of data related to situational changes in the VLRC, including a) all types of situational changes collapsed across all books and b) across countries. Instances where only one dimension of change shifts across panels is shown in c) collapsed across all books, and d) across countries. Error bars represent standard error.*

changes, but they are again reduced in panel relations from Asian comics compared to those from Europe or the United States. In addition, changes between characters were halfway between those for time and spatial location only for the Asian comics. For both European and American comics, the rates of full character changes and full spatial location changes largely did not differ, remaining under .25.

Further nuance can be seen when we look at all possible combinations of these situational dimensions. Figure 5.4a shows the breakdown of combinations of time changes (solid line) or no changes (dotted line) when coinciding with character changes (full, partial, or none, indicated by different shaded areas), or spatial location changes (full, partial, or none). This altogether creates eighteen possible shifts in meaning. A few distinct trends are noticeable.

First, several combinations of dimensions are fairly infrequent. Partial or no character changes combined with full or partial spatial location changes rarely occur. Rather, partial and no character changes typically occur when there is also no shift in spatial location. This implies that incremental or absent changes in characters typically stay within a shared spatial location. This is further indicated by changes with shifts in time. When time shifted between panels, there were also either partial or no character changes and no spatial location changes. In other words, time shifts primarily happen within the same spatial location, and with no or incremental character changes.

In contrast, shifts involving no time change occurred in contexts of full character changes. When this coincided with partial or no spatial location changes, it implies that shifts between characters also used no apparent time shift, i.e., panels merely show different elements of a scene at the same moment. But, the most frequent of these shifts with no time changes coincided with both full character and full spatial location changes. These are essentially the divisions between scenes, where all characters and locations reset, but it is unclear whether time shifts between those scenes.

The perspective again changes when comparing comics from different cultures. Given the consistency observed across countries within regions shown in the first analysis of situational dimensions, I here collapse across the broader regions of Europe, the United States, and Asia rather than analyze specific countries. Figure 5.4b depicts this breakdown across situational combinations for shifts that involve time changes, while Figure 5.4c does so for combinations that involve no time changes.

When time does shift across panels, comics from all three regions maintain largely the same patterns of frequency (Figure 5.4b). Here, time changes most frequently shift alongside those with either partial or no character changes and no spatial location changes, maintaining consistency with the proportions in the analysis across the whole corpus. The only exception is that comics from Asia use greater time shifts between panels that use full character changes, and also have no spatial location changes. Asian comics

THE PATTERNS OF COMICS

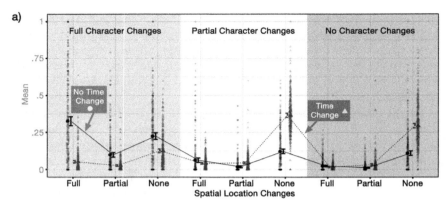

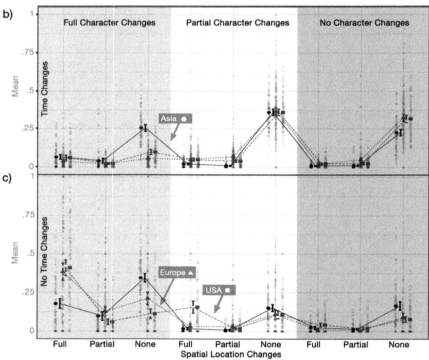

FIGURE 5.4 *Combinations of time, character, and spatial location changes between panels, both a) across the whole VLRC, and broken apart for comics from Europe, the United States, and Asia when shifts b) do involve time changes, and c) do not involve time changes. Error bars represent standard error.*

continued this prevalence when there are no shifts in time (Figure 5.4c), but again do have full character changes and no spatial location changes. These are effectively cases where different characters are shown within a scene at the same moment. Asian comics also showed a greater proportion of full *situational discontinuity*, where there were no shifts in time, characters, or spatial location (the rightmost datapoint).

With the absence of a time shift, European and American comics most frequently used full character changes with full spatial location changes. Again, these would essentially be full shifts between scenes, where all characters and locations change but time changes are ambiguous. It's noteworthy that these "scene shifts" are about twice as prevalent in European and American comics then they are in Asian comics, implying that Asian books keep their scenes in the same location longer than European and American comics. Finally, American comics alone also had a greater frequency in time not shifting along with partial character and full spatial location changes.

Altogether, these findings suggest that European and American comics focus more on shifts in time and events, while Asian comics balance shifts in time with those between characters. These findings are broadly similar to McCloud's (1993) original analysis of binary and exclusive panel transitions in comics from the United States, Europe, and Japan. There, he observed Japanese manga to use more shifts between panels of characters and environments compared to American and European comics, which more often shifted between actions. Nevertheless, our approach here provides additional nuance to these interpretations, showing how various incremental changes can occur across numerous dimensions, which may or may not coincide with each other.

5.2 Situational Runs

Our analysis of situational coherence so far has focused on the changes that occur only between adjacent panels. This gives us a sense of how all panels in a comic might differ in their overall flow of meaning. However, we can also analyze situational coherence across longer sequences of panels. For example, how long do sequences of panels go without changing in their situational dimensions? Do these lengths also differ in frequency across cultures?

Few works have investigated how sequences of images maintain, or change, in their meaning across extended sequences of panels. In an early work applying computational linguistic methods to comics, Laraudogoitia (2008, 2009) investigated how similar characters are maintained across *runs* of comic panels, i.e., contiguous sequences maintaining the same character(s) in their panels. We maintain this term of a "run" to refer to a sequence of panels that sustains some or all aspects of situational continuity.

So, a character run would be a contiguous sequence of panels with no character changes, while a spatial location run would be a contiguous sequence of panels with no spatial location changes. Additional work has characterized the "chains" of coreference that are established for characters across panels (Tseng and Bateman 2018), and experimentation has shown that maintaining these links is indeed important for understanding visual narratives (Tseng, Laubrock, and Pflaeging 2018).

Within our VLRC data, we can thus ask about the properties of runs of situational continuity in different comics. In work led by Bien Klomberg, we examined these situational runs in a few different ways (Klomberg, Hacımusaoğlu, and Cohn 2022). First, we asked about *run length*: how long are typical spans of continuous meaning across panels? We calculated average run length by dividing the total number of panels per run (run length) per book by the frequency of runs in that book. The result is depicted in Figure 5.5a, which shows run length in a logarithmic scale because there are just a few results with very long runs and most with shorter runs.

The average length overall for runs is 7.2 panels long. This is just slightly longer than the average number of panels per page (6.4 panels, as found in the last chapter). Average length of runs differed just a bit across regions, with European runs being longer (9.02 panels long) than those from Asia (5.9 panels) or the United States (5.7 panels). This suggests that European comics maintain consistency in various situational dimensions for longer than those from Asia and the United States, which thus involve more switching between situational dimensions. Note that this also aligns with more panels per page in European than American or Asian comics as well. This all implies at least some relationship between pages as segmental units and the length of runs for the continuity of the panels they contain. I'll return to this relationship between panels and layout in the next section.

The length of different situational dimensions also varied across regions. In all regions, character runs were fairly short in length, with those in Europe (3 panels long) and America (2.9 panels) extending longer than those from Asia (2.6). Given our results discussed earlier, this implies that Asian comics not only have more character changes, but they switch between characters more often. In both European and American comics, time runs were longer than spatial location runs, but this relationship was reversed in Asian comics. European time runs were the longest (17.5 panels), followed by American time runs (8.3 panels), while Asian runs were the shortest (5.9 panels). Spatial runs in Asian comics were meanwhile fairly long (9.1 panels) compared to those in European (6.4 panels) and American comics (5.9 panels). These results again suggest that Asian comics maintain within consistent spatial locations (longer spatial location runs), while not keeping a contiguous temporal flow across panels (shorter time runs) as much as sequences in European and American comics.

This discontinuity of time in Asian sequencing is maintained in our second dimension under analysis. Here, we asked about *frequency of runs*:

SITUATIONAL COHERENCE

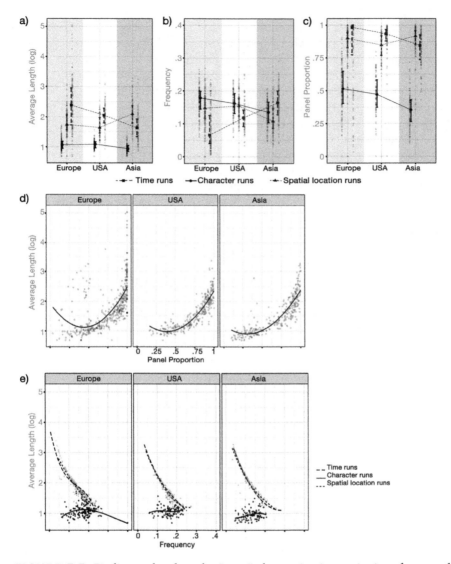

FIGURE 5.5 *Findings related to the "runs" that maintain continuity of types of situational coherence across panels. These include a) the average length of runs (logarithmic scale), b) frequency of runs, and c) the proportion of panels involved in runs. Also depicted are relationships between d) average run length and panel proportion, and e) average run length and frequency.*

how many runs occurred in each book? This was calculated by adding up the overall number of runs in a book, and then dividing it out of the total panels in a book. Frequency varied across situational dimensions between our regions under analysis (depicted in Figure 5.5b). In all regions, a slightly greater frequency of character runs occurred than spatial location runs. Time runs varied the most though. In European and American comics, time runs were actually the least frequent, while they were more frequent in Asian comics. As we'll discuss a bit more below, this should make sense: European, and to a lesser degree American, comics use time runs less frequently because they are longer and thus fill more of the book. Asian comics use them more frequently because they are shorter. We'll return to this point about the tradeoff between frequency and length below.

So far, our broad interpretation is that a lower frequency of runs might occur because more panels of a book are comprised of runs. This is clarified by looking at the *run panel proportion*: how many panels of a book were part of runs? We calculated this by dividing the total run length in a book by the total number of panels per book. As depicted in Figure 5.5c, 80 to 90 percent of all panels in a book were involved in time and spatial location runs, but character runs constituted a smaller amount within books (35 to 52 percent). This greater proportion of panels involved in time and space runs implies that these dimensions play a greater role in structuring the situational context of the sequence than characters. I will also return to this point below. In general, the relatively infrequent runs occurred because the runs were longer and constituted much of the panels in a book.

Panel proportion again resulted in a slightly different distribution across regions, with fewer panels being involved in both time and character runs for Asian comics than those in European or American comics. This once again implies that Asian comics use more discontinuity in their storytelling than European or American comics.

Some additional insights emerge if we look at the relationships between these measures, which transcend their cross-cultural differences. First off, let's consider a relationship between the average length of a run and how many panels from a book are involved in a run (run panel proportion). As shown in Figure 5.5d, these have a clear, positive relationship. When books use more panels in runs, the runs are longer. This is interesting because we could also imagine a situation where the opposite would be true: more panels involved in runs in a book could mean a greater proportion of shorter runs. In addition, despite the cross-cultural differences we discussed already, this relationship between length and proportion seems to persist in a similar way across all of our regions. This consistency across regions suggests this relationship remains more of a "universal" trait of visual narrative sequencing.

We also speculated that the frequency of runs might be smaller when runs are longer, since longer runs take up more space in a book and thus there are not as many of them. Figure 5.5e plots the frequency of runs in relation to the average length of runs. Again, it is notable how consistent this relationship is across our different regions. They all show a negative correlation between frequency and length for time and spatial location runs, but display no clear correlation for character runs. That is, as time and spatial location runs become more frequent in a book, they become shorter. However, character runs do not diminish in length with greater frequency, largely remaining at a short length.

The fact that time and spatial location runs maintain this relationship indicates that they have a more primary role in organizing the situational structure of a visual narrative sequence, while character changes shift more variably across a sequence (Klomberg et al. Forthcoming). This provides support for the idea of a hierarchic relationship between the situational dimensions of time, spatial location, and characters (Cohn 2010b, Zwaan 2004).

Earlier we saw that the overall proportions and lengths of these runs differed between comics from Europe, the United States, and Asia. But, across these dimensions they maintain fairly consistent patterns for a tradeoff between frequency and length for time and spatial location runs, but not for character runs. The relationship here between frequency and length for time and spatial location runs maintains Zipf's Law, as mentioned in the last chapter, which holds that a negative relationship exists between frequency and length (Zipf 1935). Here we see such a relationship between constituents of meaning: shorter runs are more frequent than longer runs. The consistency of these patterns, despite the cross-cultural variation shown above, implies that these trends also persist as more "universal" aspects of the structure of visual narrative storytelling.

5.3 Situational coherence and layout

Comprehending the situations depicted in a sequence of panels involves tracking changes between elements across the sequence of images. However, in comics this sequence is embedded within a spatial compositional structure of a layout, as discussed in the last chapter. Might the layout itself help structure the flow of meaning across the spatial sequence? Many approaches to layout have indeed posited that page compositions play a role in meaningful relationships between panels (Bateman and Wildfeuer 2014b, Fresnault-Deruelle 1976, Groensteen 2007, Molotiu 2012), but few previous works have analyzed such relationships through empirical analyses (Bateman, Veloso, and Lau 2021). In this section I explore some of the possibilities of these relationships within our data.

The first question we might ask is, do more complex layouts also lead to more complexity in the storytelling? To do this, we can examine whether panels that shift in their situational coherence are embedded within more complex layouts—i.e., less normative or conventional layouts. However, panels that showed shifts in time, characters, or spatial location did not differ in their layout complexity (using the metric developed in Chapter 4). In fact, there was also no difference in layout complexity between panels that involved situational shifts and those that maintained situational continuity between panels (i.e., no changes at all).

A second analysis looked at relationships between layout complexity and situational discontinuity. Comics with more complex layouts positively correlated with those using greater situational discontinuity on the whole, suggesting that books that demonstrated greater situational discontinuity also demonstrated greater layout complexity. This makes sense, since we saw that Asian comics had both greater situational discontinuity and more complex layouts. However, when we focus on the properties of the pages themselves within these comics, this correlation disappears. There seems to be no explicit relationship between the layout complexity of a page and the situational discontinuity that occurs within its panels, at least with these measures.

Despite the lack of a relationship between the overall complexity of a layout and its situational coherence, layouts and meaning may interact in more specific ways. In work led by Irmak Hacımusaoğlu, we explored one such interaction (Hacımusaoğlu, Klomberg, and Cohn 2023). Since the layout can be divided into an assemblage structure with rows and columns, we wondered whether these layout constituents might also provide groupings for meaning, such as those marked by shifts in situational continuity. Put another way, might the breaks in meaning occur at the breaks in layout at new pages, or shifts between rows or columns?

In order to examine this relationship between sequential meaning and layout, we took the proportion of situational changes within each of the layout constituent types. As we discussed in the last chapter, layout constituents differ in their frequency. Consider a page with a 3 × 3 panel grid. It would have a single shift across pages, six shifts between panels within constituents (panels within the rows), and two shifts across constituents (between the rows). This means that if we just look at the frequency of situational changes in those constituents, there will be more changes within-constituents than between-constituents, because those layout features differ in their frequency. Thus, in order to get a more equal comparison, we took the proportion of situational changes within each of those layout types: i.e., how many of each situational changes occur out of all shifts between pages? How many out of all shifts between panels within layout constituents? and how many out of all shifts between rows/columns?

Our results are depicted in Figure 5.6a, which shows how the different types of situational continuity shift across pages, between layout constituents (between rows or columns), and within layout constituents (in rows or columns). Breaking down these results across each country would be fairly complex, and we have already seen that there are fairly consistent profiles for situational continuity across each region. So, I here divided them across regions rather than countries.

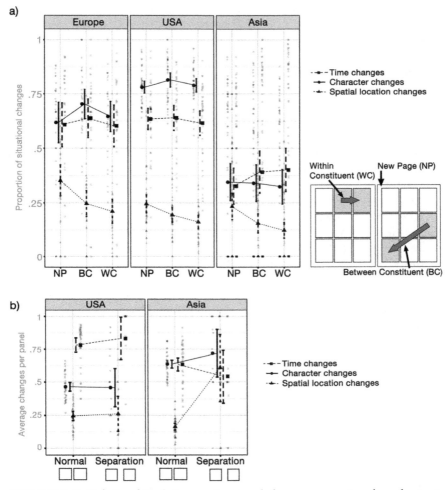

FIGURE 5.6 *Relationships between situational changes across panels and aspects of layout, including a) the shifts between different types of layout constituents, and b) across different types of gutters. Error bars represent standard error.*

Unlike in our findings earlier, in no region did time changes occur most frequently in these layout constituents. Rather, time changes appear in equal or less frequency than character changes, although spatial location changes remain the least frequent in all regions. In European and Asian comics, time changes maintain similar proportions as character changes, while character changes were even more prevalent in American comics than time changes. In Asian comics, both time and character changes remain in fairly low proportions, nearer to spatial location changes.

If we turn to describing these situational changes in the layout constituents themselves, we find some additional patterns. First off, few differences seem to arise in the contrast between and within layout constituents (rows and columns), but we do see some trends emerge in the situational shifts that occur between pages. Most prominently, shifts in spatial location occur more often between pages than within or between constituents (as seen in the bottom lines of Figure 5.6a). This pattern is pronounced especially in comics from Europe and the United States, but less so in Asia. We also see slightly more spatial location shifts between than within constituents, although this difference seems minimal when looking at the actual statistics associated with these values.

Similarly, we see slightly fewer shifts in time across pages than within or between constituents in American books, but this does not appear as prevalent in Asian or European comics. This implies further demarcation of scenes at page boundaries for American comics.

These results suggest that meaningful shifts across panels do interact with properties of layouts, albeit in a constrained way. The most prominent difference was spatial locations shift more across pages, which implies that authors use pages as a segmental cue for dividing up scenes. This is consistent with ideas that the page forms a unit (a "multiframe" or "meta-panel") that is distinct within an ongoing visual narrative (Eisner 1985, Groensteen 2007). However, this notion of "page as unit" seems to be culturally variable. Situational changes at page boundaries did not appear in Asian comics, suggesting that they do not as frequently treat pages as segmental units, with pages merely as holders for a greater flow of meaningful information.

Instead of using the page as a scene break, Asian comics may use different layout cues *within* a page to signal greater shifts in meaning. One such possibility is the use of wider gutters between panels to signal scene changes. When we look at the alignment of wider gutters (the "separation" gutter type) and our situational changes, this indeed does occur. Figure 5.6b shows the situational coherence relationships for normal gutters and for separations. European comics are excluded here because there were only three European comics (all French) with gutter separations. In both Asian and American comics, rates of situational coherence are consistent across both gutters with normal width and separation between panels. However, in Asian comics, substantially more spatial location changes, and slightly less time changes, persist across wider gutters compared to normal width gutters. These results thus support that gutter width also may provide an additional cue within Asian pages for signaling breaks in meaning, particularly between scenes.

5.4 Conclusions

Overall, this chapter has shown that meaningful information shifts across panels in consistent ways. Generally, time changes across panels more often than characters, which changes more often than spatial locations. However, this ranking is cross-culturally variable, and in Asian comics shifts between characters occur across panels nearly as frequently as shifts in time. Along with additional analysis of the runs of situation discontinuity in a sequence, these results suggest that Asian comics use more discontinuity in their storytelling across panels than European or American comics.

These cross-cultural differences also carry over to how meaningful changes manifest within page layouts. On the whole, greater situational discontinuity occurs between pages than within layouts for European and American comics, suggesting that they use pages as a segmental unit for breaking up the flow of information. However, Asian comics do not privilege pages as segmental units for situational change in this same way, and may use within-page cues, such as wider gutters as an alternative marker of segmenting scenes.

Nevertheless, situational coherence also appears to have properties that do not differ across cultures. We observed a consistent relationship between run length and proportion, signaling that when books use more panels in runs, the runs are longer. In addition, runs of both time and spatial locations demonstrated a tradeoff in length and frequency, with shorter runs occurring more frequently than longer runs. But, no such tradeoff was shown for character runs. This finding suggests that temporal and spatial information plays a greater role in the structuring of meaning than characters, and as these patterns persisted across all regions in our analysis, such organization may be a "universal" property of the structuring of visual storytelling.

CHAPTER SIX

Framing Structure

Panels are a fundamental unit of storytelling in a visual narrative, as they provide an encapsulated container for situational information such as characters and scenes that can be connected across a sequence.[1] We've already discussed some of the ways that meaning connects across panels, so it's worth returning to the ways that panels themselves express information. Here we will be concerned with how much information panels contain, rather than say, their visual composition or the way they present this information in an aesthetic way. This "information content" aspect of panels is a higher-level component of their morphology than what we discussed in Chapter 3.

Panels function like a window on a scene for how an author wants to convey information, drawing focus to different elements by what is shown (or not shown). This method of "windowing" information is analogous to what is described as the "spotlight of attention" in visual perception (McDowd 2007, Shipp 2004). In visual perception, our overall field of vision is fairly wide and takes in light and much more information than we consciously process. Our attentional system gives focus to particular aspects of that visual array for the information we select and process. By analogy, an author uses a panel to frame particular aspects of a fictitious scene, thereby drawing the readers' focus to these particular meaningful elements. Because of this, we can think of panels as "attention units" that modulate the way that an author conveys a scene to a reader (see Levin and Simons 2000 for a similar argument about film shots).

Here it might be worth repeating a bit about how people look at the contents of comic panels. The way we move our eyes around a comic panel reflects the front-end processes of comprehension. They are "front-end" because they relate to how our eyes physically seek and acquire information, which then gets sent to the "back-end" processes that involve things such as processing the flow of meaning (Loschky et al. 2020), like we discussed in the last chapter.

Front-end processes involve two primary cognitive functions. First, readers engage in *visual search* processes, which means that their eyes look around an image to find the elements that might be relevant for them to process. Next, after landing on a part of an image, they carry out *information extraction*, where these visual signals connect to the back-end processes of recognizing what these lines, shapes, and colors might mean. This process is rapid, automatic, and takes place within a few hundred milliseconds—a fraction of a second (Loschky et al. 2020, Inui and Miyamoto 1981, Laubrock, Hohenstein, and Kümmerer 2018). In fact, people seem to look at the contents of comic panels faster than they typically look at real-world visual scenes (Laubrock, Hohenstein, and Kümmerer 2018).

So, if panels are fairly dense in their content—such as with lots of characters involved in lots of actions in a big spatial scene—then it will require more searching through the image to find all that information. This should make sense, as lots of stuff in a panel will make a person look around more. But, while reading experiences may differ, by and large people do not visually explore all parts of panels while reading them in the context of a visual narrative sequence. For example, people look at characters more often and more focally than at backgrounds, where the viewing is more dispersed (Laubrock, Hohenstein, and Kümmerer 2018).

In addition, different people tend to look at the same information within panels, and this content is often only a focal part of the scene. Usually, readers look at characters' faces and the parts of their postures that are relevant for their actions (Foulsham, Wybrow, and Cohn 2016, Hutson, Magliano, and Loschky 2018). This was especially salient in a study conducted with my colleague Tom Foulsham. We first conducted a study where we tracked people's eye-movements through comic panels as they read simple comic strips, and we observed that people indeed tended to look at similar content in each panel (Foulsham, Wybrow, and Cohn 2016). We then computed which parts of the panels people looked at the most (with their top 10 percent of fixations), and enlarged this subsection of a panel to become a whole panel. So, we now had panels that showed only the content that people looked at the most. We then compared how people comprehended sequences with the original panels compared with these zoomed-in panels that were based on people's eye-movements. We found little difference in the speed that people read the original versus zoomed-in panels (Foulsham and Cohn 2021)—despite having very different amounts of information overall—and we found only minimal differences in how the brain processed the meaning of these panels (Cohn and Foulsham 2020). This showed that people mostly just focus on the primary information in a panel, and this content drives the understanding of the panel in the context of its sequence.

So, even if a panel shows a lot of content, people might not direct their focus to extracting all that information. As we will see, authors might use panels in different ways to deal with the fact that readers might only focus on some information at a time. One strategy might be to provide as many details as an author might want in a panel, and then let readers figure out what is or isn't relevant, since they'll converge on what to look at anyhow. Another strategy might be that because people only focus on a portion of a panel, panels should only show this primary-focal information, leaving out content that might not be focused on.

We can now return to this idea of panels as an "attentional unit." These strategies for framing—providing everything versus providing only focal cues—involve modulating how much information is depicted in a panel. This was also what we compared in our studies contrasting original panels with lots of information and zoomed-in panels. They "windowed" the information in different ways.

In terms of panel structure, windowing of information in a panel is modulated by two dimensions, what I will refer to here as *attentional framing structure* and *paneling structure*. These dimensions are highlighted in Figure 6.1, which depicts the *Attentional Framing Matrix* (Cohn 2014a),

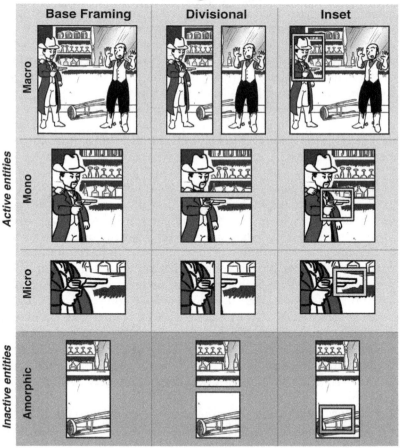

FIGURE 6.1 *The Attentional Framing Matrix. Attentional structure is depicted in rows and paneling structure depicted in columns.*

where the attentional framing structure is depicted along the rows, and the paneling structure is illustrated by the columns.

Attentional structure relates to the amount of information depicted in a panel. On this dimension, panels can be broken down into two component parts: *active entities* and *inactive entities*. Active entities are the elements that the image is about. These elements are typically the primary characters, and they are the ones that often change in their depiction across panels of a sequence. Inactive entities are what an image is largely *not* about (though they might still contribute to its overall setting and/or meaning). We can test whether entities are active or inactive through a diagnostic of a deletion test. If you can delete the active entities from a scene, it becomes much harder to understand what the panel and/or sequence is about. In contrast, omission of the inactive entities should not lead to this same type of incongruity.

Given this distinction, we can categorize panels based on the number of active entities that they might depict, as illustrated along the rows of the first column in Figure 6.1. A *macro* panel depicts multiple active entities, while a *mono* depicts only one active entity. A *micro* shows less than an active entity, as in a close up that shows only a portion of one entity. *Amorphic* panels show no active entities at all, depicting only aspects of the environment or surrounding scene. Even less than this, a panel might be *null* if it shows no information at all (such as an all-black or all-white panel), and an *affixing* panel depicts only a morphological affix with no stem. For example, a panel showing only a speech balloon in an otherwise black panel depicts only the affix (the balloon), while not showing its corresponding stem (the speaker).

It's important to clarify that these attentional categories are not the same as the classifications of *shot scale* made in film theory and practice, which categorize viewpoints by how much of a scene or figure is depicted. Shot scale range from a long shot showing figures in full within a large depiction of the setting, to a full shot showing the whole figure, to a medium shot (waist up), close shot (bust), or extreme close up (zoom into face or body part). Shot scale is largely concerned with *how* elements in a scene are presented, rather than *how many* elements in a scene are presented like the attentional categories. Indeed, a mono showing only one character could be depicted using nearly all the filmic shot scales. Similarly, an extreme close-up might depict two hands shaking, which would be a macro because it shows multiple active entities. Thus, while there may be prototypical alignments between attentional categories and filmic shot scales, they are intersecting, but different, classifications. We will explore this relationship empirically a bit later.

Paneling structure is another dimension of how panels frame information, which relates to how the information in one panel interacts with the depiction of information in other panels. Paneling is depicted across columns in Figure 6.1. The most basic distinction here is *base framing*, where each panel stands alone graphically as an attentional unit (although not isolated in narrative or in layout). *Divisional framing* depicts each panel as conveying a portion of a larger image that spreads across the panels. Here, a single image might extend across multiple panels, recognized through perception of image constancy, despite the divisions created by the gutters between panels. Another type of paneling places an *inset panel* inside another *dominant panel*, where the inset frames a subpart of the dominant panel's content.

These aspects of paneling structure can further provide ways to modulate the focus of attention. Some work has shown little difference in how people look at an array of divisional panels compared to their equivalent single-image "base" representation (Cherry and Brickler 2016), suggesting that people instead recognize the holistic connections they make across panels. Additional work has shown that people are slightly slower to read panels with insets that frame information in the dominant panel compared to panels without insets (Foulsham and Cohn 2021). This makes sense, because the insets provide an additional unit to be looked at. However, people spend much less time looking at insets that frame relevant attention-directing content in the panel compared to insets that frame less-relevant aspects of the scene. So, insets can help draw focus to the primary information of a scene.

Paneling structure can have ramifications for attentional structure. For example, as depicted in Figure 6.1, several monos might each contain a single character, but across divisional framing this might lead to the additive Gestalt of a macro with multiple characters. Monos with different characters using base framing might warrant a spatial inference to understand that they belong to a common environment, but divisional framing would provide this binding information overtly. In addition, an inset panel might highlight only a particular portion of a larger scene, thereby making that inset a micro within the macro of the dominant panel. In both cases, the non-base framing uses graphic cues to clarify the relationships between content framed by panels.

Attentional structure has been one of the focal points for cross-cultural analyses within VLT. In the first corpus study of VLT, the categories of macros, monos, and micros were compared across ten American comics and ten Japanese manga (Cohn 2011). This analysis showed that American comics used almost twice as many macros as monos, and few micros, while Japanese manga used nearly equal amounts of macros and monos, with substantially more micros. A follow-up study then analyzed ten mainstream comics from the United States and ten indie comics, again compared to ten Japanese shonen manga (Cohn, Taylor-Weiner, and Grossman 2012). Both types of American comics again used more macros than monos, but these genres did not differ. In contrast, Japanese manga here used more monos than macros, and with higher numbers of micros and amorphics.

These initial findings supported that differences persist between the framing structure of works from the United States and Japan, while also suggesting little difference in the structures across different types of American comics. With this in mind, attentional structure was a primary focus of annotations in the VLRC, alongside analysis of paneling structure and filmic shot scale. We now turn to looking at these results.

6.1 Attentional framing structure

Let's first look at how attentional framing categories are distributed throughout the corpus. Figure 6.2a shows their distribution across 357 comics in our corpus. As should be evident, macros are used the most, with monos being used about half as frequently. Micros and amorphics are used at substantially lower amounts, while there remain a small proportion of ambiguous panels (likely combining null and affixing panels, which had not yet been theorized at the time we gathered the data).

On the surface, this distribution of attentional categories makes sense given the amount of information being conveyed. Panels with the most frequency are those that convey the most amount of information, and the frequency of other panels are subsequently reduced. Nevertheless, as we will see shortly, it is potentially misleading to generalize this to some sort of universal because of the overall makeup of the corpus, and cross-cultural differences point to a more nuanced interpretation of this generalized pattern (as should already be visible by the wide dispersion of dots representing each comic in Figure 6.2a).

It is also worth highlighting the relationships between these attentional types. As demonstrated in the scatterplots in Figure 6.2b, these categories have strong relationships between each other. Overall, macros negatively correlate with all other types, while all non-macros positively correlate with each other. This means that if a book uses more macros, it will use fewer of all other attentional types. Correspondingly, as authors use fewer macros, they will increasingly use more diverse framing types that show portions of a scene. In other words, when authors show fewer scenes (macros), they use fairly diverse framing (monos, micros, amorphics) to do so, and as those scenes are shown less, the rate of all these alternative attentional types increases. As we will see in our cross-cultural analyses, these tradeoffs in the distribution of attentional types arise from certain patterns in works from around the world.

Let's now compare the attentional structure across the comics from various countries in the VLRC. In general, as depicted in Figure 6.2c, all countries use macros and monos more than micros and amorphics. This consistent pattern reflects the greater informativeness of showing multiple characters (macros) or whole characters (monos) over subparts (micros) or parts of the environment (amorphics). However, the distributions of these categories also vary in a culturally consistent way.

FRAMING STRUCTURE

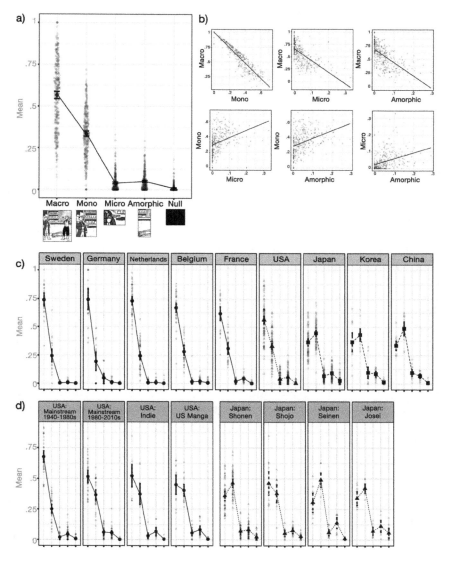

FIGURE 6.2 *a) Distribution of attentional structure in all comics from the VLRC, and b) relationships between attentional framing types (note the differences in scales), along with c) differences across countries, and d) across subtypes from the United States and Japan.*

First, European comics are fairly consistent in their distribution of these attentional categories no matter the specific countries. They have about twice as many macros as monos, and hardly any micros or amorphic panels. That is, European comics primarily focus on full scenes, which are supplemented with views of individual characters. Comics from the United

States retain a similar distribution as European comics (clarified below). However, the ratio between macros and monos here is a bit smaller, with greater quantities of micros and amorphics.

Asian books have a different distribution. Here, the frequency of macros is equal to, or less than, the frequency of monos. In addition, micros and amorphics appear more than in both the European and American comics. This distribution further shows the correlations we observed earlier: with fewer macros, all other categories are used more often. The findings here of increased amorphic panels especially align with McCloud's (1993) observations of more "aspect-to-aspect" transitions used in Japanese manga (i.e., he observed "transitions" into amorphic panels), along with other claims of manga using many close-ups or environmental panels (Tsai 2018, Shamoon 2011). These observations all relate to the prevalence of micros and/or amorphic panels.

Thus, we seem to have three primary manifestations of attentional framing: 1) a European type focusing largely on whole scenes, 2) an American type similar to this but with additional variation in non-macro framing, and 3) an Asian type with a focus on the component parts of a scene as much, if not more than, whole scenes. Because framing from different-but-associated countries have similar distributions, it implies that these countries share in patterns that are suggestive of broader shared systems—i.e., cross-cultural visual languages.

The VLRC also includes analysis of various subtypes within comics from the United States and Japan. Specifically, our American comics cut across several genres (mainstream, independent, US manga) and time periods (roughly eighty years of mainstream comics), while our analysis of Japanese manga cover four different demographics (shonen, shojo, seinen, josei). Might we find additional variation within these subtypes?

Let's begin by comparing the framing structure of the different types of American comics, along with a split in mainstream comics between those produced before and after 1980. This date is chosen as a cut-off because manga began to be imported into the American comics market with greater frequency around the 1980s, with a large influx and popularity in the 1990s (Brienza 2016, Goldberg 2010). We will take a more nuanced analysis of changes across American comics over time in Chapter 8.

American genres are compared in Figure 6.2d. First, it should be apparent that these types of comics differ in only subtle ways. Macros are still maintained more than monos throughout all American subtypes, along with a low frequency of micros and amorphics. Older mainstream comics are largely consistent with the European comics discussed above, with close to double the proportion of macros compared to monos, and few micros or amorphics. Mainstream comics after the 1980s shifted somewhat to increase in their frequency of monos, micros, and amorphics.

Consistent with previous findings, the attentional framing of indie comics does not differ much from those in more recent mainstream comics, which come from a similar time period (Cohn, Taylor-Weiner, and Grossman 2012). A slightly different distribution is maintained by US manga. On average, US manga still use macros more than monos, but this difference is marginal. In addition, micros and amorphics appear with moderate frequency. Although this distribution is not quite the same macro-to-mono ratio as most Japanese manga, it clearly shows an influence pushing them away from the patterns in other American comics. This theme of the influence of manga on American comics will be further explored in Chapter 8.

Discussion of US manga also marks a good place for us to compare different demographics of Japanese manga themselves. Subtypes here are a bit more varied. These results also appear in Figure 6.2d. The most extreme non-macro preference comes from seinen manga, where monos vastly outnumber macros. Shonen manga and josei manga maintain a slightly smaller preference for monos, but with the same overall distribution. However, shojo manga look a bit different. Here, though the frequencies are close to each other, macros actually outnumber monos, looking slightly more similar to the attentional structure of Western comics. This suggests that across these subtypes of manga, shojo manga maintain the most distinct structuring, though the overall patterns remain more similar to other Asian books than those of other countries.

The general consistency across regions (Europe, America, Asia) and within countries (America, Japan) hints at distinct patterns for the preferred framing of these different regions' panels. So, why might these differences arise? There are a few options, which are not necessarily mutually exclusive . . .

A first possibility is simple: they use different visual languages. Although comics from Europe, the United States, and Asia share historical origins in the early-twentieth century and before (Exner 2021, Gravett 2004), their structures clearly diverged across the latter part of the twentieth century in certain aspects of panel framing, resulting in the differences seen here. We will discuss a bit more about this historical change in American and some European comics in Chapter 8. However, these data suggest that somewhere in their history the patterns from various places grew more distinct. A straightforward explanation is therefore that visual languages can simply differ from each other, because varying cultural systems evolve to have distinct patterns.

Supporting this view, not only do Asian comics differ from those from America, we see here evidence of a contemporary influence of manga on American comics. US manga maintain a nearly equal proportion of macros and monos, which is more like the framing of Japanese manga than the clearly predominant macros in mainstream US comics. In addition, US manga use greater proportions of micros and amorphics, which is again closer to Japanese manga than mainstream American comics. These values suggest that the manga created in the United States by English-speaking Americans has indeed been influenced by the structure of Japanese manga.

These results imply that such conventions are transferable across cultures (Japan to America) despite differences in spoken languages (Japanese and English), and thus framing tendencies can be encoded as transmittable cognitive patterns through "language contact." This again supports that the variation across cultures may simply be attributed to patterns motivated by diversity in structures found across visual languages.

A second possibility is that cross-cultural differences arise through pressures from the physical format of the pages and/or the number of pages allotted to a given story (Lefèvre 2000, 2013). Shorter stories would need to convey more information in a smaller space, and thus would preference units that show the whole scene at once (macros) rather than showing only parts of a scene. Thus, we would predict that longer stories might have more "focal" framing (i.e., non-macro framing). But, at least cross-culturally, this constraint does not appear to be a factor, since Japanese manga (with less macros) are serialized in anthologies with page counts roughly the same as American comic books, while the European comics in our corpus (with the most macros) typically come from longer albums. In addition, these European comics (with more macros) used more panels per page than those from America (more macros) and Asia (more monos), suggesting that panel density on a page also does not motivate framing structure.

A third possibility may be the permeable influence of the spoken languages on the visual languages. Framing information with more or less complexity relates to how information is explicitly provided or left implicit. If panels only show single characters (monos), then a comprehender may need to infer more of what is not shown explicitly. A similar phenomenon occurs when sentences may or may not require subjects or objects to be obligatory. The flexible omission of subjects or objects is called *zero anaphora* (also, *pro-drop)* or conversely, languages that cannot drop subjects are said to have *obligatory subjects* (Haspelmath et al. 2001, Huang 1984). This would be like in English if you said *Reading a book* to mean *Jared is reading a book*, where Jared is inferred through the preceding discourse or the surrounding context. Because the grammatical subjects or objects are dropped from the uttered sentence, the omitted content is left inferred. The prediction would then be that because spoken languages habituate comprehenders to make these types of inferences, maybe they would be more allowing of similar omission and inference of elements in their visual sequences.

Asian languages in fact use zero anaphora more prevalently than the Germanic languages that are prevalent in our European and American comics (Haspelmath et al. 2001, Huang 1984, Dryer 2013), and indeed these Asian comics more often depict single characters (monos), compared to the macros in the European books. Could the omission of subjects have a permeable effect on the framing of panels and the inferences they sponsor? Although this might be suggested by our data, in the VLRC the cultural distinctions (Euro-American vs. Asian) are conflated with the typological (obligatory subject vs. zero anaphora), making it hard to distinguish them as independent factors in order to be confident in claiming this as a permeable influence. In future work we are already investigating this question further with a corpus on a more global scope.

Another possibility might return to the different "storytelling strategies" that I mentioned at the start, related to how an author might modulate a reader's attention. To reiterate, I described that readers typically focus their attention on only a select portion of a panel at a time. So, an author has the choice of whether to simply allow readers to direct their attention to those areas within a fairly detailed depiction (such as in more macros), or whether to constrain the panels themselves to have less information (such as in more non-macro panels).

If panel framing is connected to the direction of attention within panels, their structure might be affected by cross-cultural differences in attention itself. Psychological research has found that people from American culture, and to a lesser extent, European cultures, direct attention at the primary characters of a visual scene. Thus, if given a picture of a tiger walking in the forest, people from these cultures will focus primarily just at the tiger, but not much at the background. In contrast, people from Asian cultures fixate on the surrounding environment in the visual field as well as the primary figures (Masuda and Nisbett 2006, Nisbett and Masuda 2003). Thus, they would look at both the tiger and surrounding forest.

Bearing this in mind, authors might use storytelling strategies that adapt to the attentional preferences of their culture. Under this interpretation, American and European comics use an "objective storytelling" method with more macros, because authors implicitly expect readers to fixate on the primary elements in a panel even if there is surrounding complexity in the scene. This is idealized in Figure 6.3a, where each panel has numerous characters, and each one changes in their events across each panel in the sequence.

In contrast, panels in Asian comics use more focal framing (monos, micros, amorphics), to specifically depict the attentionally relevant information in each panel, as in Figure 6.3b. This more "subjective storytelling" simulates a reader's attention across the sequence of panels as if they were moving their eyes around a scene (Cohn 2013c), which is schematized in Figure 6.3c. In other words, reading a sequence of focally-framed panels would give a sensation that a reader was placed within a scene, with panels showing the viewpoint of their eyes as they look around at its different component parts (thus, "subjective"). In contrast, sequences with more macro panels maintain a separation that leaves the reader able to view a scene in totality (thus, "objective").

This interpretation of a "subjective storytelling" method is supported by findings that focal framing aligns with characters' viewpoints in a visual narrative (Moisich In prep). Indeed, McCloud (1993) claimed that Japanese manga specifically use more "subjective" techniques to immerse readers into

a) "Objective" storytelling

b) "Subjective" storytelling

c) Simulated scan path of subjective storytelling

FIGURE 6.3 *a) An "objective" storytelling technique showing full scenes in each panel, contrasted with b) a more "subjective" storytelling technique selecting portions of the frame at a time. Subjective storytelling which may be akin to c) where the eye scans across the parts of a scene.*

stories, such as the increased use of panels showing environmental information (in our terms, amorphic panels) that cast a "wandering eye" on a scene. He further claimed that manga's use of lines set behind an object gives the sense that the viewer is moving along with it. Indeed, psychological research has shown that such background lines enhance the sense of motion compared to regular motion lines (Ito, Seno, and Yamanaka 2010).

It should be noted that this interpretation of subjective storytelling through the increased use of focal framing does not depend on findings of cross-cultural differences in attention. These could be independent observations, despite being consistent with each other. Further experimental research could examine this relationship (or lack thereof). We will further explore this claim of a more immersive and subjective storytelling style later in this chapter. In addition, these various possible interpretations (cultural patterns, formatting, permeability, attention) are not mutually exclusive. Various pressures could be operating simultaneously, and future research aims to clarify these interpretations.

6.1.1 Framing runs

Let's now ask how attentional framing structure progresses across panel sequences. In the previous chapter, we described how *runs* of panels might maintain continuity of different situational dimensions, and we showed that there was a tradeoff between the length of both time and spatial location runs and their frequency. Despite the cross-cultural differences that we observed in situational dimensions, this relationship between length and frequency persisted in a consistent way across cultures, heralding a more "universal" tendency in line with linguistic laws (Zipf 1935). Here we can investigate similar runs of framing categories.

A *framing run* is thus considered as any contiguous sequence of panels using the same framing type. Thus, a sequence of three macros in a row, such as in Figure 6.3a would be a *macro run* with a length of three, while the three monos in a row in the middle of Figure 6.3b (panels 2, 3, and 4) would be a *mono run* with a length of three. To derive the frequency of runs for each book, I counted the total number of runs of a given framing type (like macros) and divided it out of the total number of appearances of that framing type.

The results are depicted in Figure 6.4. All framing types again display the same tradeoff in frequency and length that we saw with situational runs: shorter runs appear more frequently, and longer runs progressively appear less often. This again is consistent with Zipf's Law as observed in the structure of languages (Zipf 1935), as demonstrated by the "decaying" trendlines. The consistency of the patterning of these runs across framing types and regions, despite their cross-cultural diversity shown above, again points to a universal trait of the structuring of information across sequences.

6.1.2 Framing and situational coherence

Now that we've looked at the overall distribution of attentional categories, we can examine how they interact with other dimensions of structure. First let's look at the interaction of attentional types and the types of situational coherence that we explored in the previous chapter. In this case, we'll examine how the combinations of changes between time, spatial location, and characters align with shifts into panels with different attentional framing types.

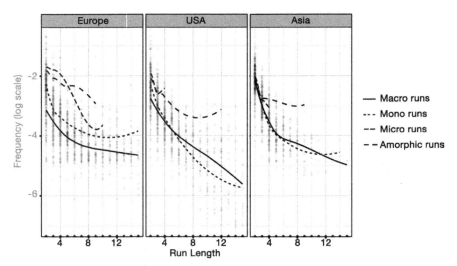

FIGURE 6.4 *The frequency of runs using different types of framing. Run frequency is plotted in logarithmic scale.*

Figure 6.5a depicts the *collocations* of all situational changes and attentional framing categories, along with their cross-cultural manifestation in European, American, and Asian comics. This figure is fairly complex, so let's take it one piece at a time. First off, for space I have omitted here some of the combinations of situational changes where there were low frequencies. As can be confirmed in Figure 5.4 in the last chapter, these included shifts involving no character changes and either full or partial spatial location changes, and those with both partial character and spatial location changes.

Let's begin by discussing what occurs when time does shift across panels, which is depicted in the left column of graphs in Figure 6.5. As in our analysis in Chapter 5, shifts in time most often involve partial or no character changes where no spatial location shifts. That is, it maintains the same spatial location while shifting minimally between characters. These situational shifts were maintained the most across macros, and only slightly less in monos and micros. These patterns were also consistent across all regions. Within these panels that shifted in time, Asian comics again deviated for having more full changes between characters where there were no spatial location changes. Although this difference occurred for macros, it was even more for monos and micros.

With time changes, this full character change with no spatial location change was most pronounced for amorphic panels, where it was the most frequent shift in situational dimensions. This should make sense, since amorphic panels depict only environmental information, and thus shifting to them from any other framing type would involve a full change to having

FRAMING STRUCTURE

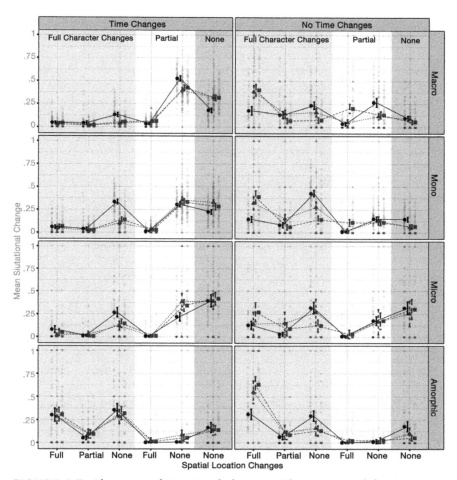

FIGURE 6.5 *Alignment of situational changes within attentional framing types. Solid line is Asian comics (circle), dashed line is US comics (square), and dotted line is European comics (triangle).*

no characters. These shifts were essentially changes between "aspects of an environment" within the same spatial location. Amorphic panels were also frequently involved with full character changes and full spatial location changes. These would be full "scene shifts" into a scene-setting amorphic panel, such as the exterior of a building. It is noteworthy that all of these situational dimensions for amorphic panels are similar across regions, despite the greater proportion of character changing in other framing categories for Asian comics.

Let's now stay with amorphic panels as we turn to discussing shifts that involve no time change, as in the second column of graphs in Figure 6.5. With no shifts in time between panels, amorphic panels largely maintain the same types of other situational changes. However, we now see some differences between regions. Here, Asian comics used more of the changes between "aspects of the environment" (full character changes, no spatial location changes). This aligns with McCloud's (1993) observations that in Japanese manga, "aspect-to-aspect" transitions (i.e., shifts into amorphic panels) have a sense of timelessness as they move between spatial aspects of an environment. In contrast, European and American comics used more amorphic "scene shifts" (full character and spatial location changes) than Asian comics, and this regional pattern for "scene shifts" persists for macros, monos, and micros as well.

We can now discuss when no time changes occur in macros, monos, and micros. In macros, monos, and micros we again see the emphasis for Asian comics to use full character changes without spatial location changes. They additionally used more partial character changes in macros with no spatial location changes. This emphasis was particularly prominent for monos, micros, and amorphic panels, suggesting that Asian books use more "focal framing" to "slow down time" and show various aspects of a scene, rather than push those scenes through temporal states.

Nevertheless, European comics used these same collocations of full character changes and no spatial location changes in greater frequency than American comics, especially for micros where they were similar to Asian comics. American comics also distinctively used more partial character changes when there were also full spatial location changes, especially for macros and somewhat for monos.

Finally, micros distinctively showed a frequent use of full *situational discontinuity* (the datapoint furthest to the right), with no time change, no character change, and no spatial location change. This would be cases that zoom in on the same character as a previous panel, while also maintaining the same moment. Also frequent with micros was this same interaction with partial character changes, essentially zooming-in on only one character from a previous panel with multiple characters. These same collocations for micros were also present when time shifts also occurred.

Let's try to summarize all of this. In all cultures, panels that contain a large amount of information (macros) shift between different temporal states more often than any other type of situational dimension, especially while maintaining the same spatial location and minimal changes in characters. Mono and micro panels were more often involved in full, partial, or no character changes while maintaining the same spatial location. Amorphic panels were the most likely to involve full spatial location changes with full character changes in "scene shifts," especially without time shifts, or to use full character changes with no spatial location change in shifting between "aspects of the environment."

Like in our sections on situational coherence in Chapter 5 and on attentional framing structure earlier in this chapter, we again see a tension between many collocations with the same trends across regions and the patterned differences arising between regions. For example, macros and amorphic panels with time shifts differed minimally between regions. However, most distinctly, Asian comics emphasize character changes more than European and American comics, no matter the framing categories. Here we again see hints at the differences in "storytelling" style across regions manifesting in the relationship between how much information panels show and how that information shifts across panels.

A final observation is also important. Here we see consistent collocations of particular situational dimensions and attentional framing structure, suggesting that meaning is not simply flowing indiscriminately across panels. Rather, patterns manifest in particular combinations of meaning and framing, heralding more specific constructions of storytelling. But, the analysis depicted in Figure 6.5 only characterizes collocations for adjacent juxtapositions of panels, and additional patterning arises in longer sequences of panels. We will address more of these *narrative patterns* further in the next chapter.

6.1.3 Framing and shot scales

We can also explore the relationship of attentional structure to filmic shot scales, which above I argued are orthogonal dimensions of presenting information in panels. So, detailing their relationships might help to show how they intersect. Within the VLRC, we annotated several different categories of shot scale (Figure 6.6a), but they also can be treated as a fairly continuous gradation, since the different shot scales gradually zoom in from a long shot into an extreme close up (Cutting and Iricinschi 2015).

To accommodate the graded nature of shot scales, here I assign values to each of the types of shot scale, assigning each of the six different categories to equal distribution going from zero to one (as in the y-axis of Figure 6.6b). Since long shots are the widest scale, I assigned them a value of one, progressing with full (.83), medium (.66), medium close (.5), close up (.33), and extreme close up (.17). Ambiguous views were given a zero. With these values, we can find the average shot scale used by each attentional framing category. The results are depicted in Figure 6.6b.

When we look at the shot scales for our framing categories collapsing across all books in the VLRC, we see a range of results. Macros use wider shot scales than monos and amorphics, and micros used fairly narrow (close up) framing. Macros of all continents averaged around a shot scale of .73, which would fall between full and medium shot scales, but ranged from long shots to medium close shots. Monos averaged more like medium shots (.6), but again with a wide range from long shots to close ups. Micros expectedly showed the narrowest scale, averaging near an extreme close up (.22), while amorphics maintained an average between a medium close and close shot (.44). However, both micros and amorphic panels had the widest

132 THE PATTERNS OF COMICS

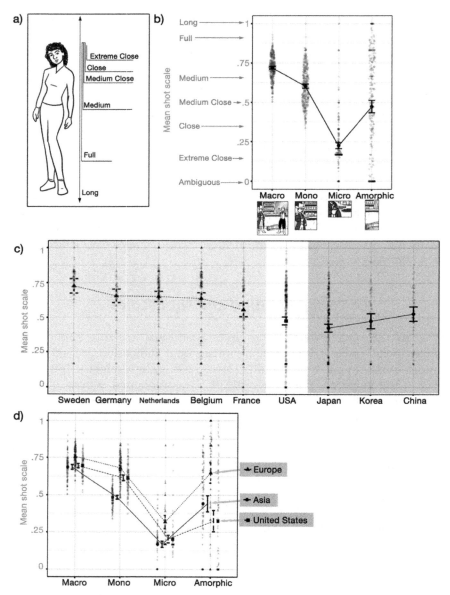

FIGURE 6.6 *Filmic shot scales a) illustrated for a human figure, and b) averaged for different attentional framing categories. Variation in shot scales are also shown for c) comics from different countries and d) crossed with attentional categories for different regions. Each dot represents a comic.*

distribution of shot scales, ranging all the way from extreme long shot to extreme close up.

Next, we can assess the overall shot scales of different types of comics in the VLRC. Overall, the average shot scale was a .53, which would be near a medium close shot. This is similar to the average shot scale of contemporary Hollywood films, which have reduced over time to arrive near an average of a medium shot, which is claimed to be optimal for both showing a figure and providing detail of the emotions on their faces (Cutting 2015).

But, shot scales varied a bit across cultures, as shown in Figure 6.6c. Panels from European countries used wider shot scales than those from Asia or the United States. The average shot scale from European comics was a .64, which would be similar to a medium shot. In contrast, panels from Asian or American comics used an average shot scale of around .45, which is between a close and a close up. So, on the whole European comics are showing a wider viewpoint in their panels than comics from Asia or the United States.

Shot scales of attentional framing categories also differ across regions. Here I again collapse across our broad regions of interest, with results depicted in Figure 6.6d. Monos from Europe were between a full and medium shot (.7), and those from the United States were more around a medium shot (.66). However, monos from Asian comics averaged more like a medium close shot (.5). Micros from Europe used slightly wider views than other regions, near a close up (.30), while those from Asian and American comics were nearer to an extreme close up (~.17). Finally, the greatest differences were shown to amorphic panels. Amorphic panels from Europe were similar to their monos (.6) as medium shots, while those from Asia (.45) and the United States (.3) fell between medium close and close shots, with all maintaining a wide variance.

Altogether, these results show that cultures differ in the presentation of shot scale in their panels. Although the attentional framing structure of panels from the United States is more similar to those from Europe, American comics use tighter shot scales that are more similar to Asian comics. In addition, other than the narrow shot scales of micros, European attentional framing categories consistently use similar shot scales around a medium shot, while framing categories in American and Asian panels remain more differentiated by their shot scales. These results reinforce that, although attentional categories may have prototypical alignments with certain shot scales, wide variance occurs between them, and attentional framing and shot scales ultimately capture different types of information.

6.2 Paneling structure

As discussed in the introduction to this chapter, paneling structure is an additional facet of how panels depict information. This dimension relates to how much the content in one panel remains isolated or whether it shares graphical relationships to other panels, as in Figure 6.1. Overall, 96 percent of comic panels use base framing, meaning that they remain spatially independent of other panels. This should be expected, since base framing is where panels stand alone, and can be considered as the default for panel framing. Divisionals (1 percent), inset panels (2 percent), and dominant panels (1 percent) were all fairly infrequent, suggesting paneling variation is rare on the whole.

These proportions were fairly disparate across countries, likely because of the small numbers of non-base framing. European comics used base framing the most (98 percent), then Asian comics (95 percent), and then those from the United States (94 percent). Divisionals were used only slightly more in Asian comics (2 percent) than European or American comics (.04 percent), while insets appeared more in comics from the United States (4 percent) than Asia (2 percent) or Europe (1 percent).

Some additional insights arise when we examine what attentional categories were used within those non-base framing types, along with their situational coherence. Figure 6.7a shows the proportion of non-base framing using different attentional categories (i.e., out of all divisional panels, what proportion used macros, monos, micros, or amorphic panels?).

Divisional panels most often used macros or monos, reflecting that they most likely broke apart larger macros. Also, although they were not as frequent overall, amorphics appeared slightly more often in divisional paneling than as inset panels. Divisional panels also typically showed character changes more than time changes (Figure 6.7b), suggesting that by breaking up a larger scene into multiple parts, each panel shifts across characters in a scene. Nevertheless, roughly 50 percent of divisionals also used time changes, suggesting that many divisionals also show a progression of events.

Dominant panels were also predominantly macros and monos, which would suggest that they show scenes or characters, while insets were mostly monos, then macros, micros, and amorphics. This is somewhat surprising, as inset panels often might show a subsection of the dominant panel, which, unless they selected out whole characters (monos), these would likely be micro panels. But, micro panels were relatively less frequent as insets compared to monos or even macros. Insets also used more time changes than character changes, predominantly reflecting the shift in events between dominant and inset panels. The prevalence of time shifts here is also surprising, since it implies that insets may not be giving a sense of simultaneity between inset and dominant panel, but rather shift in time as well as characters.

6.3 Subjectivity and framing

So far, we've shown that the attentional framing of panels differs across countries, collocates with specific changes in situational coherence across

FRAMING STRUCTURE 135

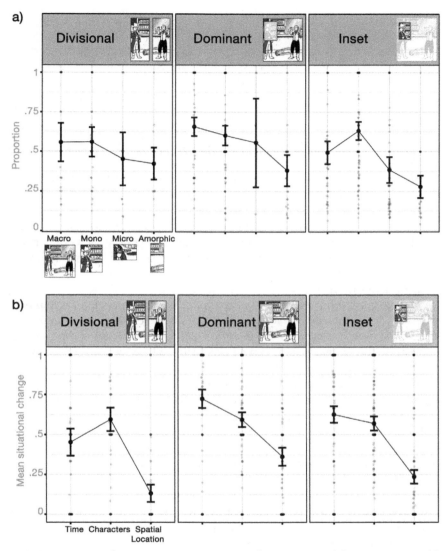

FIGURE 6.7 *Paneling structure interacting with a) attentional framing types and b) across shifts in situational coherence.*

panels, and varies in their shot scale of the representation. Earlier, I posited that certain patterns of framing lead to different types of storytelling. "Objective" storytelling shows a full scene (macros) and allows a reader to select the important active information from it, while "subjective" storytelling frames specific information into their own panels (monos, micros, amorphics), and then shifts between those elements. In subjective storytelling, I posited that this could be akin to simulating a viewer's attention, as if they were moving their eyes around a scene, with each panel looking at the primary places they look.

If subjective storytelling actually does reflect some degree of subjectivity, then we might expect it to intersect with the ways that visual narratives show character's viewpoints directly. This relates to the broader notions of perspective-taking or "focalization," which arise in narratives across modalities (Genette 1980, Maier and Steinbach 2022), and has been widely theorized in the context of comics (Mikkonen 2017, Horstkotte and Pedri 2011, Packard 2016, Round 2007, Borkent 2017, Maier and Bimpikou 2019, Thon 2016).

All images encode some aspect of perspective-taking through the ways that a visual depiction shows a perspective on a scene (Mikkonen 2017, Branigan 2012). The degree to which a picture gives a sense of subjectivity can be encoded in various ways and to varying degrees (Jahn 2021, Mikkonen 2012, 2017). Many such views depend on the viewpoint taken on a perceived object, such as framing a scene from behind a person, with the implication that the viewer of the image is looking in the same direction as a character in the scene.

The most overt representation of character's viewpoints appears in *point-of-view (POV)* or *subjective viewpoint panels*, where the visual depiction directly shows a character's perception on a scene from a first-person view, and these types of viewpoints have been analyzed within the VLRC. In some cases, panels use explicit visual cues to signal subjectivity, such as frames simulating an object being looked through, such as the keyhole in Figure 6.8a or the gun scope in Figure 6.8b. Panels may also use angles chosen to suggest a character's eyeline (Branigan 2012), as in Figure 6.8c.

Sometimes, a subjective viewpoint is created by their relationship to their adjacent panels (Thon 2016), as in Figures 6.8a, 6.8c, and 6.8d. This observation was argued even in early film theory by Kuleshov (1974), which has undergone experimental analysis with mixed results (Calbi et al. 2019, Barratt et al. 2016). In this sequential subjectivity, one panel might show the observer, and another panel shows their viewpoint, creating the inference that they are viewing that scene. Without overt cues to signal their first-person perspective, these sequentially subjective panels may no longer convey subjectivity if taken out of this context, such as if the middle panel in Figure 6.8d was shown in isolation.

As demonstrated in Figure 6.8a–d, all types of attentional framing operate as subjective panels. However, a consistent claim has been that subjective perspective, or internal "focalization" more broadly (Genette 1980), aligns with less complex framing—i.e., "focal" framing—of a representation. All attentional framing categories can be used to signal subjectivity, as in Figure 6.8, but this idea would be that more constrained framing heightens the sense of subjectivity on a scene. Similarly, divisionals have also been claimed to heighten a sense of focalization (Poharec 2018), and indeed divisionals break up an image to draw more focus to those smaller parts

FRAMING STRUCTURE 137

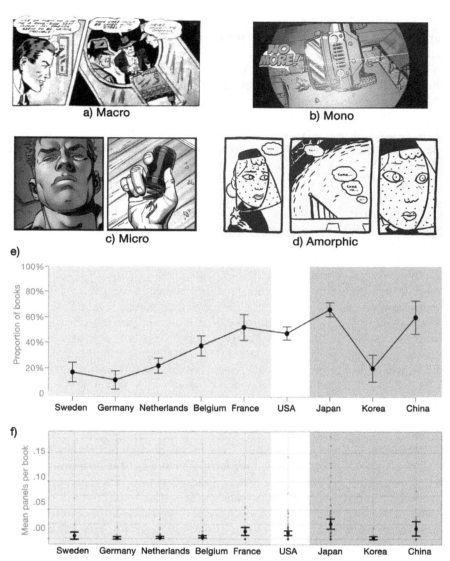

FIGURE 6.8 *Subjective viewpoint panels using attentional framing categories of a a) macro, b) mono, c) micro, and d) amorphic panel, while e) shows the proportion of books that use subjective panels across countries, and f) the proportion of panels that use subjectivity (error bars show standard error).* Captain Midnight #1 *by Jack Binder, Public Domain.* The Amazing Spider-Man #539 *by J. Michael Straczynski and Ron Garney, Spider-Man © Marvel Comics.* Heck *by Zander Cannon, Heck © Zander Cannon.*

of the scene. These ideas are directly in line with the notion that greater amounts of monos, micros, and amorphics lead to a "subjective" type of storytelling.

Some experimentation has supported the idea that focal framing invites more attribution of internal mental states. In his dissertation research, Oliver Moisich (In prep) presented participants with an excerpt of panels from David Mazzuchelli and Paul Karasik's 1994 graphic novel adaptation of Paul Auster's novel *City of Glass*. Participants were then asked to identify panels that they believed could or could not represent the point-of-view of a character. He found that more panels with focal framing, particularly micros, were chosen to convey character's internal perspectives, while no difference was shown across framing types that maintained an "external" perspective that did not show a character's perspective. In addition, despite differences in their attentional framing structure, the filmic shot scale of the panels showed no consistent relationship with attribution of point-of-view.

Subjective panels in actual comics were also analyzed in an early corpus analysis alongside attentional framing categories (Cohn 2011). Subjective panels were more prevalent in Japanese manga (1.6 percent) than in American comics (1 percent), and subjective panels overall in manga correlated positively with the rates of monos and micros. However, no analyses looked at the framing of the subjective panels themselves. These frequencies are slightly less than the rates of POV shots found in analyses of films, where they constitute 2 to 10 percent of all shots (Cutting and Candan 2015, 2013, Salt 2016). Experimental evidence with an animated film has also shown that greater attribution of internal mental states occurs with more focal shot framing (Bálint, Blessing, and Rooney 2020, Bálint and Rooney 2019).

With this context in mind, we have asked about both proportions of subjective panels in the VLRC, along with the nature of their framing (Cohn, Hacımusaoğlu, and Klomberg 2022). Following our idea that more focal framing (monos, micros, amorphics) sponsors a subjective storytelling method, we expected that more POV panels would arise in countries that use less complex framing, i.e., in Asian comics. In addition, subjective panels themselves might use more focal framing.

When determining subjective panels, the judgment was binary: panels were either deemed to show a subjective viewpoint or not. Only 42 percent (151/361) of the comics in the corpus contained subjective panels. As depicted in Figure 6.8e, the frequency of books using subjective panels did vary across countries, but no consistent pattern appeared within or across regions. The greatest frequency of books using subjective panels were found in Japanese manga (66 percent) and then Chinese manhua (60 percent), followed by French bande desinée (52 percent) and American comics (47 percent). Lower proportions of books with subjective panels appeared in Flemish comics (38 percent), and comics from Korea, the Netherlands, Germany, and Sweden (<20 percent).

FRAMING STRUCTURE

Some variety was found with the subtypes of Japanese manga and comics from the United States. Within Japanese manga, subjective panels appeared in 81 percent of shonen (boys') manga, followed by high proportions of josei (women's) and seinen (men's) manga (50 percent), and then shojo (girls') manga (46 percent). In comics from the United States, subjective panels appeared in more indie comics (67 percent) than US manga (59 percent), or mainstream comics (40 percent).

In these 151 books that used subjective panels, I then asked: When a comic has at least one subjective viewpoint, what proportion of panels use subjectivity? Overall, books had an average of 2.6 percent of panels per book that were subjective panels, which is broadly consistent with the proportion of subjective panels in previous corpus analyses of comics (Cohn 2011) and the lower end of proportions of POV shots found in corpus analyses of film (Cutting and Candan 2013, 2015, Salt 2016). This may imply a broader rate of subjective viewpoints maintained in visual storytelling across static and dynamic narratives. However, it is worth remembering that films and comics may not be considered as fully independent media as they might appear. Not only do many comics form the inspiration for contemporary films, but the shooting and editing of many films are often preceded by the creation of drawn storyboards, sometimes drawn by people who also work as comic artists, which lay a foundation for their visual narrative structure.

When looking at cross-cultural diversity of the proportion of these subjective panels, we again see no consistent trends in terms of regions (Figure 6.8f). Japanese manga and Chinese manhua used the highest frequency of subjective panels, followed by Swedish, French, and American comics. These proportions break down further for manga and American comics. Shonen manga (4.7 percent) used the highest frequency of subjective panels, followed by shojo (3.1 percent) and seinen (2.9 percent) manga, and then josei manga (1.1 percent). In American comics, indie comics used subjective panels the most (3.9 percent), followed by mainstream comics (2.1 percent), and then US manga (1 percent).

These results support the idea that Japanese manga use more subjective panels than other types of comics, and provides further evidence for the idea that they broadly use more "subjective storytelling." Interestingly, shonen manga in our sample had the most books with subjective panels, while shojo manga used the least out of all manga. However, shojo manga have often been described as conveying the emotions and mental states of their characters (Prough 2010, Takahashi 2008), typically in contrast to shonen manga. If our results are generalizable, it implies that subjective viewpoints may not be the primary technique used by shojo manga for conveying such internal states, which instead may use other techniques such as visual morphology or sound effects (Cohn and Ehly 2016, Shinohara and Matsunaka 2009, Takahashi 2008, Pratha, Avunjian, and Cohn 2016).

Let's next turn to the attentional framing structure of these subjective panels. Do subjective viewpoints often use more focal framing? As depicted in Figure 6.9a, overall, subjective panels differed in their framing types. Subjective macros (32 percent) and monos (35 percent) were more frequent than subjective micros (16 percent) and amorphics (16 percent). On the surface, this implies that subjectivity does not necessarily coincide with focal framing. However, these frequencies reflect the total number of subjective panels found across books. As we saw earlier in this chapter, macros and monos are used more than other attentional types in general, and this is thus reflected in the greater prevalence of subjective macros and monos. These frequencies are further reflected in the differences across subjective panels in different regions, as in Figure 6.9b.

To account for this difference in baseline proportions of framing types, I thus calculated the proportion of subjective panels for each framing category out of the total number of that framing category in a given book. For example, out of all mono panels, how many were subjective monos? The results of this analysis are shown in Figure 6.9c.

Here, attentional types of subjective panels again differed, but with a different distribution of frequencies. Far greater proportions of micros and amorphics used subjective viewpoints than macros or monos. The large proportions of subjective micros align with the idea that subjectivity is associated with focal framing, and is consistent with experimental findings that micros and close-ups motivate interpretations of characters' internal states (Moisich In prep, Bálint, Blessing, and Rooney 2020, Bálint and Rooney 2019). In addition, the high proportions of subjective amorphics aligns with the idea that panels showing the surrounding environment may reflect a "wandering eye" around a scene (McCloud 1993).

This same overall trend of more subjective micros and amorphics than macros and monos persisted across regions, as in Figure 6.9d. However, European comics used greater proportions of subjective micros and amorphics than American comics, which used greater proportions than Asian comics. This consistent pattern supports the overall idea that focal framing aligns with the representation of subjective viewpoints. Unlike the way that framing categories themselves differ across regions, this consistency suggests that the alignment of focal framing with subjective viewpoints is a more general typological preference.

In addition, given claims that divisionals might also heighten the sense of subjectivity to a reader (Poharec 2018), I also examined the rate of subjective panels using divisional framing. However, the rate of subjective divisionals was extremely small (.06 percent) compared even to the small proportion of non-subjective divisionals (.6 percent), or subjective insets (.2 percent). Thus, the insight that divisionals may confer a sense of subjectivity may relate to the general sense of focal framing that divisionals give to the parts of a scene compared to base framing showing the whole scene.

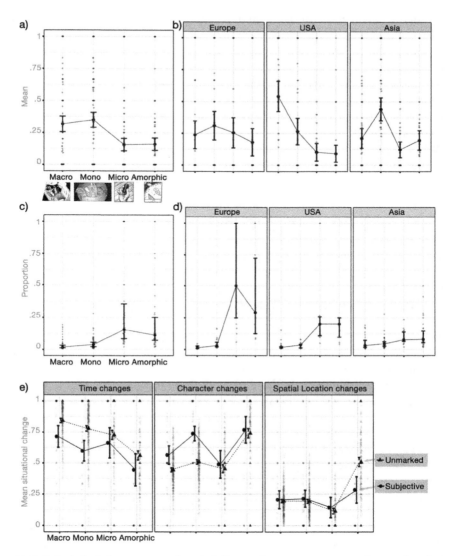

FIGURE 6.9 *Subjective panels of different framing types are shown for their frequency a) across all subjective panels, and b) across regions in the VLRC, and for their proportion within framing categories, both c) across all subjective panels, and d) across regions in the VLRC. Finally, e) shows situational changes across framing types for both subjective and non-subjective panels. Error bars represent standard error.*

Finally, we can again ask: what types of situational changes between panels might occur with subjective panels, particularly related to attentional framing? These results are depicted in Figure 6.9e. The most salient difference for subjective panels compared to their non-subjective counterparts was the decrease in the rates of time changes for subjective panels. This implies that panels showing point-of-view may not shift in time from the previous panel, but rather show a viewpoint happening at the same moment. In addition, character changes were more frequent in subjective panels, particularly subjective monos. This should make sense, since a point-of-view panel may change from a panel showing the viewer, to the subjective panel showing the character (mono) or scene (amorphic) that they look at.

6.4 Conclusion

This chapter explored the variation in framing structure within and across comics. The primary finding was that panels in comics from Europe and the United States tend to show more of a whole scene (macros) rather than depicting panels with those component parts (monos, micros, amorphics). In contrast, comics from Asia tend to use panels that depict parts of a scene as much if not more often than whole scenes. This focal framing technique was suggested as a type of "subjective" storytelling that simulates the way a person might look around a scene at different information, compared to the "objective" storytelling that shows the whole scene outright.

Further analysis of collocations of situational changes supported this "wandering eye" view of focal framing, showing that panels with single characters (monos) or aspects of the environment (amorphics) more often shift between characters than the wider views. In addition, direct subjective viewpoints constituted a greater proportion of micros and amorphics than other framing categories, aligning with experimental evidence for a relationship between subjectivity and focal framing (Bálint, Blessing, and Rooney 2020, Bálint and Rooney 2019, Moisich In prep).

Given these results, it is worth returning to the discussion at the start of this chapter about the cognitive processes related to perceiving the information in panels, and the effect this has on comprehending a sequence. When a panel shows a full scene all at once—as in cases of increased macros in objective storytelling of the European comics—it would thus create more demands in the front-end processes of actual attention. A comprehender would need to move their eyes to search more through a panel to find what is necessary to extract for its sequential meaning. But, by being more explicit about the overall information within a sequence, the back-end comprehension processes might require less effort to connect information across panels.

In contrast, by showing only portions of a scene at a time, such as characters (monos) or the environment (amorphics), each panel unit is easier to process. They require less visual search, since the panel itself frames the relevant information directly. However, by providing less information in each panel, the overall sequence may be more demanding to comprehend, and this subjective storytelling thus requires more inferencing in the back-end processes to be understood.

Thus, these patterns of framing structure will lead to different demands on how people engage and comprehend comic panels, and subsequently, how they comprehend their sequences. It is worth emphasizing that neither strategy is better or worse, and familiarity with each of these strategies may in turn modulate how they are processed. For example, if a reader is used to comprehending a more objective storytelling style, then a sequence with increased focal framing may be demanding to understand, even if the individual panels seem less complex. Indeed, readership of different types of comics affects the brain response to panels with different types of framing (Cohn and Foulsham 2020, Cohn and Kutas 2017). In other words, as we have seen throughout, comics differ in the types of structures they use, and comprehension of those structures requires fluency gained through familiarity with those types of comics. We will return to a discussion of these storytelling styles throughout subsequent chapters as we explore further dimensions of visual language structure.

CHAPTER SEVEN

Narrative Structure

Much of the research on how we understand a sequence of images, whether drawn or filmed, has focused on the ways that meaning changes between adjacent images.[1] Comprehenders have been shown to track various situational dimensions of events, spatial locations, and characters across panels (Cohn 2020b, Loschky et al. 2020), and as we discussed in Chapter 5, these dimensions may vary in how much they change across panels. However, changes in meaning alone are not sufficient to account for the structure of a sequence of images, particularly not meaningful changes that are only tracked across linear relationships between panels.

Consider the sequence in Figure 7.1a (Cohn 2013d, c). Here, the first panel shows a man in bed, followed by a panel of a clock. The third panel shows a window with the time of day, followed by a penultimate panel of the clock at a different time, and then the final panel shows the man making a phone call. There are several important traits about this sequence that make it difficult for an approach based only on meaningful relationships. First, taken at its surface relationships, this would only show character changes and/or partial spatial location changes. But, several panels have content that must connect across a distance. The man only appears in panels 1 and 5, while the clock appears in panels 2 and 4, meaning these panels need to be connected across a longer distance than just pairs of panels.

Second, this sequence actually has multiple interpretations depending on how you associate panels with each other. In the first interpretation, each panel constitutes its own "moment," which would mean that the shift in "time" for the clocks in panels 2 and 4 would occur between the shift in time for panels of the man in panels 1 and 5. As depicted in Figure 7.1b, this creates an *embedded clause* for the clock panels, which can be confirmed through deletion of panels: You can delete the outer panels (1 and 5) and the clock sequence could work on its own, or you could delete the center panels (2, 3, and 4) and the shift between the first and last panels could be their own sequence.

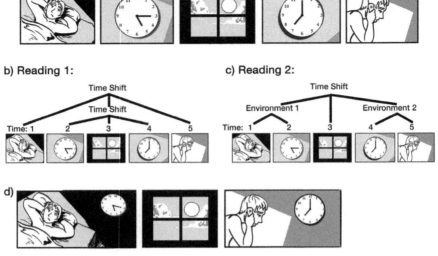

FIGURE 7.1 *a) An ambiguous narrative sequence with interpretations b) of each panel showing a separate moment, or c) with panels grouping together, while d) shows an alternative sequence showing the same meaning.*

Another interpretation of this sequence is that the first (1 and 2) and last (4 and 5) pairs of panels occur at the same time, just showing different views of the environment at a shared moment. As diagrammed in Figure 7.1c, here the man is lying in bed in panel 1 *at the same time* as the clock in panel 2, and he makes a phone call in panel 5 at the same time as the clock in panel 4. This interpretation requires us to group together these pairs of panels into common environments, and then have a single time shift between them (with the center panel being even more ambiguous for how it may be associated with the other panels). This possible interpretation can be confirmed because we can incorporate the contents of both the first and last pairs of panels into single panels, as in Figure 7.1d. With the man and clock within single panels instead of across pairs of panels, the environmental relationships become clear, and the ambiguity disappears.

Not only does this sequence have several potential ways to convey meaning, but these meanings depend on grouping elements together. A linear treatment of meaning changing across these panels would be unable to account for this structural ambiguity. Especially where the first and final panels need to connect, these relationships extend across a *distance* with several panels placed in-between. In fact, you could keep adding more panels in the middle (ex. other scenes around his room, a cat having a multi-panel adventure, etc.), and the outer panels would always need to connect to each other. We need to account for all of this structure in a theory of how we comprehend a sequence of images.

The contrast between Figures 7.1a and 7.1d also reinforces why meaningful relations alone does not fully govern the structure of the sequence. These sequences effectively convey the same overall meaning but use a different surface *presentation* in the sequence. Since the same overall meaning is conveyed but with a different sequencing structure, it suggests that an additional structure is organizing that meaning. The meaning must be separate from the structure that organizes it, or else different presentations for the same meaning wouldn't be possible.

Finally, in both of these examples, we have intuitions for how a *narrative* progresses beyond the situational dimensions conveyed by that sequence. Both of these sequences begin with panels that *set up* the overall event situation, which is then prolonged across the center panels, and has its climax in the final panel. These basic roles played by panels maintain the expectations we have of how narratives progress in canonical order of a set-up, initiation, climax, and an aftermath. These functional roles go beyond the incremental changes in meaning that may occur between panels.

All of this suggests that meaningful changes between images are not enough to characterize the ways we structure and comprehend a sequence of images. I have suggested that this role is played by an additional **narrative structure** that functions in parallel with meaning to organize and package these situational dimensions of events, spatial locations, and characters.

7.1 Visual Narrative Grammar

Visual Narrative Grammar (VNG) is my theory for the structure of sequential images. In this model, images are assigned to narrative categories based on cues within panels, and then these panels are organized into hierarchic groupings, analogous to how syntactic categories organize words into constituents at a sentence level (Cohn 2013d). Because images typically contain more information than words, the conceptual structure of the units are closer to whole sentences and thereby convey a "discourse" level of meaning. However, the principles that combine these units remains similar between syntactic and narrative structures. In essence, narrative structure acts as a "macro-syntax."

It is important to point out that the constructs of narrative grammar came about by following methods of syntactic research, not merely through theorizing alone. These methods include diagnostics for categories and constituent structures (Cohn 2015b, a), in addition to extensive use of such manipulations in experimentation (for review, see Cohn 2020b). Indeed, manipulation of this narrative structure has consistently been shown to evoke the same brain responses as manipulations of syntax in sentences, and these responses are independent of those of processing meaning (Cohn 2020b). Thus, the comparisons between syntactic and narrative structure persist at the architectural level, and are grounded in empirical evidence.

VNG is certainly not the first theory to posit a "grammatical" approach to narrative. Other such approaches have proposed formal structures for verbal stories (e.g., Mandler and Johnson 1977) and for film (e.g., Carroll 1980). These theories were based on Chomskyan phrase structure grammars (e.g., Chomsky 1965), which posit procedural "rules" for the combinations of units. These precedents also derive meaning structures from the grammar, and/or remain ambiguous about the relationship between grammar and meaning. In contrast, VNG is based on contemporary linguistic theories using *construction grammar* (Culicover and Jackendoff 2005), which posits schematic patterns stored into long-term memory as lexical items unto themselves (not procedural "rules"), along with interface-rules specifying privileged mappings to semantics (Goldberg 1995, Jackendoff 2002).

There are three primary schemas specified by VNG:

(1)

a) Canonical narrative schema: $[_{\text{Phrase X}} (\text{Establisher}) - (\text{Initial}) - \text{Peak} - (\text{Release})]$

b) Conjunction schema: $[_{\text{Phrase X}} X_1 - X_2 -. . . X_n]$

c) Head-modifier schema: $[_{\text{Phrase X}} (\text{Modifier}) - X - (\text{Modifier})]$

The first schema (1a) specifies a canonical order for narrative roles to progress. Although some categories are optional (indicated by parentheses), the categories must go in this order. The second schema (1b) specifies a conjunction, where any category (here specified as a variable "X") can be repeated inside a grouping of that same type of category (i.e., lots of Xs go in an X grouping). Finally, the third schema (1c) allows for any category ("X") to be modified in a grouping of the same type of category. This primary category ("X") is the "head" that is modified by other types of elaborative categories. Let's now explore each of these schemas and how they combine.

First, VNG argues that the meaningful cues within images can map to narrative roles, which are organized into a *canonical narrative schema*. The idea of narrative roles again comes down to abstraction: despite different meanings in panels, we can recognize that there are patterned ways that panels function in a sequence. These basic narrative categories[2] include:

Establisher (E) – sets up an interaction without acting upon it, often as a passive state

Initial (I) – initiates the tension of the narrative arc, prototypically a preparatory action and/or a source of a path

Peak (P) – marks the height of narrative tension and point of maximal event structure, prototypically a completed action and/or goal of a path, but also often an interrupted action

Release (R) – releases the tension of the interaction, prototypically the coda or aftermath of an action

These descriptions of narrative roles outline their correspondence to meaning—i.e., how *semantic* content (contained in the visual cues within images) may influence an image's *structural* role in a sequence. Nevertheless, identification of a narrative category uses both a panel's bottom-up content and its top-down context in a global sequence (Cohn 2013d, 2014c). For example, a reader might recognize a panel as an Initial, both because it shows a preparatory action (bottom-up) and because it follows a previous Establisher panel (top-down). Syntactic categories are assigned in a similar way: although syntactic categories (such as nouns, verbs) prototypically correspond to the semantics (such as objects, events) of words (Jackendoff 1990), they also rely on context within a sentence. For example, the word "dance" (semantically, an event) can play a role either as a noun (*the dance*) or a verb (*they dance*), depending on the top-down context.

The basic narrative schema in VNG places these narrative categories into a constituent ("phrase") in the specific order of *Establisher-Initial-Peak-Release*. In actual sequences, not all constituents must contain all categories, meaning that most elements are non-obligatory and can be left out without significantly affecting the sequence (as notated by parentheses). Only Peaks are obligatory, because they motivate a sequence as its "head." However, Peaks too can be omitted under specific constrained, inference generating contexts (Cohn and Kutas 2015, Magliano et al. 2015, Magliano et al. 2016, Cohn 2019a, Klomberg and Cohn 2022).

Not only do narrative categories apply to individual panels, but they can also apply to narrative constituents. Consider Figure 7.2, which I'll continually manipulate in order to show the various structures of VNG. The first panel shows a boxer reaching back to punch another. This preparatory action is prototypical of an Initial. The full punch occurs in the next panel, a Peak in relation to that Initial. An Establisher then resets the actions in

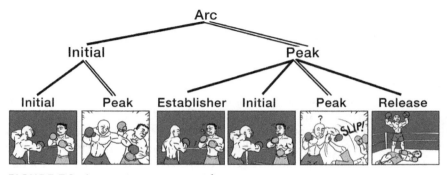

FIGURE 7.2 *A narrative sequence with two narrative constituents.*

panel 3, by setting up a new situation with the boxers passively facing off again. Panel 4 repeats the preparatory action of the first boxer reaching back to punch, again a cue for an Initial. The subsequent Peak in the penultimate panel does not depict a completed action (as in panel 2), but rather shows an interruption of the boxer's action: he slips. The final panel, a Release, shows the aftermath of this action, with the victor standing over his opponent.

If we consider only the panel-level narrative categories (*I-P-E-I-P-R*), this sequence will not conform to the canonical narrative schema. However, combining categories into groupings introduces segmental complexity into a narrative, enabling constituents to play narrative roles relative to each other at a higher level. A maximal node is considered an "Arc," meaning that it plays no functional role in a larger constituent.

Figure 7.2 uses two constituents: the first two panels form an Initial that together set up a Peak constituent of the remaining four panels. Internally, each constituent maintains the canonical narrative schema, with Peaks forming the "heads" that motivate the primary meaning of their "upstairs" phrase (i.e., each constituent is an expansion of its Peak, indicated by double-barred lines).[3] This means that individual panels and whole constituents both take on narrative roles, and the canonical narrative schema is *recursive*. This recursion means that narrative structures can continually build larger and larger structures, since the principles guiding short sequences also apply to higher "plot" level narrative structures. Thus, VNG applies not only for short sequences but also to the narrative structures of stories of any length.

Additional schemas specified in VNG increase the complexity of sequences by elaborating on the canonical narrative schema. **Conjunction**, as specified in the schema in (1b), allows categories to repeat within a constituent of the same category (Cohn 2013d, 2015b). This is structurally similar to how syntactic conjunction repeats grammatical categories (such as multiple nouns in a noun phrase: *The butcher, baker, and candlestick maker*). Figure 7.3b conjoins three panels at the outset of the sequence. Because these opening panels in 7.3b depict the same information as the single first panel in 7.3a, it suggests that they all function to introduce the scene as Establishers. Indeed, the three panels in 7.3b could be substituted for the single panel in 7.3a, which shows that they occupy a similar distributional status in the sequence.

The conjunction schema itself only specifies that narrative categories repeat within a constituent, and does not inherently specify meaningful relations. However, various conventionalized correspondences exist between *conceptual structure* and this *narrative* schema (Cohn 2013d, 2015b). For example, the conjunction in Figure 7.3b shows each character in its own panel (as monos), but nothing shows us that these characters occupy the same spatial location (as in the equivalent macro in Figure 7.3a). Thus, this spatial environment must now be inferred across these panels. Because of

NARRATIVE STRUCTURE 151

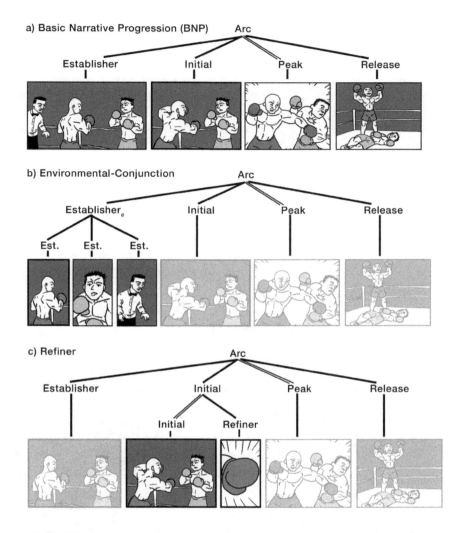

FIGURE 7.3 *Narrative schemas within Visual Narrative Grammar for a) the basic narrative progression, b) Environmental-Conjunction, and c) Refiners.*

this relationship, I call this type of construction ***Environmental-Conjunction*** or "***E-Conjunction***," since it is a conjunction in narrative structure (panels repeating the same narrative role) that leads to an inference of a broader spatial environment (notated with subscript "e" in the diagram).

Various meaningful relations are also possible using the conjunction schema. Figure 7.4 depicts several of these correspondences to a three-panel conjunction constituent, all Initials. The left tier of Figure 7.4 shows different three-panel sequences that can operate as conjoined Initials of a) *actions* or events (***Action-Conjunction***), b) characters within an *environment*

(*Environmental-Conjunction*), c) parts of a single *entity* or character (*Entity-Conjunction*), or d) disparate *categorically* associated elements (*Category-Conjunction*[4]).

In each type of conjunction in Figure 7.4, the conjoined panels on the left are semantically equivalent to (and may create inferences of) the single panels in the right tier. In other words, the single, non-conjoined image in the right tier can substitute for the three conjoined images in the left tier. This substitution serves as a diagnostic test for assessing conjunctions (Cohn 2015b). This also occurs in the clock examples at the start of this chapter,

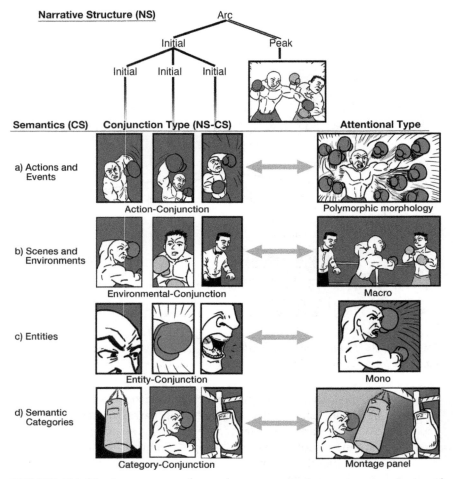

FIGURE 7.4 *Varying correspondences between narrative conjunction (repeated narrative categories, here, Initials) with semantic information (actions, characters in a scene, parts of an individual, or elements sharing a semantic category). This information could also be framed by a single image (right tier).*

where the first and last panels in Figure 7.1a could substitute for single panels in Figure 7.1d. In addition, because conjunction is recursive, these forms can also embed within each other. For example, the three-panels in Figure 7.4c could replace the first panel in 7.4b, which would create an N-Conjunction constituent embedded within an E-Conjunction constituent. Thus, the same *narrative* conjunction can have several types of *semantic* mappings.

Another modifier is shown in the third panel in Figure 7.3c, which depicts the same information as its preceding panel, only zooming-in on the puncher's fist. This is a **Refiner** (Cohn 2013c, 2015b), which modifies the information in another "head" panel (again, double bar lines) using a narrower viewpoint of the same information. These panels both play the same role in the overall narrative arc. In Figure 7.3c, the Refiner attaches to an Initial, and thus the overall constituent is also an Initial. Refiners thus use the "head-modifier schema" described above in (1c), where the "head" is any narrative category, and the "modifier" is the Refiner.

Unlike conjunction, the narrative category here is not distributed across units, but rather the Refiner modifies the head panel with added focus, while the head retains its wider viewpoint and more fundamental role in the sequence (as in 7.3a). Refiners can be placed either before or after their head (as in the head-modifier schema, above), but placement following the head is more common and preferred (Cohn et al. forthcoming). Because Refiners modify their head, they can be deleted without recourse on the sequence. If a head is deleted, the modifier takes on the role of the head (e.g., in Figure 7.3c, the Refiner would become the Initial). This is structurally analogous to phrases such as *I'll take the white*, where the adjective *white* takes on the role of a noun in the otherwise more complete *white wine*.

The canonical narrative schema, conjunction schema, and head-modifier schema constitute the three core narrative patterns of VNG and are stored in long-term memory as "constructions." These schemas are consistent with abstract combinatorial principles found at the syntactic level (Culicover and Jackendoff 2005, Jackendoff 2002), and they can combine in multiple ways to explain much of the complex sequencing found in visual narratives. However, as in human languages, visual languages do not just use basic schemas. Rather, many constructions appear in regularized ways that employ or depart from those canonical patterns. Similarly, VNG allows for conventionalized constructional patterns that may or may not use these basic schemas, so long as they are systematic within and/or across authors.

Some of these patterned constructions can arise through combinations of modifiers. Conjunction and Refiners are basic schemas within VNG that can expand canonical narrative sequences into more complicated structures, including within regularized patterns. Consider Figure 7.5a, where the **Alternation** between two boxers results in an "A-B-A-B" pattern (where the characters are "A" and "B"). This surface pattern is composed of sets of conjoined panels (Cohn 2013c), such that each pairing forms a constituent

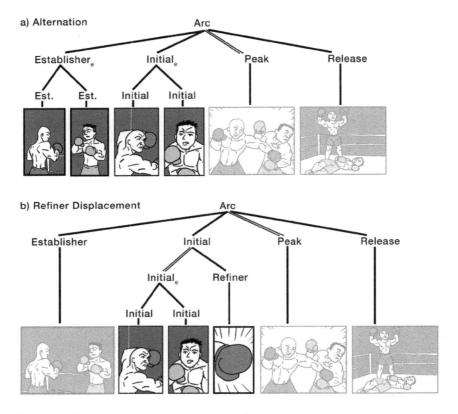

FIGURE 7.5 *Narrative patterns created by the interaction between narrative schemas within Visual Narrative Grammar, specifically a) Alternations between characters and b) Refiner Displacement.*

using Environmental-Conjunction (i.e., [A-B]-[A-B]). In Figure 7.5a, the first pairing creates an Establisher and the second pairing forms an Initial. Again, using our diagnostic for conjunction, we can confirm this interpretation because each pairing of panels can be substituted by the single panels in Figure 7.3a (Cohn 2013d, 2015b). This particular type of alternation pattern between characters is a subtype of the "crosscutting" or "multitracking" (Bateman and Schmidt 2012, Bordwell and Thompson 1997) found in films, as well as in drawn visual narratives (Cohn 2013c).

Another pattern uses both conjunction and Refiners. In Figure 7.5b, the Refiner is separated from the "head" it modifies by an intervening panel. This intervening panel unites with the head using Environmental-Conjunction, forcing the Refiner to connect across a distance. This pattern is called **Refiner Displacement**, because the Refiner is displaced away from its head (Cohn 2013c). Thus, the Refiner must connect across a distance rather than with its adjacent panels, and the coreference of this distance dependency has been shown to evoke similar brain responses as anaphoric relations in sentence processing (Cohn et al. forthcoming, Coopmans and Cohn 2022).

Note again that substitution of the conjoined panels here could be made with a single panel, which would result in the same basic Refiner sequence as in Figure 7.3c, confirming this structure.

In summary, VNG posits a basic narrative schema composed of categorical roles that can expand recursively into hierarchic constituents. This narrative schema can also be elaborated by basic modifying schemas (conjunction, Refiners) that alter and enrich the framing of attention on a scene, potentially with various correspondences to meaning. Combining these schemas can yield several complex sequences, including patterned constructions such as Alternation and Refiner Displacement. Note that in all patterns presented in Figures 7.2, 7.3, 7.4, and 7.5, the basic narrative arc persists at the top level of all structures. Complexity merely expands from this basic structure so that these substructures inherit the upper-level categories. Thus, narrative structure does not simply use a uniform process of updating meaningful relations across units of a (visual) discourse, but rather stitches together structured patterns in complex hierarchic embedding.

Bearing in mind the complexity of these schemas and their combinations, we can characterize them into three levels of "narrative complexity." At the lowest level, narrative structures depict a full scene in each panel (macros) with narrative progression across panels, as in Figures 7.3a and 7.2. This Basic Narrative Progression (BNP) should be the most similar to the iconic perception of viewing events and makes no modulation on framing or narrative pacing. It thus constitutes Level 1 of narrative complexity. The next most complex would be the schemas that modify this structure. Level 2 therefore involves Conjunction and Refiners, which still constitute basic schemas within the narrative grammar, but add complexity beyond a simple progression of a full scene. Finally, Level 3 consists of patterns emerging from combinations of these modifiers: Alternation and Refiner Displacement. These patterns arise from the interaction between modifying structures, and thus use more complexity than the basic schemas alone.

7.2 Complexity in visual narratives

We can begin our analyses by comparing the overall distribution of narrative patterns in 357 comics in the VLRC. As in previous chapters, this overall analysis only reflects the averages when collapsing across countries. As we will see below, comparison across cultures will add nuance to these aggregated analyses, but this broader view still retains some interesting observations.

Let's begin with the BNP, which is used substantially more than all the other types, validating its basic status. On average, 45 percent of adjacent panel pairs in these comics used the BNP. For sequences of three panels in a row, this only reduces to 36 percent, and four panels in a row using the BNP averages 29 percent of panels. Thus, overall, a large proportion of panels in a comic use this pattern, including across runs of panels. All other patterns were used substantially less than the basic narrative pattern by a large margin. Indeed, Environmental-Conjunction (13 percent) was used the next most, followed by Alternation (4 percent), Entity-Conjunction (1 percent), Refiners (1 percent), and Refiner Displacement (.03 percent). This wide variance across comics will become clearer in our analysis across countries.

When we aggregate patterns together into levels of complexity, we observe an expected reduction in the frequency of narrative patterns across levels. As depicted in Figure 7.6a, Level 1 patterns are used substantially more than Level 2 patterns, and Level 3 patterns hardly appear at all. We can also see some tradeoffs between these complexity levels. Specifically, if we correlate the data for complexity levels (as in Figure 7.6b), we see that the more complex patterns (levels 2 and 3) are used more often when the BNP (level 1) is used less, and vice versa.

Further insights come from comparing the specific patterns that comprise these levels of narrative complexity. Since there are so many possible contrasts between all the narrative patterns, scatterplots might get a bit overwhelming. Instead, we can depict these relationships in a network graph, as in Figure 7.7. Here, each of the narrative patterns is depicted as a node, and the shading of the node indicates its complexity level. The size and coloring of the lines between nodes represents the strength of the relationship between those patterns, with darker and thicker lines representing stronger relationships. Solid lines represent a positive relationship (i.e., when one is more frequent, so is the other), and dashed lines represent negative relationships (i.e., when one is more frequent, the other is less frequent). These negative and positive relationships are also indicated in the numbers on each line, which are the correlation values. Essentially, larger numbers (i.e., more away from zero, whether positive or negative) suggest a stronger relationship.

First, in line with the overall complexity relationships, the BNP has a negative relationship with all other narrative patterns (dashed lines): the more any complex patterns are used in a book, the less that book will use the BNP. Second, within the patterns in Level 2, only some patterns have relationships to each other. Refiners appear more when there is also more Environmental- and Entity-Conjunction, and these conjunctions also increase in frequency together (all ps < .005). Similarly, Level 3 patterns of Alternation and Refiner Displacement do increase together, but this correlation is relatively weak compared to most of the other relationships (p = .08).

Some relationships between levels are also insightful. As expected, Environmental-Conjunction (Level 2) has a strong relationship to both Alternations and Refiner Displacement (Level 3). It would be unusual if

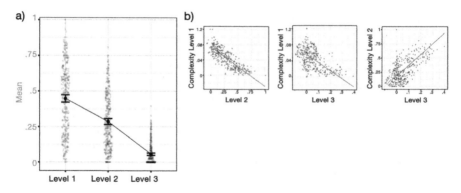

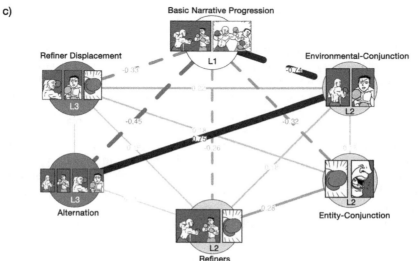

FIGURE 7.6 *a) Frequency of sequences with different levels of narrative complexity in the VLRC. The relationships between b) these levels of complexity to each other and c) additional relationships between specific narrative patterns.*

these did not have this relationship, since both of these more complex patterns are composed of Environmental-Conjunctions. However, we also see a relationship between the frequency of Refiners (Level 2) and Refiner Displacement (Level 3). Both of these patterns use Refiners, but displacements only use the basic Refiner schema at a higher level of structure, which do not show up in the adjacent panel patterns derived for these analyses. The implication is that when books use any types of Refiners, they use them in a variety of sequencing.

We can now clarify these broad trends by analyzing these patterns across the countries in the VLRC. Although our aggregated analysis suggested a reduction across complexity levels, this is not uniform when looking at the distribution of narrative complexity levels across countries, as depicted in Figure 7.7a. This descending complexity is shown quite consistently in books from Europe, where Level 1 narrative patterns are at least three times more frequent than Level 2 patterns, which are also more frequent than Level 3 patterns. This distribution becomes slightly less prominent in comics from the United States and France, but Level 1 patterns remain more prevalent. Asian books do not display this same distribution. Across Japanese manga, Korean manhwa, and Chinese manhua, Level 2 patterns are in fact more frequent than the Level 1 BNP, which is actually closer in frequency to Level 3 patterns. These Level 3 patterns are also noticeably more frequent in Asian books than those from Europe and the United States. Thus, we again see a difference here between the storytelling methods of Asian visual narratives and those from Europe and the United States.

Additional nuance comes from looking at subtypes of books from the United States and Japan, as shown in Figure 7.7b. In comics from the United States, the large decrease from Level 1, to Level 2, and to Level 3 patterns is shown primarily in the older mainstream comics (1940s to the 1980s), and we can see a drop in Level 1 patterns in the more recent mainstream comics (1980s to the 2010s). We will analyze this difference in more granularity in Chapter 8, when we discuss how comics from the United States have changed over time. By comparison, indie comics and US manga have equal frequencies for Level 1 and Level 2 patterns, and a slight increase in Level 3 patterns. When compared to the trends for Japanese manga, this difference between indie and US manga and mainstream American comics has the appearance of an influence of the storytelling of Japanese manga.

The narrative patterning of different demographics of Japanese manga is also fairly consistent. In all cases, they use more Level 2 patterns than Level 1 or Level 3 patterns, which were used near the same frequency. The exception here is shojo manga, which used slightly fewer Level 2 patterns and slightly more Level 1 patterns, despite the same overall distribution. Taken together, these results across countries, and across subtypes of comics from the United States and Japan, again reinforce that overall preferences of storytelling maintained throughout the visual language of a particular culture, despite slight variation across subtypes, and the potential influence of one visual language on another.

When turning to the specific narrative patterns, other than the BNP in Level 1, only Environmental-Conjunction (Level 2) and Alternation (Level 3) were used with substantial frequency, with all other patterns averaging below 2 percent of panels. I thus graph the frequencies of these patterns in Figure 7.7c. Reflecting the overall narrative complexity differences, Asian comics used Environmental-Conjunction and Alternation in greater frequency than in European and American comics, and they also used less BNP. In fact, the BNP and Environmental-Conjunction are used around the same frequency. Thus, the small proportions of Level 2 and Level 3 patterns overall are primarily representative of their frequency in the Asian comics.

NARRATIVE STRUCTURE

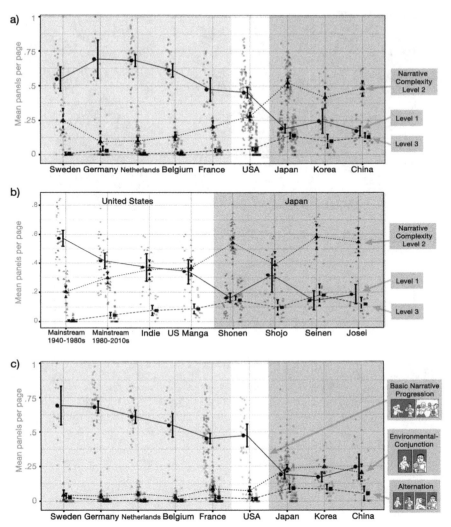

FIGURE 7.7 *The overall narrative complexity values a) distributed across countries in the VLRC, and b) in subtypes of comics from the United States and Japan. More specific narrative patterns are shown in c) across countries.*

Combined with the correlations we saw earlier in Figure 7.6b, this suggests Asian comics use more diverse narrative patterning than those in European or American comics.

As an illustration of the differences between narrative complexity in Asian and American sequencing, let's look at a few examples. Consider first a sequence from the manga *Vagabond* by Inoue Takehiko, depicted in Figure 7.8a. This sequence spans twelve panels across three pages, read

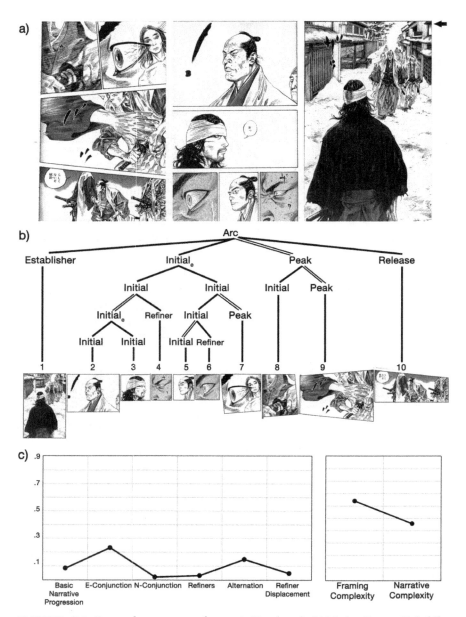

FIGURE 7.8 *Example sequence from a)* Vagabond *#195 by Inoue Takehiko (Kodansha, 2006) and b) its narrative structure, along with the c) frequency of narrative constructions, and framing and narrative complexity values for* Vagabond *#322 in the VLRC.* Vagabond © I.T. Planning Inc.

NARRATIVE STRUCTURE

right-to-left, where the protagonist Musashi (wearing the bandage on his head) encounters several samurai who are associates of a samurai he has earlier killed in a duel. The narrative structure of this sequence appears in Figure 7.8b (note that this tree structure is diagrammed from left-to-right, despite the layout order progressing right-to-left).

The characters first encounter each other in an Establisher (panel 1), before showing the primary samurai (panel 2), then Musashi (panel 3), and then a zoom of that samurai (panel 4). These three panels from 2 to 4 create a Refiner Displacement, which uses an Environmental-Conjunction (panels 2 to 3), followed by a Refiner (panel 4) that zooms in on the first character across a distance dependency (panel 2). The sequence next shows a different samurai (panel 5), and a Refiner zooming-in on his face (panel 6). These panels are Initials that set up his recollection of his dead associate killed by Musashi, here overlain on his eye (panel 7). This memory is a Peak in relation to the earlier Initials. These panels all depict events of the second samurai (panels 5 to 7) happening at the same time as the events of the first samurai and Musashi (panels 2 to 4), and together create a larger Environmental-Conjunction of the maximal Initial. In essence, all of this is the initiation of the primary events of the sequence that subsequently appears in the Peak.

In the Peak, the second samurai begins to draw his sword, an Initial for the about-to action (panel 8), which is then interrupted by the hand of the first samurai stopping the attack (panel 9), which ultimately is the primary event of the sequence. The final panel is a Release that resolves the sequence with the main samurai stopping the actions and telling the other samurai not to rush. So, across these ten panels we have characters recognizing each other, and a halted action of drawing a sword. But, this sequence involves fairly complex embedding of multiple modifiers including two Environmental-Conjunctions, a Refiner, and Refiner Displacement. At the top level though, we see the canonical progression of a narrative sequence.

This complexity of the narrative sequencing is further reflected in the data for a chapter of *Vagabond* within the VLRC, illustrated in Figure 7.8c. We can see a low proportion of panels using a BNP (8 percent), with fairly frequent Environmental-Conjunction (23 percent) and Alternation patterns (14 percent). Smaller frequencies appear of Entity-Conjunction (2 percent), Refiners (3 percent), and Refiner Displacements (4 percent), though they are present. All of this persists across 190 panels in twenty-five pages. *Vagabond* uses a fairly high narrative complexity of .45, with a framing complexity of .65 (note that almost all panels here are monos or micros). These frequencies support that the sequence in Figure 7.8a is representative of the structures in this manga, and broadly in Asian comics.

Let's now compare this to a sequence from the American superhero comic *The Savage Dragon* #187 by Erik Larsen, shown in Figure 7.9a. This sample sequence spans twelve panels across two pages, read left-to-right, and shows a fight scene with Malcom Dragon, the protagonist with the fin on his head, successively dispatching multiple enemies. The structure of this sequence is

162 THE PATTERNS OF COMICS

shown in Figure 7.9b. Although this sequence connects with panels in previous pages, I leave them out of the analysis, but indicate where they would connect in the narrative structure with ellipses (. . .).

The sequence begins with Malcom punching a monstrous villain (panel 1), which was set up by an Initial in the last panel on a previous page where he declares he'll fight them all. As it shows a climactic event, this panel is a Peak. Much of the subsequent sequence is filled with iterated Initial-Peak pairs, almost fully alternating, as he dispatches each villain one-by-one. He dodges a blast in panel 2 in an Initial that sets up his flip to kick these villains in the Peak of panel 3. The next grouping begins with Jimmy, the character with dreadlocks, punching Malcom (panel 4), an Initial, which allows Jimmy's fiery girlfriend to grab Malcom (panel 5), which only sets up Malcom to headbutt her in a Peak (panel 6). The next grouping is about how he defeats Jimmy. He grabs the fiery woman (panel 7) in an Initial only to throw her into Jimmy in a Peak (panel 8). All of this serves as an Initial to set up the subsequent Peak grouping where he approaches Jimmy (panel 9) and then delivers the final blow (panel 10) in the main Peak.

Each of these groupings (panel 1, panels 2 to 3, 4 to 6, 7 to 10) shows Malcom defeating a different character, climaxing for each one in the Peak of each constituent. Each of these constituents then comprise a Peak within a broader Peak constituent with an Action-Conjunction (marked with subscript a): effectively this is a list of Malcom's actions defeating these villains. The aftermath of these actions is shown in panel 11, where he looks at all the defeated foes on the ground in front of him. This panel is a Release to all the preceding fighting. Finally, the last panel shows two characters commenting in amazement at witnessing Malcom's actions. This is also a Release, but provides a conclusion to all the subsequent events, which then comprise another Peak.[5]

Note that in comparison to the *Vagabond* sequence, this narrative structure uses no modification of the narrative categories through Environmental-Conjunction or Refiners. The only conjunction is an Action-Conjunction, which further reinforces the successive events of the sequence. The result is a sequence more densely packed with actions and events than the *Vagabond* sequence. This character is reflected in the overall annotations for this comic, which was dominated by panels involved in the BNP (78 percent), few in Environmental-Conjunction (4 percent), and Refiners (2 percent), but no Entity-Conjunction, Alternations, or Refiner Displacement. This yields a much lower narrative complexity overall (.08), but a higher framing complexity (.94) because nearly all the panels are macros.

This comparison hopefully highlights the differences in the narrative structure across these systems. As I have said before, neither of these strategies is better or worse, but they achieve different storytelling effects. In addition, I should reiterate that the measure of narrative complexity here is based on the degree of elaboration of a canonical narrative schema with modifiers (conjunction, Refiners) and/or their interaction in constructional

NARRATIVE STRUCTURE 163

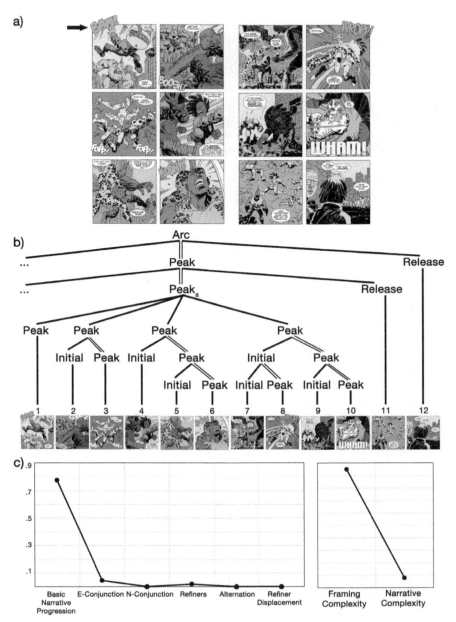

FIGURE 7.9 *Example sequence from a)* The Savage Dragon #187 *by Erik Larsen (Image Comics, 2013) and b) its narrative structure, along with the c) frequency of narrative constructions, and framing and narrative complexity values for this issue.* Savage Dragon © *Erik Larsen.*

patterns (Alternation, Refiner Displacement). The excerpt from *The Savage Dragon* has low narrative complexity in this technical sense, but it is far from simple in its narrative structure. This short sequence alone uses fairly rich embedding structures and dependencies, along with a rhythmic patterning of alternating Initial-Peak clusters in its pacing. It indeed has quite a lot of complexity within its use of the basic narrative schema, just not in the way quantified with this particular measurement.

Thus, although I emphasized narrative complexity in terms of the specific types of narrative schemas involved in a sequence, other types of complexity can also be identifiable. Future work can hopefully elaborate on these measures in ways that can capture additional types of relative complexity in further detail.

7.3 Narrative and framing structure

In this chapter we've analyzed variation across levels of complexity in narrative sequences. Similarly, in the last chapter we analyzed variation across levels of framing complexity within panels as narrative units. Thus, it is worth asking: what is the relationship between the complexity found in units and their sequencing?

Corpus research on linguistic structure has established a relationship between the structure of units such as words (morphology) and their sequencing (syntax). Using various measures of the internal complexity of words and the properties of their sequencing, typological research has pointed to a tradeoff between these structures (Ehret 2018, Koplenig et al. 2017, Bentz et al. 2022). Specifically, this work has found that less complexity of the units (words) leads to greater complexity in the sequencing (syntax), and vice versa. The explanation for this finding often evokes an argument about efficiency or optimization of distributing information (cf. Levshina 2021), with the idea being that if "less information is carried within the word, more information has to be spread among words in order to communicate successfully" (Koplenig et al. 2017, 1).

We might extend an expectation of a similar relationship to the units and sequencing in visual narratives. To tweak the quote above, we might expect that if "less information is carried within the [panel], more information has to be spread among [panels] in order to communicate successfully." To address this question, we can thus compare the framing complexity of panels and our narrative complexity discussed above.

For framing structure, I've assigned a value to each of the primary attentional categories along a zero to one scale to create a metric of *framing complexity*. A macro panel contains the most information, and thus I assigned the full level of complexity, a 1. I've thus assigned reducing values as categories become less complex, descending from macros (1), monos (.75), micros (.5), amorphics (.25), and ambiguous panels (0). With this

NARRATIVE STRUCTURE

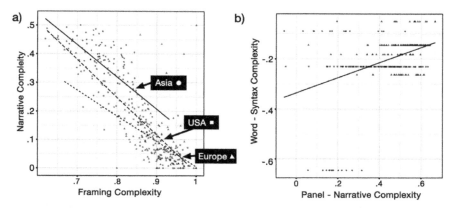

FIGURE 7.10 *Correlations between a) framing complexity and narrative complexity across comics from Europe, the United States, and Asia, and b) the difference between framing and narrative complexity plotted against the difference for word complexity and word-order complexity from Koplenig et al. (2017) for the corresponding spoken languages.*

scale, we can now calculate an average framing complexity for each comic. For narrative complexity, since we have three levels, our values ranging from 0 to 1 are distributed by thirds. The most basic values at Level 1 are assigned a value of 0, Level 2 are assigned .5, and Level 3 are assigned a 1. Using these values, we can average together the values for all narrative sequencing within each comic, arriving at a single value that characterizes the complexity of a whole comic.

In Figure 7.10a, attentional framing complexity is plotted directly against narrative sequence complexity, with each dot representing a book. Our regions of interest again cluster together, and their trendlines suggest the same types of differences we've seen for framing and narrative complexity previously. Asian books use more narrative complexity and less framing complexity (upper left), European books do the opposite (lower right), and American comics span the whole range.

But, it should be clear that overall, a strong negative relationship exists between these values, apparent in the sweeping downward trendlines. This suggests a tradeoff in the structures: when the units are more complex, the sequencing is less complex, and vice versa. This consistent tradeoff in complexity between units and sequencing is similar to that found between morphology and grammar in spoken languages (Ehret 2018, Koplenig et al. 2017, Bentz et al. 2022). This would be a type of *universal* if it applies across modalities, despite the surface differences between their representations. That is, verbal morphology and syntax differ in their representations from visual morphology and narrative structure, and yet a similar tradeoff appears to persist. Such results may imply a general optimization for the way that systems distribute information across their resources, with meaning being encoded either more into units or across sequences. If so, this distribution could reflect a cognitive constraint that pressures the way that communicative systems express information.

Given that both spoken and visual languages demonstrate this tradeoff between units and sequencing, might we posit a permeable relationship between them? In other words, is it possible that the relative allocation of complexity into units or sequences in the spoken modality might affect the way information is allocated in the visual modality? To test this, I first subtracted the narrative complexity value from the framing complexity values in Figure 7.10a, to derive a single metric reflecting their relationship. Larger numbers thus reflected works where units were more complex than sequences. I then derived a similar calculation from the open data provided from the study by Koplenig et al. (2017), which looked at the tradeoff between verbal morphology and syntax across different translations of the Bible. Here I derived values for each of the languages reflected in the countries in our VLRC data, although they had no data for Japanese. I then compared this spoken language data against our VLRC data, the result of which is plotted in Figure 7.10c.

Here we see a positive correlation between the tradeoff in units and sequencing in both verbal and visual modalities ($r = .394$, $p < .001$): comics that displayed greater unit-complexity also came from places where the spoken languages had greater unit-complexity, and vice versa. The greatest verbal and visual unit-complexity was German, and the least was Chinese. This correlation suggests that the distribution of information into units or sequences in visual languages may have a relationship to a similar distribution between words and syntax in spoken languages. If such an influence exists, it would persist as a permeable relationship between these modalities.

Despite this suggestive outcome, it is again worth exercising caution in overinterpreting these results. First, the data from Koplenig et al. (2017) lacked spoken Japanese, and thus a large source of our own data went unrepresented in this correlation. Second, tradeoffs in structural complexity are analyzed in various ways in linguistics, and other measures may be more adequate to implement than the one used here (e.g., Ehret 2018, Bentz et al. 2022). Finally, especially for analyses on permeability throughout this book, it is important to replicate such results with a wider sample than just the countries and languages represented in the VLRC.

7.4 Conclusion

This chapter examined different levels of complexity in the patterns of narrative structure. Once again, we see a tension between cross-cultural differences and more consistent and universal tenancies. Sequencing patterns vary between comics from different cultures, again with the prominent finding that Asian comics differed from those from Europe and the United States. But, we also observe a tradeoff between the complexity of units and sequences that extends across cultures. As this tradeoff also occurs in the structure of verbal languages, it possibly reflects universals in linguistic structuring that span across modalities, and there may also be a permeable influence between modalities for such structural tendencies.

CHAPTER EIGHT

Visual Languages Across Time

One of the ways that linguists have used corpora is to investigate how languages have changed over time, by seeing how words or grammar may have shifted and or how structures may have interacted across languages. We can similarly examine how visual languages have changed over time. Indeed, although comics have roots in practices of multimodal storytelling with sequential images that date back centuries if not millennia (Kunzle 1973, Petersen 2011, Mair 2019), the visual languages that are distinctly associated with comics grew with these industries emerging throughout the twentieth century (Exner 2021). Although much of the VLRC contains data about comics published between the 1980s and 2010s, extended longitudinal analyses are possible with data going back to the 1940s for superhero comics from the United States and for comics from the Netherlands and Flemish Belgium.

This chapter thereby makes inroads in the study of *historical linguistics* for visual languages. Because of the scope of our data, our primary questions here focus on how European and American comics may have changed over time across structures already discussed in previous chapters: layout, situational coherence, framing, and narrative patterns. We will additionally consider aspects of multimodality in our corpus of American comics.

8.1 Layout

8.1.1 Panels per page

Let's first consider the overall dimensions of how many panels appear per page. As we have this information for all books in the VLRC, we here show how panels per page shift across time in comics from Europe, the United States, and Asia, as depicted in Figure 8.1a. We again see the same relationship as we found in Chapter 4, with European comics using more panels per page than those from Asia or the United States. Over time, European comics show a slight increase and then decrease from the 1940s through to the 2010s, but always hovering between eight and nine panels per page. Comics from the United States meanwhile begin around six panels per page in the 1940s and reduce over time to around five by the 2010s. Finally, the VLRC only includes data for Asian comics between the 1980s and 2010s, but they sustain around five panels per page throughout that time period.

8.1.2 *External compositional structure*

Next, let's consider the external compositional structure, starting with analysis of the arrangements of panels. Here we will look specifically at mainstream comics from the United States alone. As in Figure 8.1b, horizontal staggering was the primary organizing structure for American layouts in the 1940s, yet it declined steadily over time. Its initial decline in the 1970s corresponded with an increase in using the pure grid, which still maintained a row-based structure. As horizontal staggering further declined in later years, the rate of pure grids largely grew stable, alongside a strong increase in whole row panels. In other words, instead of multiple panels in a row, whether staggered or not, there was one large panel constituting the whole row. In addition, embedded columns (blockage) have also steadily increased over time, marking the primary deviation from the row-based layout structure.

Shifts in the directionality between panels further reinforces a reduction in the Z-path overall and an increasing use of vertically stacked panels, as depicted in Figure 8.1c. Across the eighty years spanned in this corpus, rightward directions have steadily decreased (i.e., the directions between panels within rows), while downward directions have simultaneously increased (i.e., the directions between panels within columns). Correspondingly, downward angles (i.e., directions between rows) have gone down only slightly, while upward angles (i.e., direction between columns) have slightly increased. This aligns with other empirical observations that grid structures have reduced in time across American comics' layouts (Bateman, Veloso, and Lau 2021).

Altogether, these shifts in directions and arrangements imply greater conventionalization of American page layouts towards expectations that readers will know how to navigate pages. For example, horizontal staggering, which is also prevalent in European comics, emphasizes a row-based structure that clearly defines the rows through the staggered gutters. Although readers do not do it (Cohn 2013b, Cohn and Campbell 2015), a pure grid at least presents physical ambiguity of a reading path and could be read either as rows or columns. Shifting from layouts with horizontal staggering to pure grids shows a confidence that readers will

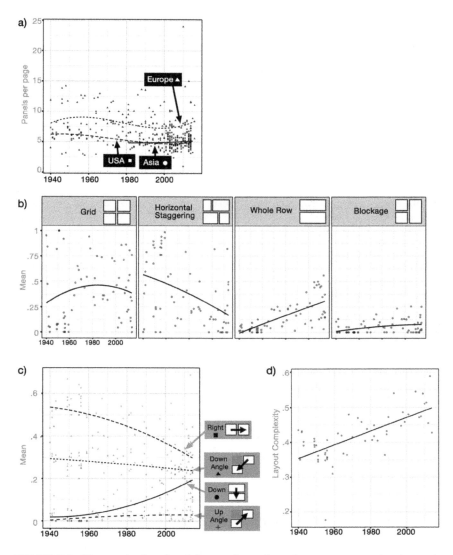

FIGURE 8.1 *Changes in time for a) the numbers of panels per page over time in comics from Asia, Europe, and the United States. For comics from the United States specifically, changes over time for a) the different arrangements of panels in layouts, b) the navigation directions between panels in layouts, and c) the overall layout complexity.*

know the proper reading order without the explicit cues guiding them into rows.

A similar conventionality is present in the increasing use of columns. The shift toward greater verticality may have occurred mostly because of the increasing amounts of panels spanning whole rows. When these panels are stacked on top of each other, they are read vertically, despite appearing as single-panel rows. This would especially reflect the trend in the 2000s for "widescreen" panels (Mazur and Danner 2014).

A smaller influence may be the increase in embedded columns (blockage). Despite claims that embedded columns confuse readers for the reading order, particularly when placed left of a single panel (e.g., Abel and Madden 2008, McCloud 2006), readers overwhelmingly order panels in blockage in a vertical fashion (Cohn 2013b, Cohn and Campbell 2015). As we saw in Chapter 4, vertical columns are more characteristic of Chinese and Japanese comics, and thus the increase in blockage over time can at least in part be attributed to the influence of manga's influx into the American comics market in the 1980s and 1990s. This influence will be a recurring theme throughout this chapter. Overall, these trends demonstrate an increasing conventionality and consolidation of the layout styles in mainstream American comics.

Nevertheless, although the layouts appear to become more conventionalized, they also appear to take on more complex features than simple Z-path grids. Like before, we can also combine the characteristics of layouts into a common metric of layout complexity, which incorporates information about the normativity of panel shapes, arrangements, directions, and gutter widths. With this metric, we saw previously that Asian layouts (a value of ~.47 along a 0 to 1 scale) were slightly more complex than those from Europe (~.41), while American layouts fell in the middle (~.45). Now we can ask: Do these American mainstream comics change in complexity over time?

Figure 8.1d shows this change, where an increase in complexity is clearly visible from the 1940s through to the 2000s. Complexity rises from ~.35 in the 1940s to ~.5 in the 2010s. This analysis implies that not only are layouts becoming more conventionalized over time, but they are also becoming more complex in their features overall.

8.1.3 Assemblage Structure

Next let's examine the assemblage structure corresponding to these arrangements. In Chapter 4 we saw that constituent structures across cultures maintained a relative consistent proportion. Shifts within constituents occurred more often than those between constituents, and these occurred more often than shifts between pages. As we discussed, this should be expected, because a single page with a 3 × 3 grid of nine panels would only have a single shift between pages, two shifts between the three rows, and six shifts within the rows (two per three rows). As depicted in Figure 8.2a, these relative proportions also maintain consistently across time with minimal change. This suggests that not only are these proportions consistent across cultures, but they are across time as well.

VISUAL LANGUAGES ACROSS TIME   173

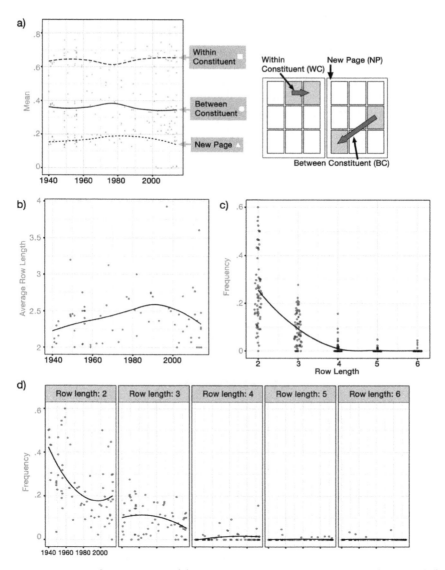

FIGURE 8.2 *The structure of layout constituents over time including a) shifts within and between constituents and between pages, b) change in the overall length of rows, c) the overall frequency of row length, and d) change in different length of rows over time.*

Additional insights come by examining the properties of rows specifically. Although our analysis related to panel arrangements and directionality indicates that rows have decreased in frequency over time, they still persist as the primary constituent structure of American page layouts. In Chapter 4, we showed that the length of rows overall maintains a Zipfian distribution

(Zipf 1935), with the frequency of rows correlating with their length: shorter rows are more frequent than longer rows. When collapsing across publication dates, we again see this distribution in this data for row length, as in Figure 8.2c.

But, despite this more universal tendency, when these lengths are extended across time, we can see changes in the proportions of different lengths of rows. As in Figure 8.2d, the shortest rows of only two panels long have decreased in their frequency, while those with three panels remained steady until the 1970s and then decreased by the 2010s. A subtle increase occurred for four-panel long rows. The result of these changes is that overall panels have increased from an average of around 2.2 panels per row in the 1940s to around 2.6 panels per row in the 1990s, before waning again in the 2010s (Figure 8.2b).

These findings suggest that authors were filling multi-panel rows with more panels over time. This data excluded single-panel rows (whole rows), which as we saw above increased in frequency in this same time frame. Given that the numbers of panels per page overall remained steady, these results imply that as rows with single panels increased, multi-panel rows became longer to compensate, while maintaining a similar overall density of conveying information. As we will see in our next section, the content of that information has also shifted over time.

8.2 Storytelling

Let's next examine the changes that have occurred over time in relation to the visual storytelling. As we covered in the past three chapters, these structures are situational coherence, framing structure, and narrative structure. Our longitudinal data in the VLRC for these structures includes both American and European comics. For European comics, those before the 1980s primarily came from Dutch and Flemish comics, while after the 1980s it included all the European countries in the VLRC.

8.2.1 Situational coherence

In Chapter 5, we saw that American and European comics used more time changes across panels than any other situational changes, followed by character changes and spatial location changes. In contrast, Asian comics used comparable amounts of changes of time and characters, again with spatial location changes being used the least. Now consider how these situational changes have changed from the 1940s through to the 2010s, as depicted in Figure 8.3.

Both American and European comics maintain the same general distribution of situational coherence changes described earlier, descending

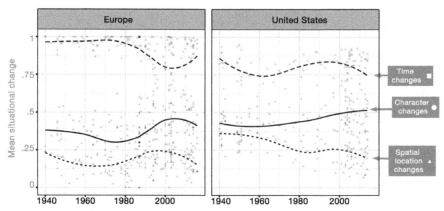

FIGURE 8.3 *Shifts in situational coherence between panels from the 1940s to the 2010s in American and European comics.*

in frequency from time to character to spatial location changes. However, shifts over time have occurred in both regions. In American comics, the clearest change is an increase in the amount of character changes starting since around the 1980s, along with a decrease in the spatial location changes. Time changes appear to have oscillated, falling and rising in frequency over the years.

A somewhat similar shift has occurred in European comics, where again we see an increase in the frequency of character changes over time starting around the 1990s. Here, we see a clearer trend related to time changes, which decreased since the 1990s. Finally, spatial location changes have oscillated, declining slightly and then increasing in the 1990s.

In both cases a primary finding was the increase in character changes over time, and concurrent decreases in time and/or spatial location changes. The most compelling explanation for these developments is that they have resulted from an influence of Japanese manga. As discussed, Japanese manga, like other Asian comics, use a near equal amount of character and time changes, and reduced amounts of spatial location changes. These characteristics are consistent with the shift in situational coherence in American (since the 1980s) and European books (since the 1990s), which is when manga correspondingly began their increasing influx into the Western markets. We will see this influence persist throughout the framing and narrative structures below.

8.2.2 Framing

Let's next examine the attentional framing structure of panels over time. To reiterate our findings from Chapter 6, European comics had almost double the proportion of macros as monos, and very few micros or amorphics, a structure consistent in American comics, which had just a slightly smaller macro-mono ratio, with increased numbers of micros and amorphics. Finally, Asian comics used as many if not more monos as macros, with greater proportions of micros and amorphics. Let's now examine how the American and European comics may have shifted over time.

Changes over time for the attentional framing categories are depicted in Figure 8.4a. American comics show the most dramatic shifts. Macros rapidly decline in frequency from the 1960s until the 1990s, where they then rebound in frequency into the 2000s. Inversely, monos increase in frequency since the 1960s, apexing in the 1990s after which they also rebound slightly. Finally, micros and amorphics both gradually increase since the 1960s as well.

Here we again see a possible influence of manga, with the peaks in changes occurring in the 1990s, right at the initial influx of manga into the American comic industry. But, unlike in the changes in situational coherence, it is worth pointing out that these shifts in framing do not begin in this period, and indeed appear to begin earlier, around the 1960s. This suggests that, even if manga drove the largest stylistic shifts in framing, they were already developing gradually for several decades before, possibly motivated by changes in page size, book length, or other aspects of formatting (Cohn, Taylor, and Pederson 2017). In addition, this change over time clearly rebounds following this apex in the 1990s, suggesting a "return" to a pre-manga framing of American comics following a period of influence from manga in the 1980s and 1990s.

By comparison, European comics appear to have fewer of these shifts over time. Rather, we see a fairly consistent distribution of attentional framing categories over time, with only a minor increase in macros, which apexes in the 1980s before waning again into the 2000s. This latter waning of macros accompanies a concurrent increase in monos and a small increase in micros and amorphics. This latter shift occurs after 2000, perhaps suggesting a delayed and only slight influence of manga. Overall though, these results suggest that, unlike in American comics, the framing structure of European comics has remained more stable over time, just like the stability in their panels per page. If manga have had an influence on framing in European comics, it has occurred later and with relatively less impact so far.

These differences between cultures can be seen even more clearly when collapsing these categorical values into a single value for framing complexity. As depicted in Figure 8.4b, the overall framing complexity of European comics is fairly high and has a relatively stable arc across time. In contrast, American comics start with the same level of complexity as European books, then descend starting around the 1960s, apex in the 1990s, and rebound back to near European levels of complexity by the 2010s. These values again imply not only distinguishable cultural characteristics, but distinctive developments over time for these visual languages.

VISUAL LANGUAGES ACROSS TIME

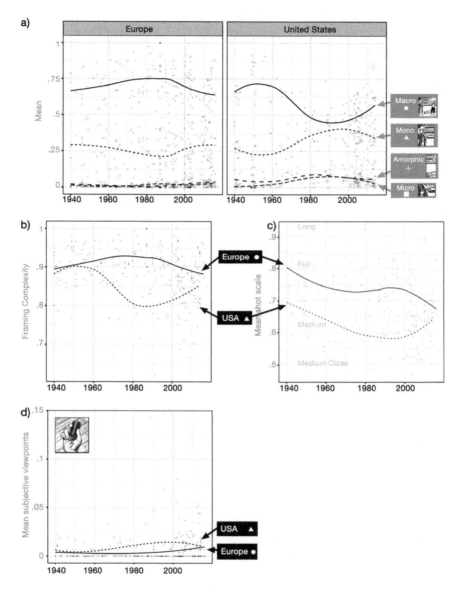

FIGURE 8.4 *Changes over time related to framing structure in American and European comics, for a) different framing types, b) overall framing complexity, c) filmic shot scale, and d) subjective viewpoints.*

178 THE PATTERNS OF COMICS

Differences also persist in how the filmic shot scales have changed over time. As depicted in Figure 8.4c, the shot scales of panels from American comics somewhat reflect their overall framing, with a gradual decline since the 1940s. Shot scales average around a medium shot in the 1940s, then become tighter (more like close shots) into the 1990s by rebounding in the 2000s. But, unlike the relatively stable framing structure in European comics, the shot scale here has gradually declined across this time span, averaging around full shots in the 1940s, and then progressing down to average medium shots by the 2010s. This implies that European comics have shifted more in how they present content in panels (shot scale), even though the information structure of panels has remained consistent (attentional framing). This difference between the change in shot scale and attentional framing helps further confirm that these classifications pick up on different aspects of panels.

We can also consider the changes that have occurred for subjective panels over time. As described in Chapter 6, subjective panels are more prevalent and frequent in Japanese comics than in other cultures. As depicted in Figure 8.4d, we can see that subjective panels have indeed shifted in frequency over time in both American and European comics. American comics have a greater frequency of subjective panels overall compared to panels in European comics. In addition, American comics again have a characterizable increase in subjective panels starting around 1980 and becoming steady around 2000, again consistent with the influence of manga shown elsewhere. European comics also have a slight increase, although it only begins around 2000.

Finally, it is also worth mentioning how these developments compare to those observed in changes across Hollywood movies over the past 100 years, carried out in corpus work by psychologist James Cutting. He observed that the number of characters in film shots (framing) has decreased over time, while their shot scales have also become tighter, arriving at an average shot scale around a medium shot (Cutting 2015, Cutting and Candan 2015). These changes are consistent to what we have generally observed in comics, with reduced framing over time in American comics, and tighter shot scales in both American and European comics. This consistency between comics and movies should not be overly surprising, as they have both influenced each over time, and movies are often preceded by storyboarding, which is another context of the use of visual languages (and indeed are often created by comic creators). Nevertheless, these consistent shifts reinforce that changes in visual storytelling may have persisted broadly in media across the past 100 years.

8.2.3 Narrative patterns

To conclude our examination of changes in visual storytelling, let's finally look at the changes in the patterns of narrative structure. In Chapter 7, we observed that the sequencing in Asian comics used more complex narrative sequencing than in American comics, while European comics used the least complex sequencing. Here let's begin by looking at our generalized value for narrative complexity across time.

Figure 8.5a depicts narrative complexity for American and European comics, which both increase over time. Once again, both cultures begin with similar levels of narrative complexity and then deviate, with American comics overall having greater complexity than European comics. Over time, American comics show a gradual increase in complexity starting in the 1960s and then apexing around 2000 then plateauing. In contrast, European comics maintain only a slight gradual increase starting around the 1970s, which appears to be leveling off in the 2000s.

Further detail appears in specific narrative patterns, as in Figure 8.5b. In American comics, we again see the characteristic trends as elsewhere, with a gradual reduction of the BNP starting in the 1960s, apexing in the 1990s, and rebounding in the 2000s. Simultaneously, the more complex narrative patterns—particularly Environmental-Conjunction and Alternation, which

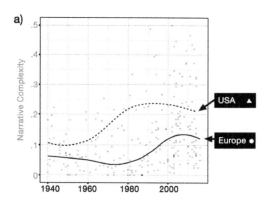

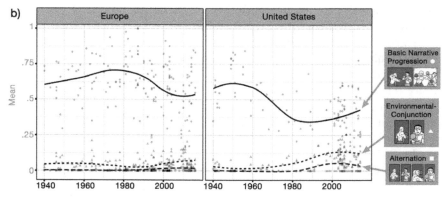

FIGURE 8.5 *Changes over time related to narrative structure in American and European comics, for a) the overall narrative complexity, and b) specific constructions of the Basic Narrative Progression, Environmental Conjunction, and Alternation.*

were the only ones above 5 percent overall—have increased from the 1980s into the 2000s. Meanwhile, European comics first show an increase in the BNP from the 1940s to the 1970s, and then a long gradual decline into the 2000s. Here, only Environmental-Conjunction appears to have increased, starting an ascent only in the 2000s. This use of more Environmental-Conjunction aligns with the increase in character changes observed previously.

Once again, these results support the idea that Japanese manga have influenced the structure of American comics in the 1980s and 1990s, although they may have been gradually developing in narrative complexity for decades prior. By comparison, European comics had a slow increase in narrative complexity of their own, and if there has been an influence on the narrative structure by manga, it has occurred later than in American comics, starting around the 2000s.

8.3 Multimodality

Although the structure of visual storytelling has changed over time in American and European comics, their visual languages are not the only meaningful structure contributing to the overall storytelling. Comics are typically *multimodal* documents, combining the visual language of the graphics with the verbal language of the writing. The full storytelling is achieved through the relationship between these modalities. In the VLRC, we analyzed the multimodal relationships between text and images across time in mainstream comics from the United States specifically (Cohn, Taylor, and Pederson 2017). This original analysis used the framework introduced in Cohn (2016b), although I here adapt the terminology to changes in the theory introduced in Cohn and Schilperoord (2022b). The question here would be how storytelling may have changed not only with regard to the visual properties of panels and their sequencing, but also with their interactions with the written language.

A first question was about which modality carried the *semantic weight* of the multimodal expression. Semantic weight is defined as the relative contribution of modalities to the overall gist. A modality would thus carry more relative semantic weight if it conveyed more meaning, making it an *imbalanced* semantic weight overall. A *balanced* semantic weight would then occur if both modalities equally contributed to the overall message.

Semantic weight was assessed by annotators using a deletion diagnostic (Cohn 2016b), by testing whether the overall gist of a panel stayed the same when imagining if each modality was omitted. If the gist remained similar when a modality was missing, the non-deleted modality was inferred as more semantically weighted (visual-weight, verbal-weight), since it could be said to carry more of the overall meaning. However, if the gist was not retained when either modality was missing, meaning was inferred to be shared between modalities (balanced-weight).

Consider the two excerpted sequences in Figure 8.6, which both come from *Lady Luck* by Klaus Nordling (1949). Figure 8.6a uses a substantial amount of text, and the visuals largely just support this text by showing who is talking. If we were to delete the text, as in Figure 8.6b, we would have little understanding of what this sequence is about, but if we were to delete the pictures, at least some general gist would remain. This suggests the semantic weight is imbalanced in this sequence, but weighted more towards the verbal than the visual. The opposite occurs in the sequence in Figure 8.6c, where the text provides minimal information and the sequence could easily be understood without it (Figure 8.6d). The visuals here largely convey the meaning, suggesting a more visual weight.

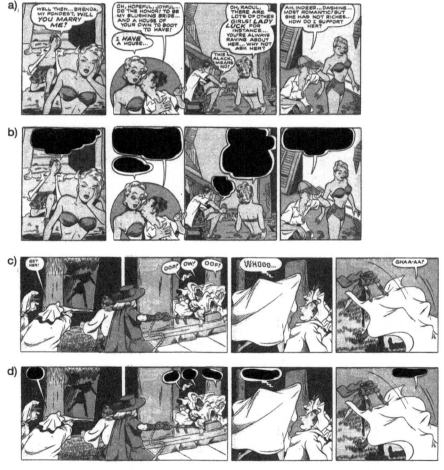

FIGURE 8.6 *Multimodal sequences that have imbalanced semantic weight from* Lady Luck *by Klaus Nordling (1949), a) where the text carries more semantic weight, which is then b) deleted, or c) where the visuals carry more semantic weight, which is then d) deleted.*

Figure 8.7a shows how semantic weight has changed over time in Mainstream American comics from the 1940s through to the 2010s. Overall, books had a higher frequency of panels with verbal-weight, which were more frequent than those with balanced-weight, which in turn were more frequent than visual-weighted panels. However, these classes overall had clear changes over time. Although panels with balanced-weight maintained a fairly constant frequency over time, those with verbal-weight progressively reduced over time and those with visual-weight increased over time. By the 2010s, these three categories appear to converge to the same frequency. The overall message is that balanced-weight has remained

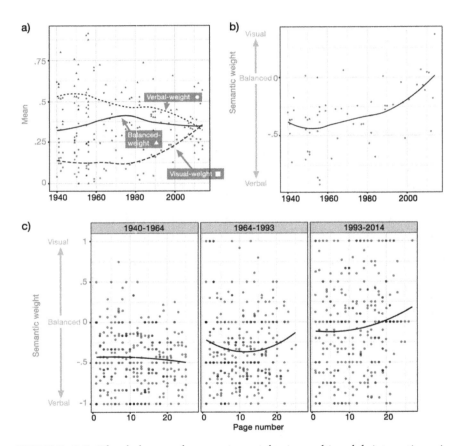

FIGURE 8.7 *The balance of semantic weight in multimodal interactions in Mainstream American comics from the 1940s through to the 2010s, shown through a) the frequency of balanced-, verbal-, and visual-weight, and b) the average semantic weight across a one (visual) to −1 (verbal) scale, and c) semantic weight distributed across the pages of comics.*

constant, while panels rely less on meaning from text, and more from meaning in the images.

Another depiction of this relationship is offered in Figure 8.7b. Here, I've given these categories values that reflect this idea of semantic *weight* as a type of balance. So, balanced-weight was given the value of 0, with more positive values leaning towards visual-weight (1) and more negative values leaning towards verbal-weight (–1). With this, we now have a single value to reflect the overall semantic weight of a comic. Here we can see that in the 1940s, comics were much more verbally-weighted (a value around –.04), but over time the semantic weight shifts away from this verbal focus. By the 2010s, the overall semantic weight is more balanced (near 0).

The implication here is that older American comics indeed carried more of their meaning in the text than the visuals. Over time, American comics grew to carry more meaning in the visuals, and to distribute meaning throughout across both modalities. We can see a bit more nuance in Figure 8.7c, which shows how semantic weight changes across the twenty-five pages of comics, divided across three spans of dates in the eighty years of American comics we analyzed. Across the time periods we see the gradual shift of semantic weight from more verbal (negative numbers) to more visual and balanced (positive numbers), just like in Figure 8.7b.

In the older books (1940 to 1964), semantic weight remains fairly constant across the pages of the book, remaining with a verbal-weight from start to finish (–.05). In the middle grouping of books (1964 to 1993), we see slightly the most verbal-weighting in the middle of the books, approaching more balanced-weight at the beginning and end of the comics. Finally, more contemporary books (1993 to 2014) begin more balanced and become more visual as the story progresses. These results imply not only that semantic-weight has shifted over time, but it has also changed in how it progresses across the pages of comics.

Perhaps more striking is that these spans of dates were not chosen by me explicitly, but rather were pulled out by my statistical software in groupings that it thinks best characterize the data. What's notable though is how they roughly correspond to significant eras in mainstream American comics history (Duncan, Smith, and Levitz 2015). The first grouping spans from 1940 to 1964, which is roughly the Golden Age, the end of which is marked by the rise in prominence of Marvel Comics in the early 1960s. This second grouping spans roughly the Silver and Bronze Ages of US comics (Duncan, Smith, and Levitz 2015), until 1993, the year after Image Comics was founded (1992) and when Japanese manga flooded into the American market. Given that the rise of Image Comics led to a boon in creator-owned comics in the United States, it makes sense that there would be a shift to more visual storytelling, since artists were given more independence in the creation of their comics. That these groupings were selected as notably different on the basis of the data suggests that they have distinguishable features in contrast to each other, and indeed may mark notable periods of change in visual storytelling across comics in the United States.

Multimodality not only involves relationships between meaning, but also between grammar. We also judged the relative contributions of grammatical structures for each modality, a distinction that we call *symmetry* (Cohn and Schilperoord 2022b). Where semantic weight was about the relative contribution of meaning of each modality, symmetry is about the relative complexity of the grammars used by each modality. For the text, sentences (with syntactic structure) used a complex grammar compared to the simple grammar of single words (such as onomatopoeia). For visuals, we assessed whether the sequence used a narrative grammar or whether it was a visual sequence with a non-narratively associated "list" of images (a simple grammar).

The symmetry of grammatical structures was determined using diagnostic tests (Cohn 2015b). If both modalities used a complex grammatical structure (syntax, narrative), it was deemed as *symmetrical* (technically, symmetrical-complex). These are essentially parts of a comic where the panels tell a story across a sequence, and the text has full sentences. If only one modality used a complex grammar (syntax, narrative) and the other used a simple grammar (a single word, a visual list), it was an *asymmetrical* interaction. These would be panels that are all visual except single words such as sound effects, or would be panels with sentences across panels that visually show only a non-narrative list of associated elements. Finally, panels using only text or only visuals were considered as *unimodal*.[1]

If we return to Figure 8.6, we can see examples of these interactions. The panels in Figure 8.6a would largely be considered symmetrical, because the speech balloons all have full sentences and they are embedded into a visual sequence with a narrative progression. In contrast, most of the panels in Figure 8.6b use only single words. As these single words use only a simple grammar, when combined with the narrative sequencing they create an asymmetrical multimodal relationship.

Let's now examine how these relationships appear in American comics over time. Figure 8.8a shows the distribution of grammatical symmetry in multimodal interactions for comics in our corpus. Symmetrical interactions between sequential images with full sentences were by far the most frequent, followed by asymmetrical interactions with images using single words. Both of these types appear to reduce slightly over time, although symmetrical structures rose in the 1960s through to the 1980s, implying a greater number of wordy panels. Unimodal expressions of panels with only visuals were used the least, and these changed the most dramatically over time. Visual-only panels began almost completely absent in comics in the 1940s, but increased in frequency through the 2010s. This is consistent with what we just observed with the visuals carrying greater semantic weight over time.

This overall observation of the grammatical symmetry can be captured using a single value. Here, I've assigned the most complex interaction of symmetry the value of 1, asymmetry a value of .5, and unimodal panels a value of 0. By averaging these values for each panel, we can arrive at a single score for the overall complexity of the grammatical symmetry in a comic. The result is depicted in Figure 8.8b, where we can see that the complexity began fairly high (more symmetrical), rose a bit in the 1960s, and then descended steadily until the 2010s with its lowest complexity. This again reflects that storytelling on the whole has shifted to being more visual, and using panels with less full sentence structures.

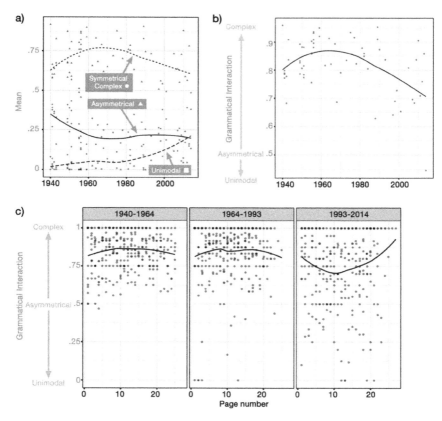

FIGURE 8.8 *Symmetry of the grammatical structure (syntax, narrative) in multimodal interactions in Mainstream American comics from the 1940s through to the 2010s, shown through a) the frequency of symmetrical complex, asymmetrical, and unimodal expressions, and b) the average complexity of the grammatical interaction across a one (complex) to zero (unimodal) scale, and c) grammatical interactions distributed across the pages of comics.*

As with semantic weight, we can also see how these interactions progress across the pages of a comic. Comics from 1940 to 1993 all appear to have a similar arc of symmetry across their pages, remaining steady with a high complexity of symmetry (again, more sentence structures). More contemporary comics (1993 to 2010) appear to begin with more symmetrical interactions, then become more visually focused throughout the middle of the comics, and return to more complex sentence structures at the end of the comic.

To further analyze whether these multimodal interactions were affected by the quantity of words, we also counted the total number of words per panel. We then averaged these values for each panel across a whole book to find the average words per panel of those books. Figure 8.9a shows the average words per panel for comics over time. As should be evident, there's an arc to the trend over time.[2] In the 1940s, books averaged around fifteen words per panel, then this rose to around twenty-five words by the 1960s through to the 1980s, and then fell again to around ten words by the 2010s. Notice that this arc is similar to the pattern of symmetrical structure across time (Figure 8.8a), and to the generalized symmetrical complexity over time (Figure 8.8b).

Just to provide some details, the wordiest comic in our corpus was *Wonder Woman* #289 by Roy Thomas and Gene Colan (DC Comics, 1982), which averaged 39.6 words per panel. You may recall from Chapter 3 that this book was also the one with the most carriers per panel (3.3 on average), which makes sense that word count and carriers would go together. By contrast the least wordy comic was *The Punisher* #5 by Nathan Edmunson

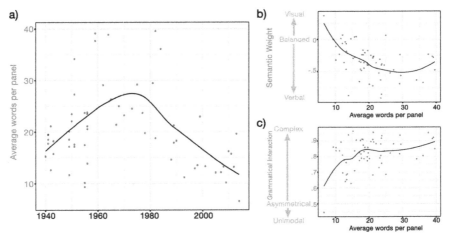

FIGURE 8.9 *Within Mainstream American comics, a) the average number of words in panels from the 1940s to the 2010s, and the relationship between this word count and b) semantic weight, and c) grammatical interactions.*

and Mitch Gerads (Marvel Comics, 2014), with only an average of 6.6 words per panel, since this book had many panels with no words at all (the most in a panel was forty-seven words). These comics are thus representative of the furthest peak of wordiness from the 1960s to 1980s, and its subsequent lowest decline into the 2010s.

Additional confirmation of the relationship between words per panel and both semantic weight and grammatical symmetry are in Figures 8.9b and 8.9c. Semantic weight has a negative correlation with the words per panel: As there are more words per panel, the meaning is more guided by the text. Similarly, as there are more words per panel, the grammatical complexity goes up, since symmetrical structure by necessity involves more complex sentences with multiple words.

8.3.1 Multimodality and visual storytelling

The analyses above suggest that mainstream comics from the United States have become more weighted in meaning towards visuals, with an increasing amount of interactions between text and images where the visuals play a greater role, either on their own or with minimal text. In the section before that, we also saw that American comics have decreased in the complexity of their framing, while increasing in their narrative complexity. Given these two sets of results, we can now ask if they might be related. For example, when images tell a story on their own, maybe there is an increase in the complexity of their properties? Observations like these have been linked to oral storytelling traditions, where the greater complexity and communicative weight of drawings and/or gestures rise when speech is used less (Wilkins 2016, Goldin-Meadow et al. 2008).

Let's first consider the overall framing complexity (averaged from macros to amorphics) of these comics related to their semantic weight and their grammatical symmetry. Previously, we saw that these American comics reduced in their framing complexity over time, peaking in the 1990s, and then rebounding somewhat in their framing complexity into the 2000s. Figure 8.10a shows this similar pattern when we look at framing complexity broken apart into different semantic weights of panels. Both balanced- and verbal-semantic weight show this characteristic curve with complexity reducing the most around the 1990s before rebounding. This pattern is also shown for visual-weighted panels, but the framing complexity is reduced. This implies that panels with less complex framing (micros, amorphic) are where visuals carry the most meaning.

Looking at the overall value of semantic weight across individual framing categories confirmed that less complex framing aligns with visual-weight. As a reminder, 0 would be balanced-weight, while more positive values are more visually-weighted and more negative values are more verbally-weighted. The most verbal were macros (−.29) and then monos (−.25)

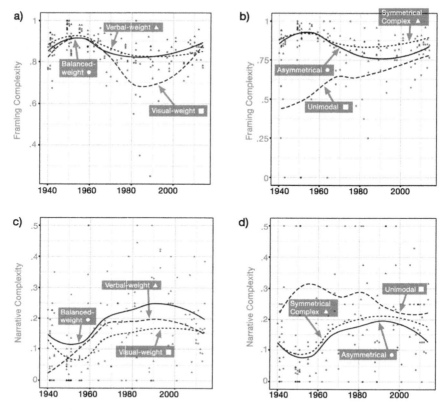

FIGURE 8.10 *Dimensions of storytelling over time for a) framing and semantic weight, b) framing and grammatical symmetry, and c) narrative complexity and symmetry.*

compared to the more balanced/visual micros (−.09) and amorphics (.08). This confirmed that less complex framing aligns with more visually-weighted storytelling.

If we then look at the symmetry of structure across the sequences in relation to framing (Figure 8.10b), we again see this characteristic dip in the framing complexity around the 1990s for symmetrical and asymmetrical structures. But, a totally different trend across time is shown for the unimodal panels. In these panels, which contain no text at all, framing complexity was its lowest in the oldest books, and complexity of panels grew steadily up through to the 2000s. The implication here is that older comics used wordless panels with less framing complexity (micros, amorphics), which might focus on that specific visual content relevant for the storytelling that predominantly was conveyed verbally or in a balanced manner. Over time, panels without words also began to carry more information on their own (macros, monos).

This interpretation is supported further by looking at these dimensions in relation to narrative complexity. As depicted in Figure 8.10c, narrative complexity grew for all types of semantic weight, peaking in the 1990s and 2000s, similar to what we saw in the analysis of narrative complexity more generally. However, if we look at the symmetry of structure, we only see this increase and peak for the symmetrical and asymmetrical structures. Unimodal expressions again maintain a different pattern, where narrative complexity peaked around the 1960s, and then declined again into the 2000s.

My interpretation is that in these earlier comics, narrative complexity was greatest when the images were on their own, despite text carrying more meaning and emphasis overall in this time period. This would be consistent with the idea that, when written language dominates, shifting to visuals alone allows them to carry more meaning. However, in more contemporary comics, narrative complexity overall grew, and with it the ability for more complicated structures to persist even in multimodal interactions. In other words, when the visual language took on more narrative complexity throughout, then that complexity permeates across all multimodal relationships, not just the ones where text is absent.

8.3.2 *Multimodality and morphology*

Given our focus here on multimodality, it is worth closing this section by turning to the morphology most associated with multimodality: the *carriers* of text. As discussed in Chapter 3, we can abstract elements, such as word balloons, thought bubbles, sound effects, and captions into an abstract class of "carriers" that hold text. These can be characterized by their underlying meanings in terms of which characters have access to the contents of the carrier, beyond what its surface features may look like. That is, a "speech balloon" may not always indicate speech, just as a "caption" may actually show someone's thoughts like a thought balloon.

We can see that the overall rates of carriers changed in comics from both the United States and Europe over this eighty-year span. As was reported in Chapter 3, comics from the United States used more carriers than those from Europe, but this use also changed over time. As depicted in Figure 8.11a, American comics began using about 1.5 carriers per panel, rising to more than two carriers per panel between the 1960s and 1980s, and then descending back to around 1.5 into the 2000s. European comics began using around 1.5 carriers per panel as well in the 1940s, although they rose steadily to use slightly more carriers per panel into the 2000s.

More nuances can be seen when we look at the change across time for specific types of carriers, as in Figure 8.11b. In American comics, Public carriers ("speech") were used the most, and maintained a fairly constant rate near 1.25 carriers per panel over time. Private carriers ("thoughts") had

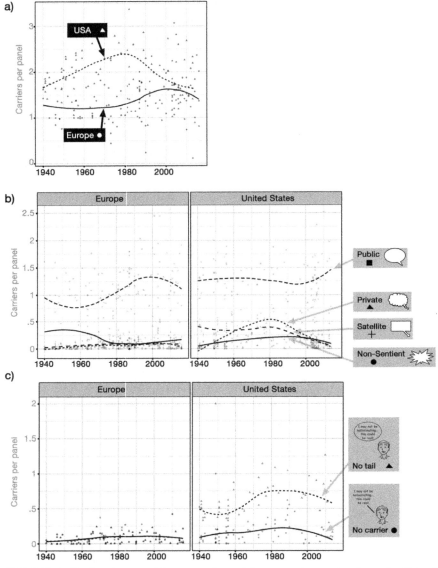

FIGURE 8.11 *Carriers used for more than eighty years in comics from the United States and Europe, both for a) total carrier use, b) specific types of carriers, and c) the rate of having no depicted carriers or tails.*

perhaps the most notable change over time, starting in the 1940s with fairly low frequency, then rising in prevalence to a peak around 1980 of about .5 per panel, only to fall again into the 2000s. This difference likely accounts for much of the shape of the overall trend of carriers changing over time (Figure 8.11a). Similarly, Satellites ("narrative captions") maintained steadily until the 2000s and then declined. Finally, non-sentient carriers ("sound effects") seem to have increased slightly over time, though without being too frequent overall.

European comics displayed a fairly different trend over time. Public carriers were again the most frequent, but increased in time from around one carrier per panel in the 1940s to 1.5 in the 2000s. Both Private and Satellite carriers were infrequent in the 1940s and rose slightly in frequency into the 2000s. Finally, Non-sentient carriers in the 1940s used .5 per panel and actually decreased further across the eighty years of the corpus.

Finally, the overall presentation of carriers has changed over time as well. Figure 8.11c shows the frequency per panel that carriers omit their carriers (the physical boxes or balloons) or omit their tails, plotted across the eighty years of our corpus. As we saw back in Chapter 3, European comics used few instances where carriers or tails were omitted, and indeed this mostly stayed constant with only a slight rise over time. In contrast, American comics showed a steep increase for omitting tails from the 1960s to the 1980s, which then waned somewhat into the 2000s, but this frequency was far greater for the omissions of carriers over time.

Altogether, we find that although both American and European comics maintain Public carriers more often than all other types, they have increased in frequency in European comics since the 1940s, while all other types remain infrequent. These European carriers have also largely retained both carriers and tails in their physical presentation. Over this same time, American comics maintained a fairly constant use of Public carriers, but with a rise and fall in the use of Private carriers and a reduction in other types. In addition, there has been a shift in the depiction of the carrier and tails. Once again, we find that comics differ in how they use and present visual conventions, and these differences suggest changes in the multimodal relationships over time and their manifestation in visual storytelling depending on how often they convey characters' speech or thoughts, or general sound effects or captions.

8.4 A shifting visual language

Throughout this chapter we have described ways that both European and American comics have changed across eighty years of publications. In particular, our data about layout, visual storytelling, and multimodality illustrates how the Kirbyan AVL may have shifted over time in comics from the United States.

One way to summarize these changes is simply to look at each of the trends we've observed throughout, as we've done in each of the previous sections. However, we can also tie together these observations using statistical measures, such as the clustering analysis that has been used in previous chapters. I again used the clustering approach to find groupings motivated by the properties of the data itself, rather than imposing preconceived categories on the data. In this case, we can see if books from similar time periods group together to form characterizable "styles."

To analyze these data, I entered nearly all the information that was analyzed throughout the sections of this chapter into a k-means clustering analysis. This included framing information (macro, mono, micro, amorphic), subjective panels, situational changes (time, spatial location, characters), narrative patterns (BNP, Environmental-Conjunction), semantic weight (visual, verbal, balanced), symmetry (unimodal, asymmetrical, symmetrical), word count, panel directions (lateral, down, up-angle, down-angle), and panel arrangements (grid, horizontal stagger, whole row, inset, blockage).

The clustering analysis resulted in three clusters, with the first two consisting of nineteen comics and the last of fourteen comics. To see if these clusters then reflected "styles" in how American comics have shifted over time, I compared how many books from each cluster appeared within each decade. To be clear about the prediction here, if books from each decade were to appear in equal amounts or randomly, it would suggest no clear stylistic trends. However, if they did differ across decades, and if those differences follow a systematic distribution, then we might identify them as showing some sort of patterning.

Indeed, statistical analysis showed that these clusters did differ in how they appeared in different decades (χ^2 = 37.9, p < .001). As can be seen in Figure 8.12a, clusters also follow consistent trends across decades. Comics from the 1940s and 1950s split into clusters 2 and 3. This persists into the 1960s, when one book from cluster 1 appears at the end of the decade (*Nick Fury Agent of S.H.I.E.L.D.* #1 by Jim Steranko in 1968). Cluster 1 persists in small amounts through the 1970s and 1980s, while cluster 2 diminishes. By the 1990s and 2000s, all comics belong to cluster 1. Finally, in the 2010s, all comics belong to cluster 1, except for one (*Green Lantern Corps* #42 by Peter Tomasi and Patrick Gleason in 2010).

This distribution of clusters across decades suggests that clusters 2 and 3 characterize the properties of older comics, while cluster 1 characterizes the emergence of the contemporary Kirbyan AVL. The next question becomes, what are the characteristics of these different clusters?

We can compare the properties of these clusters based on their dimensions of structure. However, the full list of elements put into this analysis was fairly extensive, so I instead characterize the traits of these clusters using our averaged complexity assessments. Thus, instead of looking at all four framing categories that were included in the analysis (macro, mono, micro, amorphic), I instead characterize these clusters in terms of their framing complexity scores. I also provide information about their situational discontinuity, narrative complexity, semantic weight, grammatical complexity, and layout complexity. We can see how the different clusters are characterized across each of these dimensions in Figure 8.12b to i.

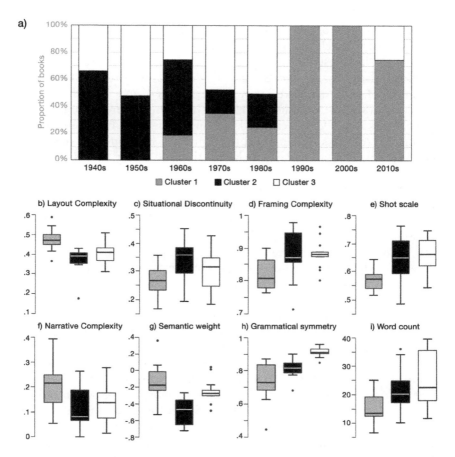

FIGURE 8.12 *Results of a cluster analysis of Mainstream American comics for how they distribute into a) clusters into different decades, and their characteristics of a) layout complexity, b) situational discontinuity, c) framing complexity, d) shot scale, e) narrative complexity, f) semantic weight, g) grammatical interactions, and h) word count.*

Let's begin by describing the properties of the clusters associated with older comics. Clusters 2 and 3 are characterized by lower framing complexity (8.12b), greater situational discontinuity (8.12c), fairly high framing complexity (more macros, 8.12d), wide shot scales (8.12e), and low narrative complexity (8.12f). Where these clusters deviate from each other seems to be primarily in their multimodal interactions. Books in cluster 2 use more verbal semantic weight than those in cluster 3 (8.12g), while those in cluster 3 have more grammatical symmetry (i.e., more sentences interacting with narrative sequences, 8.12h). Comics in cluster 3 also used more words compared to those in cluster 2 and cluster 1 (8.12i). Thus, it seems that clusters 2 and 3 largely share the same structures in their visual languages, but differ in how those visual structures relate to text.

By comparison, cluster 1 deviates from the other clusters in almost all structures. This cluster displays higher layout complexity (8.12b), lower situational discontinuity between panels (8.12c), lower framing complexity of panels (8.12d), narrower shot scales (8.12e), and greater narrative complexity (8.12f). Multimodal relationships also differed from those in both clusters 2 and 3, with cluster 1 demonstrating more balanced semantic weight (8.12g), less symmetrical grammatical relationships (i.e., more asymmetrical and unimodal panels, 8.12h), and fewer words per panel (8.12i).

Overall, this analysis suggests that Kirbyan AVL has developed from a predominant older structure with more varying multimodal relationships (clusters 2 and 3), to a more contemporary visual language with consistent multimodality (cluster 1). The older Kirbyan AVL had more complex panels with wider shot scales, placed within less complex layouts and narrative sequences, while on the whole using more words and verbal-weight. This shifted to a visual language with less complex panels, with narrower shot scales in more complex layouts and narrative sequencing, and with a more balanced semantic weight with fewer words.

Since this is all a bit abstract, it can be useful to examine the structures in examples. We can highlight this change in the structure across comics from the United States by comparing the data for books by two of the most exemplary comic artists of the mainstream American comic industry. First is *Captain Marvel Adventures #1* (1940), an early work by Joe Simon and Jack Kirby, the namesake of "Kirbyan AVL." Second is a page from *Amazing Spider-Man* #328 (1990), written by David Michelinie and drawn by Todd McFarlane,[3] one of the most popular and best-selling American comic artists of the 1980s and 1990s. In both cases, it is attested that Kirby and McFarlane did the primary storytelling, while the writers largely added the text. A sample page from each is shown in Figures 8.13a and 8.13b, while data for the properties of these comics are provided in Figure 8.13c to i.

I won't discuss every detail about these comics, but it should be immediately apparent in the graphs that they differ in all the same ways as we saw in the clusters. Kirby's visual language uses greater framing complexity (more macros), with a wider shot scale (between a full to medium shot), more time changes, and more BNP in storytelling, with a row-based layout that primarily uses a pure grid or horizontal staggering. The multimodality of the older comic is also verbally-weighted. We can see all this in the sample page as well: it has a horizontally staggered grid with panels showing full scenes, progressing in basic actions and with substantial text in each panel.

Compare this to McFarlane's structure: it has reduced framing complexity (fewer macros, more of all other categories), with a narrower shot scale (between a medium to close shot), more character changes, less BNP, and

VISUAL LANGUAGES ACROSS TIME

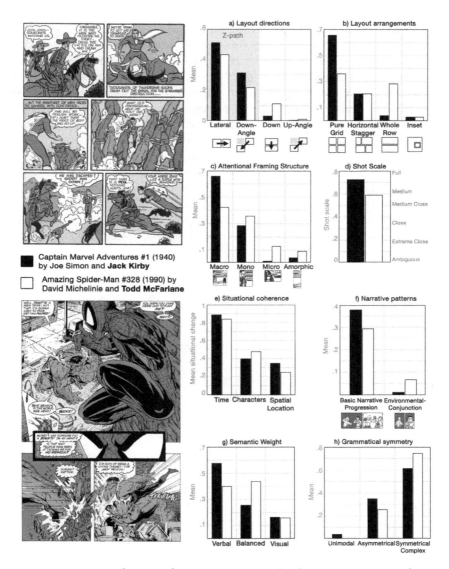

FIGURE 8.13 *Sample pages from* Captain Marvel Adventures #1 *(1940) by Joe Simon and Jack Kirby, and* The Amazing Spider-Man *#328 (1990) by David Michelinie and drawn by Todd McFarlane, along with data corresponding to their a) layout directions, b) layout arrangements, c) attentional framing structure, d) shot scale, e) situational coherence, f) narrative patterns, g) semantic weight, and h) grammatical interactions. Spider-Man © Marvel Comics. Captain Marvel Adventures is public domain.*

more Environmental-Conjunction. The use of pure grids is greatly reduced, along with an increase in panels spanning a whole row. In other words, the panels show less information, while more information connects across panels, and it does so within more complex non-grid layouts. This should be visible in the example page, which has two whole row panels, two micro close ups, more shifting between characters, and less rapid narrative progression across panels. The text-image relationships also maintain a more balanced semantic-weight. It is worth noting that despite their multimodal differences, these books maintain a similar average word count (*Captain Marvel Adventures*: 18.7, *Amazing Spider-Man*: 18.3).

Altogether, this analysis suggests that the gradual shifts across time in various structures in American comics have given way to more distinctive overall varieties. Although more nuanced changes may have indeed occurred over time and within these clusters, by looking "bottom-up" from the properties of the data there appears to broadly be a distinctive shift between an older to a contemporary variety of Kiryban AVL.

8.5 Implications

This chapter has shown that the structure of visual languages can change over time, and they do so in ways that may be culturally distinctive. Our primary focus across multiple structures was how the Kirbyan AVL used in mainstream comics from the United States has shifted between the 1940s and the 2010s. This analysis overall found a shift from an older AVL to a more contemporary structure that began slowly emerging in the 1960s and reaching fruition in the 1990s, and then continuing as the dominant patterning of American comics.

The full fruition of this contemporary variety of AVL in the 1990s might be telling. This period saw the rise of mainstream creator-owned comics, which allowed more independence from the editorial guidance of the major publishers. Along with this, factions arose in this decade with older creators often critical of the storytelling of younger creators. Although some socio-cultural factors were likely at play (such as the younger creators vastly outselling many older ones), such criticism may also be a byproduct of the change in the visual language. Essentially, it is a visual language equivalent of "kids these days are ruining the language," despite the changes merely reflecting the apex of a gradual historical shift in structures.

It is also noteworthy that the 1990s marked the influence of Japanese manga into the American market at a large scale, which seems to have influenced the AVL. This would be an example of language contact, which often accompanies language change. For example, although they maintained a row-based structure, embedded columns increased in the 1980s and 1990s. In addition, we see a reduction in framing complexity, an increase in narrative complexity, and an increase in changes between characters and spatial locations at the expense of time changes. Although these storytelling trends have gradually progressed since the 1940s, they apexed in the 1990s. However, it is noteworthy that after the 1990s several of these dimensions show a slight rebounding of frequency, suggesting perhaps a return away from the peak of this full manga influence and a return towards more "American" storytelling.

It is worth considering that this influence of manga has often been said to result in a type of "decompressed" storytelling (Cicci 2015, Mazur and Danner 2014). This may be reflected in manga using fewer time changes and more character and spatial location changes than American and European comics, along with lower framing complexity. The shifts in time for American comics towards these properties would indeed create a type of "decompression" relative to the storytelling in older comics. Such decompression is further reflected in less meaning and complexity being carried in the text, along with less words, with an increase towards balanced text-image relationships or visually dominated storytelling. But, this decompression does not seem to have rendered an increase in panels per page, indeed suggesting that more pages may be required to achieve this decompression of information.

In contrast to the trends of American comics over time, European comics appear to have undergone fewer changes in structure across the past eighty years. Indeed, these works reflected more consistency with the older American comics. They have maintained consistent panels per page, and only a slight shift in storytelling, with an overall decrease in time changes and an increase in character changes. The framing structure across time has remained relatively stable, except for a slight shift after the 2000s. If manga have had an influence, it is delayed compared to American comics.

Altogether, we clearly show shifts in the structure across these eighty years for both American and European comics. But, at the same time, American and European comics largely begin with similar proportions of data for situational coherence, framing, and narrative patterns. Despite this common origin, cultures diverged into more distinctive patterns. Although we have no data here for Japanese manga before the 1980s, given that early manga originally was based on American newspaper comics in the early-twentieth century (Exner 2021, Gravett 2004), we would also expect consistency between Japanese structures and the patterns in American and European comics shown here. Nevertheless, as our cross-cultural data in earlier chapters suggests, Japanese manga (along with other Asian comics) have developed distinctively from American and European comics, which has subsequently influenced those works in more recent decades. The question then is how and why deviation from this common origin occurred more for only some traditions (America, Japan), while less for others that remained more stable over time (Europe). These analyses can thus hopefully provide a foundation for future work to more thoroughly examine historical changes across visual languages, whether used in comics or in other contexts.

CHAPTER NINE

Cross-Cultural Visual Languages?

Throughout this book we have examined several structures that constitute the visual languages used in comics, and in each case, we have found systematic variation across different populations. By and large, these distinctions have yielded recognizable patterns corresponding at least somewhat to the different regions represented in the VLRC: Europe, Asia, and the United States. Given this result, we could potentially make the claim that there are distinct visual languages corresponding to these places: a European Visual Language, Asian Visual Language, and American Visual Language.

Nevertheless, such an interpretation assumes that the data from within those regions maintain a fairly uniform characteristic. The previous chapters attempted to address cross-cultural variation by summarizing results in a "top-down" way. These analyses have used pre-assigned categories for our comparisons, based on the places that these comics came from, their genres or demographics, and/or their publication dates. Although these categories have yielded identifiable differences between groups, adhering to such categories may also hide similarities that cut across these comics. Indeed, languages are not specifically bound to the confines of countries, and this is also true of the visual languages that persist largely in print cultures.

In addition, we have already discussed cases where cultures have been influenced by each other, meaning that it is possible for people in one place (such as the United States) to potentially be drawing in a visual language that originated in another place (such as Japan). This would mean that data associated with the comics from the United States may actually contain different visual languages. This is not to mention the cases where authors from one country might be working in the comic industry of another country.

So, is there another way to identify potential visual languages? We have already used such an alternative approach with a more "bottom-up" method in the form of statistical clustering analyses. Again, this approach takes the raw data with no classifications (such as countries), and the analysis clusters the data in a way that best reflects how it should go together. Essentially, books with similar structures will be sorted together, regardless of where they come from. Then, we can see if those groupings match classifications we can recognize. This sort of clustering analysis should better reveal the boundaries of visual languages—if there are any—based on how the data itself indicates it should be grouped, rather than by the inferences we draw from top-down categories, such as countries or genres.

An additional advantage of this approach is that it allows us to look beyond one or two dimensions of structure, like we've done in each of the chapters so far. Rather, we can combine data across numerous structures to see how they combine in systematic ways. Although we're able to do this analysis with the VLRC data, it does have a few limitations. Since not all comics were annotated in exactly the same way, some structures are uneven across the books. Because of this, I'll constrain my analysis to the annotations we have across the widest range of books: how information is conveyed within panels and across panels. This data is present in the largest number of books in the VLRC, and can thus offer the widest scope.

9.1 Visual languages?

My overall clustering analysis included the data related to storytelling. This included the three primary distinctions of change in situational coherence discussed in Chapter 5: time, spatial location, and character changes, along with the overall means for situational continuity. It also included the aggregated means for framing complexity (averaging across values for macro to amorphic panels), shot scales (averaging across values from long shot to extreme close up), and the mean rate of subjective panels, as covered in Chapter 6. Finally, the analysis also incorporated the measure of narrative complexity (averaging across levels 1 through 3) discussed in Chapter 7.

I used the same type of k-means (neighborhood-based) clustering analysis that I have used in previous chapters. In this case, I analyzed all 357 comics stories in the VLRC that included these annotations. Based on measures indicating the adequacy of the statistical outcomes, I settled on an analysis with three clusters that had roughly an equal number of books in each cluster.

As can be seen in Figure 9.1a, clusters aligned with our primary cultural regions of Europe, America, and Asia. Cluster 1 is largely made up of Asian comics, occupying the predominant proportions of Korean, Japanese, and Chinese comics. This cluster also includes about 13 percent of the comics from the United States and France. Cluster 2 is composed mostly of American comics, but also has the widest overlap with other countries. It consists of 72 percent of the comics from the United States along with at least some proportion (10 to 50 percent) of books from every other country.

Finally, Cluster 3 is primarily made up of European comics, and includes 15 percent of the American comics and only one Japanese manga from all of the Asian books (specifically, the shojo manga *Kocchi Muite! Miiko* by Eriko Ono).

These clusters predominantly divide the three primary regions of the world represented in the VLRC, again supporting the idea that they exemplify three primary visual languages represented in the corpus. We might posit these as Asian Visual Language(s), American Visual Language(s), and European Visual Language(s). However, it is important to emphasize that the distribution of books into clusters is not a uniform, one-to-one match with global regions. At

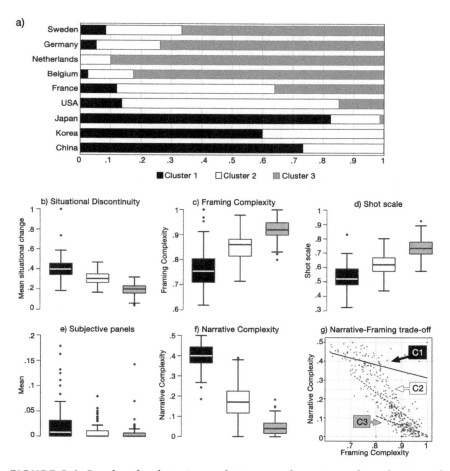

FIGURE 9.1 *Results of a clustering analysis across dimensions of panel units and storytelling, resulting in clusters that a) cut across comics from Europe, the United States, and Asia. These clusters differ in their b) situational discontinuity, c) framing complexity, d) shot scale, e) subjective panels, f) narrative complexity, and maintain g) a tradeoff between narrative and framing complexity.*

least some books from each region cut across clusters, implying that this analysis picks up on patterns of storytelling rather than global distinctions specifically. This is again consistent with the idea of a linguistic system that transcends cultural boundaries.

Now that we know what books these clusters consist of, we can examine their properties to see how they differ. Across most dimensions, we see an incremental distribution of Cluster 1-2-3, starting with situational discontinuity (Figure 9.1b). Although not pictured here, this 1-2-3 distribution occurs for the situational dimensions of time changes and character changes. Cluster 1 uses frequent amounts of character changes and low frequency of time changes, while Cluster 3 uses lots of time changes and few character changes. Again, Cluster 2 is in the middle. A slight difference arises for changes in spatial locations, where Cluster 2 seems to have the most, and Clusters 1 and 3 both use substantially fewer.

We also see this 1-2-3 distribution for framing complexity and shot scale, where Cluster 1 has the lowest framing complexity (fewer macros, Figure 9.1c) and tightest shot scale (near a medium close shot, Figure 9.1d), compared to Clusters 2 and 3 that are progressively more complex. Cluster 1 also has higher proportions of subjective panels than either of the other clusters (Figure 9.1e). Finally, the reverse pattern occurs for narrative complexity, where Cluster 1 has the highest narrative complexity, followed by Clusters 2 and 3.

This inverse relationship between framing and narrative complexity also reflects what we saw in Chapter 7: Higher degrees of framing complexity meant lower narrative complexity, and vice versa. In Figure 9.1g, we see a scatterplot similar to the one in Chapter 7, with a distribution of books (dots) spanning from the upper left to bottom right showing this tradeoff. Back then, we saw that cultures largely overlapped along this broad distribution, reflected in the tight trend lines (Figure 7.10a). Here, we now see that the trendlines have separated, and the clusters partition the books into fairly clean groups. Cluster 1 (mostly Asian comics) uses the most complex narrative sequencing, with framing of the simplest units. Cluster 3 (mostly European books) meanwhile has the simplest narrative sequencing, but the most complex framing of units. Cluster 2 (American and others) falls in the middle.

Altogether, this analysis implies three different systems of storytelling, manifesting in visual languages broadly aligning with the regions of Asia, the United States, and Europe. As has been discussed in previous chapters, the Asian strategy (Cluster 1) may reinforce a more "subjective" storytelling, focusing more on the parts of a scene (low framing complexity) with more situational discontinuity as if a viewer was looking around a scene (character changes), emphasized with subjective viewpoints. By showing less information in each frame, more complex narrative patterns are required across panels to package the meaning, which overall sponsors greater inference to connect this discontinuous meaning.

At the opposite side, the European strategy (Cluster 3) appears to be more "objective" in its storytelling. This involves showing the full scene more often (high framing complexity), which in turn requires less complex narrative patterning to connect this information across panels, manifesting as greater amounts of time changes between panels. This also involves less subjective viewpoints. By being more explicit within frames, less inference is required across panels to construct the overall sequential meaning.

Finally, a middle range also appears within Cluster 2. This cluster typically falls halfway between Clusters 1 and 3, and implies a blended storytelling style. A bit more insight here can be found by looking at the proportion of comics from the United States allocated to different clusters from each decade. Consider the graph in Figure 9.2, which shows the proportion of American books from each decade that constitute each cluster. As we can see, Cluster 2 persists in large quantities throughout all the decades, indicating that it may be characterizing an "American" style of storytelling. Older comics have more books constituting Cluster 3 (i.e., more like European comics), but we only begin to see Cluster 1 (i.e., more like Asian comics) begin in the 1980s, sustaining through the 2010s—precisely the timeline that manga rose in influence in the US.

These analyses suggests that Cluster 2, exemplified by comics from the United States, reflects a storytelling strategy that blends the objective and subjective methods of Europe and Asia. It uses moderate framing and narrative complexity, along with moderate amounts of changes in situational coherence across panels.

Altogether, these results suggest variation between three primary storytelling styles, which we might identify as indexing different visual languages. This raises questions about how homogenous these clusters might be, particularly within the countries we analyzed. Might there be varieties of visual languages within comics from particular places? Throughout earlier chapters, we've compared different subtypes of Japanese manga (shonen, shojo, seinen, josei) and comics from the United States

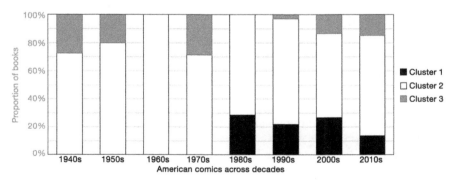

FIGURE 9.2 *Proportion of American comics per decade allocated to each cluster from the global cluster analysis.*

(older and newer mainstream, indie, US manga). Just how distinct are these subtypes if we only analyze the data from those places?

9.2 Japanese Visual Language(s)?

We can start with the subtypes of Japanese manga, which cut across demographics. Back in Chapter 3, I argued that the visual languages stereotypically used in shonen and shojo manga might be subvarieties of a broader JVL. This was posited because most of the morphology was shared between these groups, despite some morphological patterns appearing more frequently in one type or the other. What if we look across types of manga for our storytelling features, like above?

I used the same clustering approach that I described across all the data in the VLRC up above. Here, any computations that generated four or more clusters contained at least one cluster with fewer than five books. As this number was below the minimal sample per subtype (which was ten books), I deemed these clusters too small to be representative. However, it is worth noting that one cluster persisted within only five books, which were all shonen manga. This left a maximal number of three clusters, which is noteworthy for being below the number of possible subtypes (which was four: shonen, shojo, seinen, josei).

Figure 9.3a shows how books from different types of manga distributed into these clusters. To distinguish these clusters, created from Japanese books alone, from the clusters we discussed above, I'll refer to these as Clusters J1, J2, and J3. The first thing to notice is that all clusters contain all the types of manga. This hints at the overarching similarities between these types of manga, perhaps suggesting a broader JVL. Indeed, statistical analysis of this distribution did not show differences between how clusters distribute across manga demographics (χ^2 = 10.7, p = .097), implying that these clusters do not cleanly map to types of manga specifically. Nevertheless, there are a few noteworthy features we can describe.

First, although Cluster J1 has some books from all demographics, it is dominated by 54 percent of the shojo manga and 25 percent of the josei manga. This hints that at least some traits of Cluster J1 are distinctive to manga aimed at female readers. This cluster overall had the largest framing complexity (more macros, 9.3e) with the widest shot scale (9.3f), along with the lowest narrative complexity (9.3g). Otherwise, its situational dimensions resembled those of Cluster J3 (9.3b to d). Clusters J1 and J3 also seem to differ between the framing/narrative and situational dimensions. These clusters share the traits of less complex framing (9.3e) and greater narrative complexity (9.3g), but Cluster J2 differs from both J1 and J3 in situational dimensions (9.3b to d). Cluster J2 contains the largest proportion of books from all different types of manga, while J3 has a small sample of all types, but slightly more seinen manga.

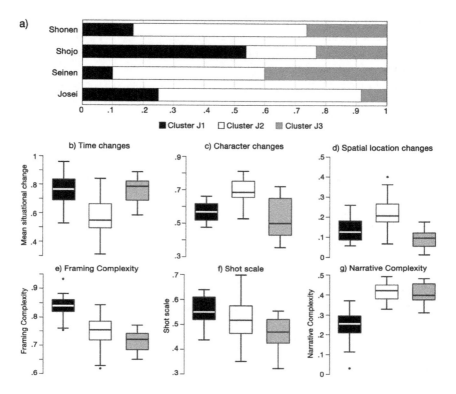

FIGURE 9.3 Results of a clustering analysis of Japanese manga resulting in clusters that a) cut across demographics of manga (shonen, shojo, seinen, josei). These clusters differ in their situational dimensions of b) time changes c) character changes and d) spatial location changes along with their e) framing complexity f) shot scale and g) narrative complexity.

Altogether, along with the dispersion of these clusters across different demographics of manga, these overlapping patterns again point towards a broader shared system. These three clusters are all similar to each other in at least one dimension of structure. Out of three clusters, J1 and J3 overlap in some dimensions (situational coherence), while J2 and J3 overlap in others (framing/narrative). These intertwining patterns of features suggest that, although there may be some distinctive subvarieties (possibly exemplified by shojo manga?), they all maintain patterns characteristic of an overarching JVL. This JVL, in turn, appears consistent with the visual language(s) across Asia, in light of the clustering across the broader VLRC data above.

We can now compare this to our comparison of varieties in Chapter 3. Here our statistical analysis showed no difference for the distribution of clusters between demographics. This is different from the results of the clustering with morphology in Chapter 3, where we saw clear statistical divisions between clusters. The implication is that a broader JVL maintains fairly consistent grammatical and panel-level structuring of information, while varieties may differ in their morphology, whether that is the open-class morphology of the graphic "style" of drawings or the closed-class morphology analyzed in Chapter 3. This is also consistent with the ways that many varieties differ: they often differ in some of their vocabulary, while sharing an overarching similar grammar.

9.3 American Visual Language(s)?

Let's now analyze the variation in comics from the United States. Here, the subtypes in the VLRC are not so much demographics, but they differ either across time, and/or genre. I here contrasted mainstream American comics from independent (indie) comics, along with an additional distinction for US manga, which ostensibly are created with, or at least influenced by, the JVL discussed above. I also split the mainstream comics into two groups, each reflecting a forty-year span, with "older" comics (1940s to 1980s) contrasting "newer" comics (1980s to 2010s). As explored in the last chapter, there is indeed nuance across these dates, but this partitions them into two primary groups supported by our analyses in the last chapter. Compared to the demographics of manga above, might we see more evidence of distinctive groups here?

I again used the same clustering approach as before. When optimizing the model to four clusters or above, there were again always clusters with less than five comics in them (although, unlike the small cluster of shonen manga above, these clusters were not from a single subtype). Thus, three clusters again were the maximal number that maintained all clusters without outliers, and which still had good measures of statistical adequacy. To distinguish these clusters, I'll refer to them as Clusters A1, A2, and A3.

As depicted in Figure 9.4a, these clusters had somewhat distinctive traits, and indeed statistical analysis here did show differences across this distribution ($\chi^2 = 41$, p < .001). First, Cluster A1 mostly consisted of the US manga and Indie comics, with few mainstream comics from any era. These appear to be the books most influenced by JVL and maintain those features, with the lowest framing complexity (9.4e), highest narrative complexity (9.4g), and the highest situational discontinuity (9.4b–d). These are presumably the books that clustered with Asian comics in Cluster 1 of the analyses above, and those that differentiated starting in the 1980s (as in Figure 9.2).

US manga and indie comics also appeared the next most prominently in Cluster A2, which was otherwise dominated by 68 percent of the newer mainstream comics. This cluster reflects the medial "American" style in Cluster 2 of the analyses above (Figure 9.1), with mid-range scores across

CROSS-CULTURAL VISUAL LANGUAGES? 207

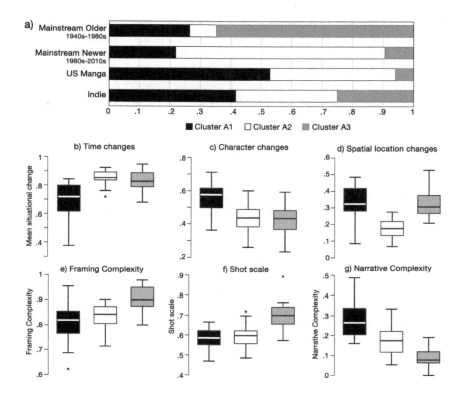

FIGURE 9.4 *Results of a clustering analysis of comics from the United States, resulting in clusters that a) cut across genres of older and newer mainstream comics, manga created by English-speaking Americans, and indie comics. These clusters differ in their situational dimensions of a) time changes, b) character changes, and c) spatial location changes, along with their e) framing complexity, f) shot scale, and g) narrative complexity.*

nearly all dimensions. It is noteworthy that this cluster, which is made up of primarily contemporary mainstream comics, also has the second largest proportion of US manga. Finally, Cluster A3 has the most prominent proportion of older mainstream comics (64 percent of them), and only a few of each of the other types. This cluster had the characteristic traits of older comics discussed in the last chapter, with higher framing complexity (9.4e), lower narrative complexity (9.4g), and lower situational discontinuity (9.4b to d). Note that these are also the traits of the more "European" style discussed above (Cluster 3 in Figures 9.1 and 9.2).

Overall, comics from the United States maintain more distinctive clusters than those from Japan. Unlike the intertwining similarities of structures displayed in clusters from manga, the clusters of American comics largely show incremental differentiation across their structures, with clusters that are more distinctly focused around one particular trait. Specifically, mainstream comics differ primarily between older and newer comics, which are distinguished from those books influenced by Japanese manga. It is also noteworthy that the books we classed as "indie" appear to have the widest dispersion across these clusters, and thus reflect the subtype with the most stylistic diversity (Cohn 2013c).

9.4 European Visual Language(s)?

With works from the United States and Japan, we asked about variation between the visual languages used in comics from within a single country. We can also invert this question to ask: to what degree might different countries be distinctive from each other? This issue particularly arises in the properties of the books from Europe, consistent with our questions related to morphology between Dutch and Flemish comics back in Chapter 3. In the VLRC, we have comics from five different European countries: Belgium (Flanders), France, Germany, the Netherlands, and Sweden. Is there an overarching European Visual Language, or might we find patterns that distinguish these countries?

I again carried out the same clustering analysis on the 158 comics in the VLRC from across Europe. Because the primary question was whether countries would correspond with clusters, and because there were five countries in the VLRC, I fixed the analysis to create five clusters. This again yielded some clusters with only a small numbers of books (four and seven), but I here retained them given the research question. The results are depicted in Figure 9.5a. I'll refer to these clusters as Clusters E1, E2, E3, E4, and E5.

As should be visible, no clusters cleanly grouped with any countries, although an overall statistical difference did arise for this distribution (χ^2 = 65.6, p < .001). This difference was likely motivated by some clusters occupying greater proportions for certain countries. For example, 75 percent of the Swedish comics were grouped into Cluster E5, but this cluster also contained substantial proportions of books from all other countries. Similarly, 48 percent of the French books appeared in Cluster E1, more than in any other cluster, while this same cluster also included books from all other countries. In addition, books from Sweden and France appeared in all five clusters. Somewhat more consistency appeared between books from the Netherlands, Flemish Belgium, and Germany, which all had few comics in E1, and then otherwise split their proportions between E3 and E5. Nevertheless, in all cases, clusters persisted across countries, suggesting no distinctive national visual languages.

Some clarification on these results can be offered by looking at the structures used in these clusters. Often, clusters were defined by fairly distinctive features. For example, Clusters E2 and E4 are both fairly small in

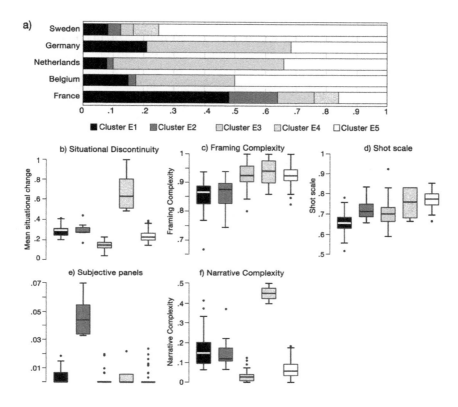

FIGURE 9.5 *Results of a clustering analysis of comics from Europe, resulting in clusters that a) cut across countries. These clusters differ in their b) situational discontinuity, along with their c) framing complexity, d) shot scale, e) subjective panels, and f) narrative complexity.*

their proportions within countries (together, only 16 percent of all European books), and these seem to correspond with outliers in the data. Cluster E2 corresponds to books with higher proportions of subjective viewpoints (9.5e), while E4 corresponds to books with higher narrative complexity (9.5f) and greater situational discontinuity (9.5e, note: I do not show them here, but character and spatial location changes largely follow the distribution of situational discontinuity, and time changes show the inverse distribution).

Besides the greater frequency of subjective panels in E2, it largely resembles E1, with slightly lower framing complexity (9.5c) and shot scales (9.5d), and slightly higher narrative complexity (9.5f), making them somewhat more akin to contemporary American comics. Meanwhile, E3 and E5 maintain similar structures, with the lowest situational discontinuity (9.5b), highest framing complexity (9.5c) and widest shot scale along with

E4 (9.5d), and lowest narrative complexity (9.5f). These are the traits most typical of the "European" cluster in our original analysis of all comics in the VLRC, and E3 and E5 together account for 75 percent of the European comics.

Overall, these results suggest that, although there is variation between books in Europe, such variation does not suggest distinctive national visual languages. Indeed, other than the outliers in certain structures, the overall range of values in each of the structures remains fairly constrained. This implies that the variation observed here may reflect consistency within a particular range, subsuming a broader European Visual Language. Of course, it is important to again be cautious about overextending this conclusion to all of "Europe." Here we have analyzed only five countries from Europe, which includes more than forty countries. Comparison with the structures in other countries is therefore necessary to better assess whether a pan-European visual language exists, or whether there may be further nuance that we are unable to capture with this particular corpus.

9.5 Comprehension

These analyses suggest that at least three storytelling strategies persist in systematic ways across comics from Asia, Europe, and the United States. Within Japan and Europe, varieties appear to use less distinct structures, although within the United States more characteristic properties seem to emerge. It is worth making a few reminders at this point.

Firstly, although these patterns may suggest distinct visual languages, these analyses only apply to particular structures within the broader architecture of visual languages (morphology, grammar, semantics). Analysis of additional structures may offer further nuance and diversity across visual languages that are not captured here, as we saw in the differences between closed-class morphology within and between different systems in Chapter 3.

Secondly, it is worth reiterating that none of these strategies are better or worse in any qualitative sense. No language has any inherent qualities of greater value than another in terms of structural properties, and this applies across all modalities. However, most theories of comprehension of visual narratives posit a somewhat "universalist" characterization on how we process a visual sequence (Cohn 2020b, Loschky et al. 2020, McCloud 1993), where the stages of processing are assumed to be similar no matter the type of visual sequence being processed. Given this universalist viewpoint, it is worth considering how these varying patterns might place different demands on comprehension of a sequence. This is easiest to describe in terms of the extremes of the objective and subjective storytelling strategies most exemplified by the visual languages associated with European and Asian comics respectively.

In the objective storytelling of European comics, the front-end processes of extracting information from a panel would be more costly, since each panel contains much more information. Here, readers need to search through these complex images in order to pick out what is relevant and what is not. This process may be aided though by Western cultural trends, where readers will be inclined to direct their attention towards the primary actors in a scene (Nisbett 2003, Nisbett and Masuda 2003). This can be seen in Figure 9.6, which diagrams my example sequence of an extreme form of objective storytelling. There are multiple characters here in each panel (each given a letter), and it would be demanding to search through each image and extract this information (here suggested by the number of descending lines coming from each panel).

But, with more information conveyed within each panel, the complexity of connecting that information across panels is then reduced. This extracted information will be incorporated into a situation model of the scene, which is the mental organization of the ongoing scene. Less complex narrative patterns are required to link panels together, while fewer situational discontinuities require inference across panels. In Figure 9.6, we see that all characters maintain co-referential mappings across situation models (white lines), while basic temporal changes persist between each situation model (dark lines), requiring little inference to understand the sequence. So, altogether here the sequencing may require less costs to be understood, but there is greater demand on the initial engagement with the information in the panels themselves.

Nevertheless, there is the potential for additional back-end costs across a sequence if this is taken to an extreme, as in this particular sequence. When a lot of information is shown repeated across each panel, greater costs may be placed in maintaining all of these elements in working memory and tracking them across the sequence. For example, with six characters in each panel in Figure 9.6, and with each character carrying out actions across the panels, comprehenders face the challenge of tracking all their activities in memory. This is visible in the number of white lines connecting each update of the situation models.

Compare this to the more subjective storytelling of Asian comics. The units are simpler in their content (lower framing complexity), and would require less "front-end" processes of decoding and extracting the information, and thus these panels would be able to be comprehended easily and quickly (Laubrock, Hohenstein, and Kümmerer 2018, Loschky et al. 2020). This is diagrammed in Figure 9.7, which contrasts the same scene as in Figure 9.6. Here, other than the first panel, each panel requires relatively few elements to be extracted, placing less demand on the engagement with each unit. As discussed in Chapter 6, such sequencing may simulate the ways that a viewer's eyes would look across a scene, heightened by greater proportions of close ups (micros) and views of the environment (amorphics), along with direct representations of character's viewpoints (subjective panels).

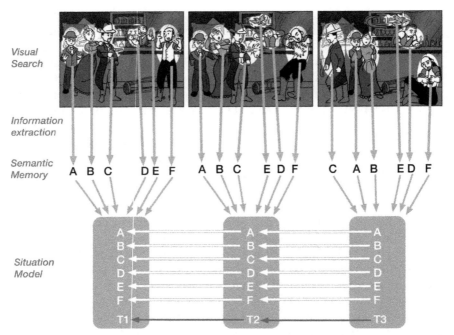

FIGURE 9.6 *Diagram of processes related to comprehending a sequence with objective storytelling.*

By showing less information in each panel, it would require a greater demand of inferencing in order to connect the meaning across panels. For example, at minimum a reader would need to maintain the spatial inference that the events in panels 2 and 3 take place within the same environment. Readers would need to familiarize themselves with these more complex narrative sequencing constructions to ameliorate relying solely on the bottom-up semantic processes. This is represented in Figure 9.7 by the connections between situation models.

Because each panel does not show all characters, only select portions of situation models are engaged at a time (white letters), leaving the non-depicted elements to remain held in memory (dark letters). Characters' appearances might extend across non-juxtaposed panels, thus requiring more distance connections, such as character C (gunslinger) in panels 2 and 4, character F (victim) in panels 3 and 5, and characters E and F (bartender and bird) only in the first and last panels. Meanwhile, some temporal relations remain ambiguous, such as the relation between the final two panels, which remain unclear whether they happen at the same or different states. All of these issues in the "back-end" processes would be more demanding for constructing a situation model of these scenes, and for guiding that comprehension through narrative structures (Cohn 2020b, Loschky et al. 2020).

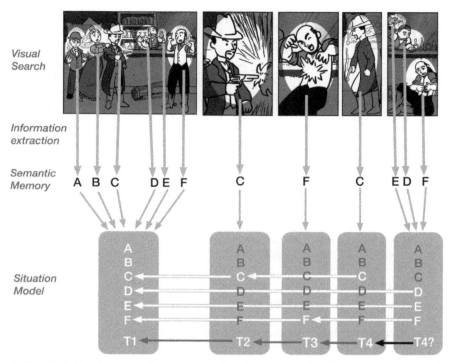

FIGURE 9.7 *Diagram of processes related to comprehending a sequence with objective storytelling.*

Thus, both of these strategies offer costs and ease to comprehension, allocated at different parts of the reading process. Neither is inherently better or worse, but both require a reader to gain fluency in the particular features of these strategies (Cohn 2020a). Because of this, engagement with an unfamiliar system may challenge fluency. For example, if you are only used to reading European comics or older American comics with fairly strict objective storytelling, the subjective approach of Asian sequencing may pose challenges to comprehension for not being overly explicit with each panel. By comparison, readers more familiar with Asian comics may find objective storytelling to be overbearing in the quantity of information in each panel. In both cases, the unfamiliar nature of the patterns may be disparagingly labeled as "bad storytelling," but such judgments are entirely relative, and would arise because of the comparative fluency of the comprehender, not because of properties of the visual language itself.

9.6 Implications

What are the implications of these analyses? As reinforced throughout this book, these results further suggest that different visual languages persist in comics. These visual languages align to some degree with the global regions represented in our corpus of Europe, the United States, and Asia, although the visual languages themselves cut across these regional boundaries. This is similar to spoken or signed languages: we associate a particular language group with a specific country or geographic origin, but ultimately, those linguistic systems can transcend those boundaries.

In addition, the presence of such consistent patterns implies that creators and readers encode this information, not that they are merely momentary creative choices or spontaneous construal that lie outside conventionalized systems. People often talk about a generic "comics medium" as if authors simply make different conscious decisions in the course of creating a visual narrative (McCloud 2006), or that there are no encoded patterns and all comprehension occurs from inferences construed solely by context (e.g., Bateman and Wildfeuer 2014a, Forceville 2020). When such consistent patterns are observed, they are then explained in terms of vague notions of wider artistic or cultural traditions (e.g., McCloud 1993), if they are attempted to be explained at all.

VLT provides a simpler explanation: regularized differences between systems are encoded as patterns in the minds of creators and readers. Although creators may indeed make choices in the process of authoring comics, they are guided by the systems they have internalized through their experience with particular visual narratives. At the same time, comprehension of a comic involves similar proficiency guided by exposure and practice with visual narratives, as suggested by a wealth of neurocognitive, cross-cultural, and developmental evidence (Cohn 2020a). In other words, creators and readers gain fluency in different *visual languages*.

Indeed, these findings also reinforce that there is no uniform, general "comics medium" except at the most superficial level. Although basic components of visual languages may persist across systems (panels, layouts, narrative patterns, etc.), subsuming all systematic variation into a generic "comics medium" disregards the conventionalized patterning present in different systems. Rather, this relationship between common structural principles and their emergence in distinct systems is precisely the relationship that exists in spoken or signed languages. Although there are shared, general structural properties of languages, these structures might be allocated in diverse ways across linguistic systems. I'll return to this point at the end of the book.

Finally, as discussed, this variation in structure may place different demands on readers' processes of comprehension. Although the general cognitive properties of comprehension may be similar (ex. front-end perceptual processes vs. back-end semantic and narrative processes), how they are distributed may depend on the particular structures of a given visual language. Readers may thus gain fluency in these different structural and comprehension strategies, habituating them to the particular ways that certain comics tell their stories. Thus, not only are there different visual languages, but readers gain fluency in those visual languages to comprehend them.

CHAPTER TEN

The Visual Language of
Calvin and Hobbes

Thus far we have focused on comparisons of visual language used in comics between and within different cultures. Before we close out our discussion of the VLRC, we can take a slight detour from cross-cultural analysis to analyze one additional source of data. Beyond the cross-cultural focus of the VLRC, we have also annotated the entire run of the beloved comic *Calvin and Hobbes* by Bill Watterson. This comic featured the adventures of an imaginative (and mischievous) boy Calvin and his best friend Hobbes, a walking, talking tiger when interacting with Calvin alone, but who appeared as a stuffed animal whenever anyone other than Calvin was around.

Our analysis of the *Calvin and Hobbes* comics allowed us a way to contrast the properties of a comic strip compared to those in longer comic books. In addition, since we had analyzed the changes that took place across eighty years of comic books from the United States, we thought it would be interesting to explore the changes in time that may have occurred in the structure produced by a single author. So, let's take a brief diversion from our cross-cultural comparisons to analyze the idiolect of one person's visual language and how it changed across a ten-year span.

The strip appeared from November 1985 to December 1995. Watterson took two sabbaticals, first from May 1991 to February 1992, and then from April 1994 to December 1994. After these sabbaticals his strip took on more creative layouts and storytelling, which we will examine throughout this chapter.

There are a few traits about the graphs in this chapter that I should highlight. First, I do not show the data from every strip, which would be a bit overwhelming, and instead I averaged across the values for strips that were produced within the same month. Thus, within the graphs I show throughout this chapter, each dot represents an average across strips of a particular month.

216 THE PATTERNS OF COMICS

Second, most of the graphs here depict the change in properties over time, which means that I place the dates along the bottom, x-axis, as we did in Chapter 8. But, because of Watterson's sabbaticals, if I were to maintain coverage of the full ten years of the strip within these graphs, we would have large gaps in the middle where no strips were released. I leave out these gaps, so readers should remember that the graphs implicitly maintain some jumps in time, with only a few months' worth of data in the years 1985 (since the strip began in November), and then again in 1991 and 1994 (sabbatical years).

10.1 Hobbes

Let's kick off our analyses with a question less related to the broader structures, but instead about the central "gimmick" of the *Calvin and Hobbes* strip: how often in the comic strip was Hobbes depicted as a real, live tiger compared to being depicted as a stuffed animal?

Figure 10.1a shows the change in frequency over time for both Daily and Sunday strips for Hobbes in different depictions. First off, Hobbes is shown much more as a real, living character than as a stuffed animal. Second, roughly the same trends persist in both Daily and Sunday strips, suggesting that Watterson made use of his character in a similar way no matter the format of the strip.

The strip begins with depictions of Hobbes as a stuffed animal in around 10 percent of panels, but then reduces over the first several years of the strip to being only around 1 to 2 percent of panels. Because Hobbes is typically only a stuffed animal when people other than Calvin interact with him, these proportions also imply that this is largely how often Hobbes is shown in panels with characters other than Calvin. This greater proportion of stuffed Hobbes at the start of the strip might reflect Watterson's establishment of the gimmick of the comic. In contrast, Hobbes depicted as a real tiger first rises and then reduces again before once again slightly rising. The reduction of Hobbes does occur around the time of Watterson's sabbatical in 1991. By showing Hobbes slightly less often, it implies more panels of only Calvin or (less often) of other characters. Nevertheless, overall Hobbes, when both real and stuffed, appears steadily in around 40 percent of panels, showing a consistent presence in the strip as one of the titular characters.

10.2 Layouts

Calvin and Hobbes had fairly distinctive layouts as a newspaper comic strip. It is well-known that the strip began using a typical grid-formatted layout in its Sunday strips. This grid format was standard for newspaper strips, since

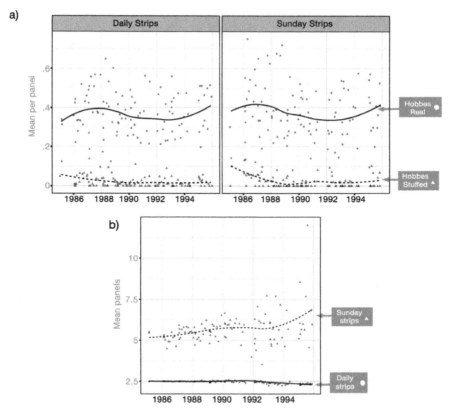

FIGURE 10.1 *Across both Daily and Sunday strips, a) the frequency of Hobbes depicted in* Calvin and Hobbes, *and b) change of the average number of panels in* Calvin and Hobbes *strips.*

it could easily be manipulated by newspapers to fit the constraints of their Sunday comics sections. The rectangular panels could be arranged in a grid, in a row, or in a column, given the needs of the newspaper. However, Watterson found this artistically limiting. As he describes in an essay in *The Calvin and Hobbes Tenth Anniversary Book* (Watterson 1995), after several years working on the strip, Watterson grew frustrated with the constraints of 1980s newspaper formats and sought more creative control afforded to him as one of the most popular cartoonists of the era. After his sabbaticals, the Sunday strips began featuring more creative layouts, taking up a whole canvas space. Through an empirical analysis, we can show this change in the properties of layouts of Sunday strips directly.

As we analyze the properties of layout, we can see clues about a shift from a standard grid into more creative layouts across numerous dimensions of structure (Caldwell 2012). First off, the overall length of strips changed. As in Figure 10.1b, Sunday strips progressively grew longer over time starting around ten panels and then increasing to a maximum of thirty-three panels long! The daily strips, in contrast, maintained a constant length with an average of 4.4 panels, although one strip reached a maximum of seven panels.

This shifting length is evidence of Watterson being unconstrained by the formatting. When Watterson began creating this strip, Sunday comics were often square panels that would give flexibility to newspapers for rearranging them onto a page (Watterson 1995). The changing length is thus indicative of a shift in formatting that would be less able to be manipulated after his creation. He speaks to this directly, saying that "with this new format I've drawn many strips I never could have drawn before . . . I've been able to draw large panels or as many as twenty small panels" (Watterson 1995, 15). We see these alterations in the layout further as we turn to more specific characteristics of the layouts.

Let's begin with the physical shapes of panels, which would then be arranged and ordered. As depicted in Figure 10.2a, we see a dramatic shift in the depiction of panels. The strip begins using square panels, which decrease in frequency into the latter years, becoming consistent by 1992. Concurrently, we see an increase in rectangular panels, again stabilizing around 1992. Although they are all fairly infrequent, we also see a slight increase in non-rectangular panel shapes over time, mostly visible in the datapoints themselves rather than the trendlines. Similarly, as depicted in Figure 10.2b, although panels with borders are by far the most frequent, we see a reduction in panel borders and an increase in borderless and bleeding panels, only here starting around 1987 and then stabilizing. This reflects Watterson's attempts "to escape the tyranny of panels" in the format of Sunday strips (Watterson 1995, 36).

These shifts again reinforce Watterson's rebellion against the formatting of typical Sunday strips. Square panels would be more manipulable across layouts in different formats, being able to be shifted between different grids, rows, or columns. So, the shift to rectangular panels may have a variety of dimensions that cannot be altered in this way. Nevertheless, it is worth pointing out that these panel shapes are still mostly rectangular in nature even if they are not squares. Despite increases in panels of other shapes, or those lacking a shape altogether because of having no borders, four-sided panels largely persist as the primary panel shape.

We can see additional changes in layout in the directions between these panels in Figure 10.2c. Z-paths would be reflected in rightward and down-angle (down-left) directions. Indeed, these directions are by far the most used, particularly rightward directions that occupy roughly 70 percent of directions between panels, with only a hint of increasing across time. In contrast, at the outset of the strip, down-angle directions are used roughly 20 percent of the time, only to plummet to around 5 percent of directions, with a clear drop-off occurring around 1991. Given that the down-angle direction would reflect the shift between rows, these proportions suggest

THE VISUAL LANGUAGE OF *CALVIN AND HOBBES* 219

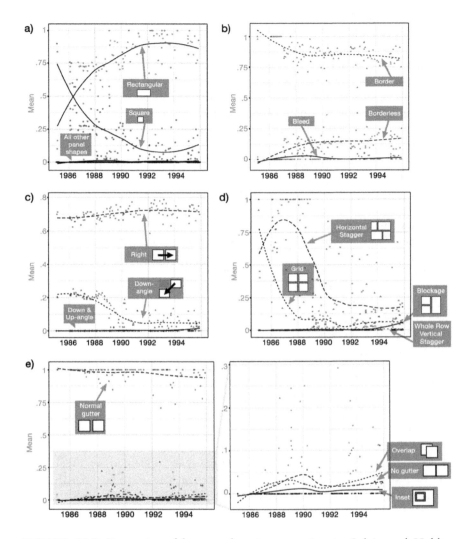

FIGURE 10.2 *Properties of layouts changing over time in* Calvin and Hobbes *Sunday strips, across a) panel shapes, b) panel borders, c) directionality between panels, d) arrangements of panels, and e) gutter widths.*

that, although Watterson might retain rows in his layouts, he less frequently places those rows on top of each other.

This interpretation is further supported by changes in the arrangements of panels, shown in Figure 10.2d. At the outset of the strip, pure grids constitute the highest proportions of how panels are arranged, followed by horizontal staggering. Pure grids would most reflect the possibility of uniformly shaped square panels able to be rearranged. In the first years of the strip (roughly before 1991), we see an initial shift as the proportion of pure grids then plummets and horizontal staggering rises. Staggering of this type requires retaining a row-based grid structure, but with rectangular panels that may have different dimensions since the vertical gutters between rows may not line up. This would mark a first shift towards having layouts less able to be altered. Following this period, we then see the proportion of horizontal staggering also rapidly decline, while there are slight increases in other panel arrangements, such as using embedded columns (blockage).

If arrangements largely went away from the row-based pure grids and horizontal staggering, but they maintained rightward directions, what replaced these types of layouts? Further insight is offered by looking at the panel gutters, as in Figure 10.2e. As should be visible, a normative proximity between gutters slightly decreased over time, while other gutter widths increased. I here "pop out" the non-normal gutters into a second figure to zoom into these trends. As should be visible, in two separate waves Watterson increases his frequency of using overlapping panels, no gutters, or inset panels. These aspects of panels' proximity make sense for being highly salient parts of Watterson's layouts, especially given his critique of newspapers wanting to move around his panels into different layouts: if panels overlap, have no border, or are inset into each other, they cannot be easily rearranged.

All of these changes are visible if we examine a sample of layouts from the strip. Figure 10.3 shows the page layouts from *Calvin and Hobbes* with the contents omitted from its first and last Sunday strips, and the first Sunday strip of each year. As should be visible, the first two strips (1985 to 1986) maintain the same layouts with a pure grid of square panels. The next few years see the introduction of rectangular panels (1987 to 1990), some borderless panels (1988 to 1989), or several additional smaller panels (1991), all of which are changes that work within the rearrangeable grid structure. Note that all of these strips (1985 to 1991) open with either an opening panel with the title or a decorative panel with the title.

Starting in 1992 we then see more diverse features. Here, there is no sign of a grid, but an increase in both rectangular and circular panels, lots of overlapping and insets, and embedded columns. All of these features in these sample strips well align with the changes highlighted in our data. These layouts are more structurally complex, more decorative, and serve as a whole composition rather than a sequence composed of rearrangeable parts.

Altogether, empirical analysis of the characteristics of layout of *Calvin and Hobbes* illustrates how the strip shifted over time from a fairly conventionalized grid pattern to a more creative and dynamic layout. That the layout changed is not surprising, as Watterson himself has discussed this, and it is fairly evident in looking at select examples of the strip over time. However, seeing these shifts in the data provides insight into the ways in

THE VISUAL LANGUAGE OF *CALVIN AND HOBBES* 221

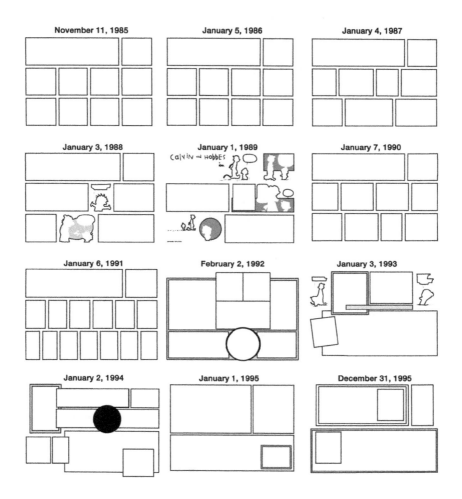

FIGURE 10.3 *Sample layouts from* Calvin and Hobbes *from its first and last Sunday strips, and the first Sunday strips of each year in between.*

which his creativity changed. It's also noteworthy that these shifts are quite different from those observed in American comic books observed in Chapter 8—they are unique to the development of this particular comic strip.

10.3 Storytelling

Given these developments in the layout of the strip, we can also ask: do we also see similar changes in the visual storytelling, and do they follow the same timing as changes in layout? So far as I've been able to find, the potential of shifts in the storytelling of the comic are less discussed than the shifts in layout. Watterson describes how the change in Sunday format "opened up new ways of storytelling" (Watterson 1995, 15), but how is only minimally described. Shifts in dimensions of situational coherence, framing, and narrative patterns are also less immediately apparent from the surface representations of the strip, unlike layouts that can be seen with a brief glance at a strip. In this next section, I thus analyze how the visual storytelling itself has changed, and then following this I examine multimodality.

10.3.1 *Situational coherence*

Let's begin by looking at the changes in situational coherence across dimensions of time, characters, and spatial location. As depicted in Figure 10.4a, we see similarities between the situational changes over time in Daily and Sunday strips. Time changes were used at extremely high rates, nearly across every panel, while character changes and then spatial location changes were comparatively less frequent. This overall distribution of time

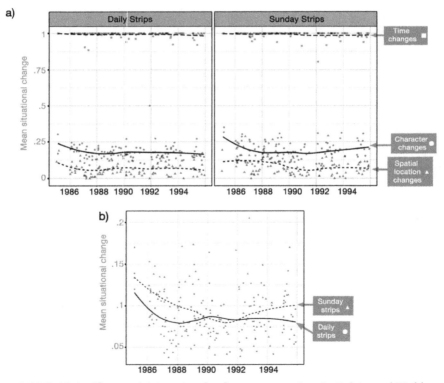

FIGURE 10.4 *Changes in situational coherence over time in* Calvin and Hobbes *across a) dimensions of time, character, and spatial location changes, and b) full situational discontinuity.*

changes being greater than character changes being greater than spatial location changes is consistent with what we observed in European and American comics, although with an even more extreme emphasis on time compared to characters and spatial locations. In addition, other than a slight reduction in character changes across the first few years of the strip, these relative frequencies between situational dimensions persist over time in a consistent way.

A bit more development in the storytelling can be observed in the rates of full situational discontinuity, which occurred when shifts between panels included no change in time, but did shift in characters and spatial location. First off, as depicted in Figure 10.4b, these types of full discontinuous shifts are relatively rare, constituting on average between 7 and 15 percent of shifts between panels. But, we do observe that Daily strips reduce in their situational discontinuity in the first few years of the strip, and then sustain to a steadier rate. Sunday strips also change over time, starting with more discontinuity than Daily strips, but then reducing in frequency more gradually before rebounding back up in frequency slightly.

It is also worth highlighting an additional observation about the direction of this change over time. In *Calvin and Hobbes*, we see a general *reduction* in discontinuity over time. This differs from what we saw in the changes in both European and American comic books across their development, where they largely shifted to use more situational discontinuity.

10.3.2 Framing

Next let's consider the framing types of panels, as in Figure 10.5a. First, it should be noticeable that the framing in Daily and Sunday strips are comparable to each other in their overall proportions and distributions. Overall, we see a predominance of macros compared to monos, with few micros or amorphic panels used throughout. This demonstrates that the majority of panels in the strip show a scene with multiple interacting characters, followed by those with only single characters.

It is worth highlighting a few consistencies in this data with what we saw in Chapter 6. First, this relative proportion of framing types is consistent with those of comics from the United States and Europe. If we return to the arguments in Chapter 6 about the constraints on formatting for framing, this relative distribution might make sense. A comic strip has limited space to convey its information, whether a typically four-panel Daily strip or a potentially longer Sunday strip. Thus, filling those units with more information (macros) rather than less would optimize the space available for conveying the ideas of the sequence.

It is interesting then that minimal difference arises between the shorter Daily strips and the longer Sunday strips, implying that the length of these strips is not sufficient to vary the information density of the units. However,

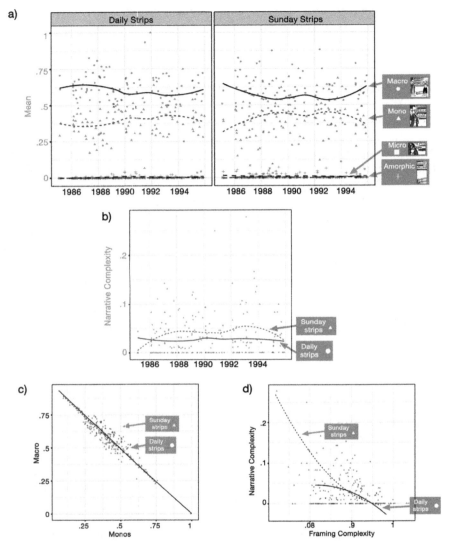

FIGURE 10.5 *Change in* Calvin and Hobbes *strips over time, across the a) attentional framing types of panels, along with b) the overall narrative complexity, along with c) the tradeoff of macros and monos, and d) the tradeoff of narrative and framing complexity.*

although I don't show the analysis here, a negative relationship held between framing complexity and maximum strip length (r = -177, p < .05), which suggested that longer sequences within *Calvin and Hobbes* led to a reduction in framing complexity. In other words, longer sequences afford more space and thus more simple panel framing.

Although the relative distribution of framing types is consistent over time, we do see some shifts. A slight reduction occurs for macros, concurrent with an increase in monos, over the first years of the strip, then by the end a slight rebound returning to more macros. This first reduction in framing complexity occurs near the time of Watterson's sabbatical, suggesting that not only has layout changed, but so is the framing of the amount of information within panels. But, unlike layout, framing complexity then rebounds again in the latter years of the strip.

Finally, it is interesting to note that throughout macros and monos maintain an inverse relationship to their trends: when one goes up, the other goes down, and vice versa. This is depicted in Figure 10.5c, which shows the correlation between macros and monos, collapsing across publication dates. Consistent with what we saw in Chapter 6, macros and monos maintain a robust tradeoff between each other, and this relationship does not differ between Daily or Sunday strips. We thus show here for a single author the same trends that are appearing across cultures for the way information is packaged by panels.

10.3.3 Narrative Patterns

Finally, let's consider the complexity of narrative patterns. Here I report only the aggregated narrative complexity score rather than each of the narrative patterns. Figure 10.5b depicts this metric across time, where we can see a slight increase in the complexity of Sunday strips across time, apexing in 1988 and then remaining steady. Daily strips maintain the same level of complexity throughout the publication history. Note however that this complexity is fairly low on our scale, with an average of .05 complexity compared to scores of European (.09), American (.2), and Asian (.4) comics.

As in Chapter 7, we can also compare the relationship between narrative complexity and framing complexity. There, we found a tradeoff between the complexity of the sequencing (narrative) and the units (framing), and because of its resemblance to similar findings in spoken languages, I speculated that it potentially reflects a universal property of how our cognition organizes information. Figure 10.5d graphs this relationship between narrative and framing for *Calvin and Hobbes* strips, which again displays a similar tradeoff, both for Daily strips and Sunday strips. Daily strips overall have lower narrative complexity and greater framing complexity, with the Sunday strips having a wider range overall along these dimensions. Nevertheless, the same overall tradeoff occurs here between these structures, replicating in an individual author's work what we saw persisting across cultures in Chapter 7.

10.4 Multimodality

In the previous sections, we saw that the layouts of *Calvin and Hobbes* shifted over time, reflecting the changes Watterson claimed to carry out after his 1991 sabbatical. However, we then saw that various changes in the situational coherence, framing, and narrative structures also occurred over time, some also aligning with Watterson's sabbatical. In this section, we next ask whether such changes not only occurred for the visual expression in this strip, but also for its full multimodal interactions. Indeed, he expressed that one consequence of his change in formatting was a new freedom in storytelling, including creating "many wordless Sunday strips now, because the drawings can finally hold their own" (Watterson 1995, 15). So, let's examine these changes.

As with our discussion of multimodality in mainstream American comics, we have three primary measures that we will use: semantic weight, symmetry, and word count. First let's look at the semantic weight, which is an assessment of whether either modality might motivate the gist of the whole sequence, or whether they maintain a balanced contribution. As in Figure 10.6a, we again see similarities between Daily strips and Sunday strips (except the overall arcs of balanced and verbal semantic weight), which again reinforces that Watterson's storytelling trends persist between the formats of the strip.

In both types of strips, balanced semantic weight is the most frequent type of storytelling, which in Daily strips rose throughout the earlier years and then slightly declined in the later strips. In Sunday strips, this frequency of balanced-weight panels only slightly declined in the later years of the strip. The frequency of verbal-weight maintains an inverse relationship to the balanced-weight. When balanced-weight goes down, purely verbal-weight goes up, and vice versa. In Daily strips, this manifested as most panels using verbal-weight in the early years of the strip, and then declining dramatically until around 1992, when it rebounded again just slightly until the end of the strip. Sunday strips show a similar decline and rise, but with a much smaller magnitude. Here, panels balancing meaning in text and image were clearly the most frequent.

By comparison, the frequency of panels with visual-weight appears unaffected by this inverse relationship between balanced- and verbal-weight. Instead, panels carrying most meaning in the visuals maintain a steady rise in frequency across the earlier years of the strip and then plateau. This implies that when Watterson is not equally distributing the meaning between modalities, he tends to let the verbal carry the meaning. Meanwhile, his use of more visually meaningful panels remains independent of strips with a greater verbal contribution.

Additional insight comes from looking at the average semantic weight of strips, as depicted in Figure 10.6b. Here, negative values represent that text carries more meaning (verbal-weight), positive values represent that the visuals carry more meaning (visual-weight), and zero represents balanced-weight. With this measure, Daily and Sunday strips do look different from each other. Daily strips start out much more verbal, and then rise toward being more visual/balanced. Sunday strips instead minimally change over time, maintaining a more consistent, balanced weight. After 1990 though, both Daily strips and Sunday strips use similar, balanced weight, before slightly waning towards being more verbal.

These data suggest that in the early years of the strip, Daily strips provided a place for words to carry more of the meaning, while the Sunday strips were an outlet for more visual or balanced expressions. In later years, both Daily and Sunday strips became more balanced in their meaning overall.

Next let's consider the symmetry of the structure in the sequence. As a reminder, symmetry describes the degree to which each modality might use a complex combinatorial structure. Symmetrical structure means that the text uses a complex syntax in full sentences, while the visual sequence maintains a narrative grammar. Asymmetrical structures typically use a visual narrative sequence with only single words (usually onomatopoeia), or sentences with visuals that have no narrative progression and instead show a "list" of related images (Cohn 2016b, Cohn and Schilperoord 2022b). Unimodal structures are panels with only visuals and no text.

As in Figure 10.6c, Daily and Sunday strips again used similar trends of symmetry across time. These trends are also consistent with those in the semantic weight. Overall, symmetrical complex interactions were used more than asymmetrical ones, which were more frequent than unimodal ones. This same distribution is what we saw in mainstream American comic books in Chapter 8, despite being a different genre, longer sequences, and different formats.

These types of interactions also changed over time. Daily strips began with similar proportions of symmetrical complex and asymmetrical strips, before rapidly deviating. Here, symmetrical complex interactions increased only slightly but overall maintained a similar frequency across the span of the strip. Asymmetrical interactions began with high frequency and then declined greatly. This decrease in asymmetry is less prominent in Sunday strips, where they begin with less frequency to begin with, and then remain more constant. By comparison, in line with the findings of visual-weight, unimodal picture-only sequences began infrequently, then rose in the 1990s and maintained a similar frequency through the rest of the strip. These rates of picture-only panels persisted for both Daily and Sunday strips.

Overall, these data suggest shifts from verbal to more balanced storytelling, while wordless panels increased and then maintained a steady presence in strips. Indeed, the rapid rise and then consistency of panels with only visuals, in combination with the rise of those with visual-weight, echoes Watterson's reflection that enhanced flexibility in his Sunday strip formatting allowed him to "do many wordless Sunday strips . . . because the drawings can finally hold their own" (Watterson 1995, 15–16). But,

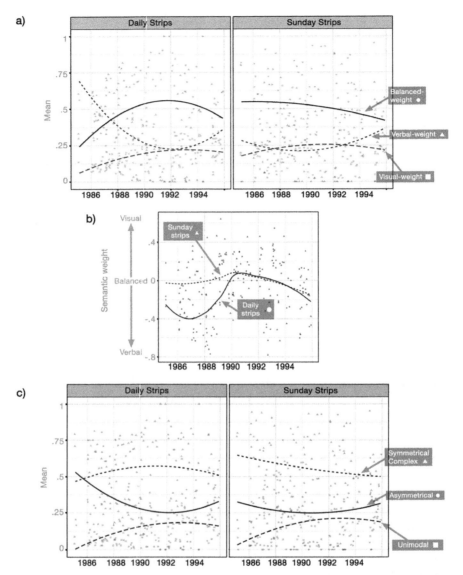

FIGURE 10.6 *Change in the multimodality of* Calvin and Hobbes *strips, both for a) how panels allocate meaning to either the visuals, text, or balanced across them, b) their overall semantic weight, and c) how panels balance their combinatorial structures across the pictures and text.*

interestingly, we see in the data that not only did the number of wordless panels in Sunday strips increase, but concurrently so did wordless panels in Daily strips. This suggests that the creative shifts Watterson made in his Sunday formats also affected his storytelling more broadly, including in the terser Daily strips.

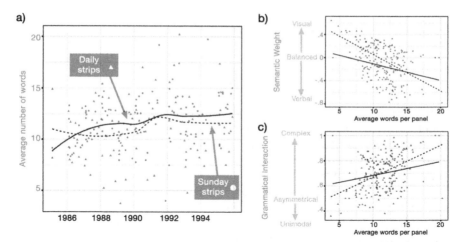

FIGURE 10.7 *The number of words used in* Calvin and Hobbes *strips, a) changing over time for Daily (solid line) and Sunday (dashed line) strips, and the relationship between this word count and b) semantic weight, and c) grammatical interactions.*

Finally, let's consider the overall number of words used in these strips. Figure 10.7a depicts the average number of words per panel over time. In both Daily and Sunday strips, the number of words per panel actually increase over time. This increase is interesting, especially given that unimodal panels (with no text) and asymmetric panels (with only single words) have gone up in time, suggesting an increase in less wordy panels.

The average number of words per panel also related to the overall semantic weight and grammatical interactions.[1] As illustrated in Figure 10.7b, a negative relationship persisted between the number of words and semantic weight, with fewer words in panels aligning with more visually weighted panels, and more words with verbally weighted panels. In contrast, as in Figure 10.7c, greater quantities of words were used in symmetrically complex panels, while fewer words were used in asymmetrical panels. These analyses confirm that wordier panels typically carry more meaning in the text and use more complex grammars.

The word count in *Calvin and Hobbes* are also interesting in contrast to the findings for American comics over time in Chapter 8. There, we saw a gradual decrease in words across the eighty years of mainstream American comics, our corpus. But, the actual number of words per panel being used in *Calvin and Hobbes* is comparable to those used in panels of mainstream American comics in this same time period (1980s and 1990s), i.e., roughly ten to fifteen words per panel. The consistency between *Calvin and Hobbes* and mainstream comics is particularly interesting given their differences in formatting. More information needs to be packaged into a short strip than in a multi-page comic. However, despite these differences, these word counts suggest that by the 1980s, American comic creators across formats had arrived at a similar word-per-panel ratio.

10.5 Conclusion

This chapter has explored the changes in structure that occurred for the comic strip *Calvin and Hobbes* across its ten years in publication. This let us contrast analyses of the visual language(s) used in American comic books over time in Chapter 8, with those for a single author's work with the differing format of comic strips. Doing so also highlights what can be learned about an author's work as a case study using empirical methods, rather than purely theorizing. In this case, we see in the data a direct reflection of Watterson's experience as a creator, where his sabbaticals and documented tension with his syndicate led to changes in the structure of the strip.

Indeed, changes did happen over time across most of the structures analyzed here. We clearly see shifts in the characteristics of Watterson's page layouts, storytelling, and multimodal interactions as his creative constraints were relaxed midway through the decade span of the comic strip. Some of these were intuited by Watterson's own descriptions of using more creative layouts, increasing the numbers of panels, and using more wordless, purely visual strips.

At the same time, other aspects of the strips remained more consistent, such as framing types and situational changes, which showed relatively minimal shifts across time, and did not necessarily align with Watterson's sabbaticals. These more constant trends also seemed to reflect the tendencies observed in American comic *books* from the same period (1980s to 1990s). Watterson's structures in terms of situational dimensions, proportions of framing types, and the overall number of words per panel all reflected similar patterns to those in mainstream American comics. This suggests that features of a shared AVL may persist in the United States despite the differences in formats between comic strips and books, although this would require further comparison with other strips and genres.

In addition to the idiosyncratic aspects of structure in *Calvin and Hobbes*, and to the consistencies it shows with the structures of other types of comics, we also observed some more universal tendencies of structure. As in our previous analysis of framing structure in Chapter 6, we observed a tradeoff between the frequency of macros and the frequency of monos. In addition, *Calvin and Hobbes* again shows the same tradeoff in the complexity of units (framing) and sequencing (narrative) observed in Chapter 7, which were consistent with tradeoffs between the structure of units (words) and sequencing (syntax) in sentence structures. This replication provides additional credence to such tradeoffs reflecting fundamental aspects of how our cognition structures information more than culture- or author-specific patterns.

Finally, these analyses also raise questions about focused longitudinal analyses of other single authors and how their works have changed over time. Comic strip authors often spend many decades working on the same strip, and while graphic style changes are often easy to see, subtle changes in storytelling may be less forthright without this type of empirical analysis. Similar author-focused analyses could investigate how structures have changed across long-running long-format comics or across multiple different works by authors spanning their careers. Such analyses could also focus on a single title that has shifts between multiple creative teams to see if structures also change in such ways. In other words, using empirical methods can provide insights into the characteristics of the structures of comics, no matter the format, beyond pure theorizing and speculation.

CHAPTER ELEVEN

Towards a Visual Language Typology

Just what are the patterns found in comics? This book has sought to explore this question by analyzing data of the structures in comics from Europe, the United States, and Asia, along with a case study of the American comic strip *Calvin and Hobbes*. By pursuing an empirical analysis driven by data, we have been able to at least initially address (if not answer) this primary question, but also various others: Are there indeed different visual languages? To what degree is there variation in the structures of visual languages used in comics cross-culturally, and to what degree do they maintain universal tendencies? What are the relationships between the structures of visual languages? Are there relationships between the structures in visual languages and those in spoken languages? Let's reflect on what this analysis has informed us about each of these dimensions . . .

11.1 Visual languages

A primary hypothesis of VLT is that different visual languages persist with systematic and distinctive structures. The notion of "visual language" on the whole is akin to saying, "spoken language" or "sign language," but this abstract notion is posited to manifest in varieties divided by particular social, cultural, and/or contextual usage. This systematic nature contrasts with the idea that pictorial information is tied to our perceptual abilities, and that images are therefore not "coded" (e.g., Forceville 2020). Indeed, although surface-level comparisons between the lexicons of graphic systems are recognized as "language-like," the regularities of other linguistic structures, such as their grammar, have been less acknowledged (Davies 2019, Forceville 2020), perhaps because such patterning and cross-linguistic variation is less overtly apparent.

Investigating the systematic variation between structures has been a central question of this book, and indeed we see evidence of such variation in all the structures we analyzed. In most of these cases, we saw systematic differences between the structural variation in the visual language(s) used in comics from Europe, the United States, and Asia. In addition, despite these cultural associations, clustering analyses showed that systematic patterns were not merely defined by regional borders, but rather cut across cultures. This is exactly what we would expect of different (visual) languages: although they may be associated with particular contexts (such as regions or cultures), they are not constrained to them, and can ultimately extend beyond those boundaries.

Within the visual languages used in Japanese manga and American comics we also saw more subtle differences suggesting evidence of varieties, corresponding to genres or demographics. With regard to manga, I investigated the hypothesis that an abstract JVL extends across varieties that correspond to different demographics of shonen, shojo, seinen, and josei manga. Analysis across structures supported this idea. The primary evidence for variation between varieties came from visual morphology, where, despite sharing most visual morphemes, clear differences in proportions between morphemes used in shonen and shojo manga suggested reliable variation between these groups. Some minimal differences between varieties also arose in layouts. However, structures related to storytelling (situational coherence, framing, and narrative structure) largely did not differ, and clustering of these structures found no distinct correspondences between derived groupings and demographics. This suggests that the differences in these varieties may be more lexical in nature (i.e., visual morphology), while more subtle features of panels as information units and their sequencing—i.e., their morphosyntax—persist throughout a broader system.

In contrast, more variety appeared in the visual language(s) used in comics from the United States. Although contemporary American comics from the mainstream and indie genres largely maintained the same features in their framing and storytelling, they differed in their layouts. These books also likely differ in graphic style, although we did not analyze this here. These both differed from older mainstream comics, which maintained structures closer to those found in the visual language(s) used in European comics. In addition, greater differences from these American structures were observed in works more influenced by manga. Works classified as US manga, and several of those within the indie genre, maintained structures more like those from books from Japan and other Asian countries. This suggested that these works were indeed influenced by JVL, and thus structurally reflected this influence.

Indeed, one reason for the dispersion of visual languages across cultures is the influence of systems on each other. This is particularly evident in the influence of Japanese manga on creators from other countries. Within Asian books, Korean manhwa and Chinese manhua both resembled the structures in Japanese manga. In the comics from the United States, storytelling and layout structures appeared to have been influenced by the influx of manga in the 1980s and 1990s. Although this influence was overt in structures of works classified as US manga, more subtle evidence persisted in the structures of mainstream American comics more generally. This influence reinforces that, although they might be associated with cultural origins, visual languages are indeed not constrained to national or cultural borders as systems of patterns encoded in the minds of creators and readers, and acquired through exposure and practice.

Throughout, I have emphasized the distinct patterns used across the visual languages in the comics analyzed here. We have seen these distinctions both in systematic contrasts between countries, and in the more abstract comparisons clustering works together to suggest visual languages. This emphasis on systematic diversity contrasts with theories that seek to describe the properties of a general "comics medium" or have no accounting for the differences in structure between cultural systems. This patterned diversity also contrasts with statements that superficial similarities or historical origins between systems warrant no differentiation between comics of the world (e.g., Exner 2021). Indeed, psychological work has suggested that experience and proficiency in the patterns of particular visual languages influences how they are comprehended (Cohn and Foulsham 2020, Cohn and Kutas 2017).

Nevertheless, despite this focus on distinct patterns, these visual languages may ultimately belong to a shared visual language family. This is also consistent with the history of comics in the past centuries. For example, although older Japanese graphic traditions did use sequential images on scrolls, they did not seem to contribute to the structures of the contemporary JVL used in manga (Cohn 2010a). Rather, the history of contemporary JVL was largely influenced through imitation of newspaper comics from the United States in the early-twentieth century (Exner 2021, Gravett 2004). As a result, the JVL characteristic of contemporary manga is likely closer in structure to visual languages used in other contemporary comics around the world than it is to the visual languages used in twelfth-century Japanese scrolls or eighteenth-century woodblock prints.

The common origins of visual languages used in comics across the world render them as both historically and typologically related. Thus, the visual languages described here might be more analogous in their typological relationships to languages that all come from the same *language family*. Within language families, such as Germanic or Romance languages, some degree of mutual intelligibility may exist across languages because of their shared representations, despite maintaining distinct structures. At the least, languages within a family share more intelligibility than with languages from other families. Thus, the visual languages discussed here share many features belonging to the same overall visual language family, although also using distinct representations.

We might look to historical common origins to name this visual language family. For example, the comic strip *The Yellow Kid* by Richard F. Outcault is widely attributed as the start of using speech balloons in panels, while this multimodal integration was further popularized along with many other morphological conventions in Rudolph Dirks' strip *The Katzenjammer Kids* (Exner 2021, Smolderen 2014). We might dub this broader visual language family **Dirksian** visual languages after the latter's influence on creators both in the United States and abroad (Exner 2021, Gravett 2004). To be clear, I'll use the term Dirksian to capture the commonalities spanning across all the visual languages analyzed throughout this book, similar to describing Germanic, Slavic, or Austroasiatic language families. Thus, the Dirksian family might include various visual languages, including, at the least, American Visual Language(s) (and their varieties), Japanese Visual Language (and its varieties), European Visual Language(s), and others.

All of these Dirksian visual languages used in (and outside) comics would be further contrasted with those from different visual language families, like those used by Aboriginal Australian sand narratives (Cohn 2013c, Green 2014, Wilkins 2016) or the myriad historical visual languages created all around the world. Indeed, several works on historical visual languages have already begun to examine the linguistic structures of visual languages used by the Maya (Wichmann and Nielsen 2016), medieval European tapestries (Díaz Vera 2013b, a), Egyptian wall paintings (Werning 2018), and others. All of these use visual languages that remain distinctive in their structures from the Dirksian ones discussed here, which are used in (and outside of) contemporary comics.

At the same time, many visual languages outside comics maintain structural similarities to those used within comics. Consider the structural properties of many contemporary instruction manuals or safety cards. They may use distinctive graphic structures, with a clear line style with simple figures and shapes, often with orthogonal or oblique spatial projection. Although they may use simple linear grammars for the sequencing of their content (Cohn and Schilperoord 2022b), their layouts often maintain grid structures comparable to those in comics, if sometimes simplified (Wildfeuer et al. 2022, Martin and Smith-Jackson 2008). The Instructional Visual Language(s) thus may also fall within the broader Dirksian family, perhaps as cousins to the more robust visual languages used in comics. Exploring these relationships across visual languages would require more extensive corpus analyses, both within and across social contexts.

This view of visual language families allows us to acknowledge the systematic nature of different graphic systems and their relations, while also distinguishing them from each other. This renders a more nuanced view than recasting historical artifacts such as Egyptian wall paintings or medieval Japanese scrolls into contemporary labels such as "comics" (McCloud 1993), and the same could be said for the (mis)labeling of "comics" to the use of contemporary visual languages outside this context (such as instruction manuals, picture books, etc.). Certainly, many visual languages across time and contexts should share common typological properties, because they are all visual languages. But, their specific historical and societal contexts should still be acknowledged as such, and this is possible with the notion of visual languages and their families. Exploring such contemporary and historical relationships between the typological structures of visual languages would make for an extensive and illuminating research project, on par with similar efforts related to such relationships in spoken languages.

Along these lines, if it is the case that visual languages used in comics largely came from similar Dirksian origins, the questions arise: how and why did they end up diverging in their structures? At what point did the visual languages from Asia (primarily Japan) begin to differentiate from those of America or Europe? We might also ask to what degree do countries in Europe differ in their visual languages, or might there be a uniform European Visual Language? Such questions carry over to visual languages in other populations, such as about varieties found in Asian or American visual languages(s), or populations left unexplored by the VLRC. Addressing this question requires more analysis of comics from worldwide and over time than the VLRC contains, including analysis of how they have developed over the past 100+ years.

Finally, it is worth emphasizing that such systematicity in structures of visual languages does not imply internal uniformity, nor does it mitigate the individuality of comic creators. Indeed, the spread of individual contributions should be evident throughout the graphs provided in this book. Rather, in line with any other languages, creators find their own idiolects within the constraints of the visual languages that they use. In some cases, what appears to be "unique" or "innovative" pertains to particular structures, such as having a distinctive drawing "style" and layouts in the graphic structure, despite morphological or grammatical structures remaining consistent with a broader visual language. We saw this with Watterson's *Calvin and Hobbes* (Chapter 10) and Todd McFarlane's *Amazing Spider-Man* (Chapter 8). Both of these creators are recognized as exemplary in their (and other) time periods—and they certainly had idiosyncratic graphic "styles"—but many of their general structures across measures in the VLRC remain consistent with those of the wider population.

This notion of consistent visual languages may understandably grate on people invested in the predominant cultural assumptions that place value in the individuality and innovativeness of people's drawings (Cohn 2014b, Wilson 1988), despite the questionable and infelicitous origins of these notions (Willats 2005). However, the linguistic view offered by VLT both reflects more accurately the cognition of what people actually do, and can offer a different type of social value: Individuals find their idiolects within a broader *community* of users, which offers a sense of identity and commonality with those sharing common visual languages. Indeed, distinctiveness can arise more from how authors *use* their visual languages rhetorically or with "what they say/draw" rather than how the visual languages themselves differ. This is again on par with other languages: exemplary authors do not necessarily create their own unique vocabularies and grammars, but rather use those languages in rhetorical or creative ways.

11.2 Typology and Universals

Beyond the cross-cultural differences found between visual languages, we also observed patterns that transcended these systems. We might classify these into two types. First, some trends suggest relationships between different structures within visual languages broadly. These types of relationships would be akin to the *typological universals* posited in studies of cross-linguistic diversity in linguistics (Greenberg 1966, Croft 2003). A second trend might suggest consistent structuring beyond visual languages alone. In these cases, the structure not only transcends cross-cultural differences within one modality, but is also consistent with findings made for trends within other languages, hinting that they are *cognitive universals* that persist across modalities.

We saw indications of various typological universals spanning visual languages in the relationships between various structures. In these cases, patterns of structuring persisted across the diversity between systems. For example, situational coherence relations broadly followed a regular pattern with time changes being more frequent than character changes, which were more frequent than spatial location changes. These situational coherence changes were also related to framing structures, with time changes being consistently related to macros, but with the absence of time changes occurring with more focal attentional categories (monos, micros, and amorphics). Lower framing complexity (micros, amorphics) also aligned with greater subjective viewpoints, in line with other experimental findings (Moisich In prep). Greater situational discontinuity also aligned with increased narrative complexity.

These trends and relationships point to abstract regularity in the structures of visual languages, despite specific variation in different systems. Some work in linguistic typology has tried to define such universals numerically or formally, such as Greenberg's original forays into articulating universals (Greenberg 1966). Although I will refrain from such specifics, these types of observations throughout this work can at least provide the foundation for further work articulating these types of visual linguistic universals. On this note, I again reiterate that these universals are about broad tendencies of the structures in visual languages, and not a statement that they occur in all cases, or that exceptions do not exist. Rather, they provide likelihoods, and more extensive analyses of visual languages both within and outside of comics can provide further clarity on how such tendencies operate.

We also observed places where visual languages may tap into cognitive universals, which are the dimensions where we might posit similarities between languages across modalities. For example, we found Zipfian distributions demonstrating a tradeoff between the length and frequency of sequencing of various phenomena (Zipf 1935). We observed these distributions persisting across several domains, including for the number of panels that constituted a row within page layouts, for the runs of situational coherence for continuity of time and spatial locations, and for runs of all framing categories. The consistency of these findings in visual languages alongside findings in other modalities suggests that this relationship between length and frequency relates to more general aspects of human communicative systems and/or cognition (Piantadosi 2014).

Another potential cognitive universal arose in the observation of a tradeoff in complexity between units (framing) and sequencing (narrative). Not only did this observation hold across comparisons of the cultural and clustered data, but it was also evident in the focused corpus of *Calvin and Hobbes* comics where formatting constrains the sequencing of shorter strips. In all cases, lower complexity in units aligned with greater complexity in the narrative structure, and vice versa. This finding is consistent with the tradeoff of morphology and syntax in spoken languages (Ehret 2018, Koplenig et al. 2017). Thus, we might posit a general, universal trait of communicative systems broadly for seeking a balance between the complexity of their units and their sequencing. Such a constraint would be a feature of human cognition more broadly, rather than specific to linguistic systems in any particular modality.

11.3 Permeability

We also sought evidence for relationships between structural properties of spoken languages on those of visual languages. This idea was that of *conceptual permeability*, where the structuring of concepts in one modality might be shared with the structuring of concepts in another modality (Cohn 2016a). Three domains suggested the potential for permeability.

First, in Chapter 3 we analyzed the paths of motion events depicted in comics across their source, route, and goal. Spoken languages have been observed to follow different constructional patterns for the way that they encode motion events, with a contrast between verb-framed and satellite-framed languages being the primary distinction (Talmy 1985, Zlatev et al. 2021). Since satellite-framed languages place the primary motion and manner information in a main verb, they have been hypothesized to place more salience to the motion events and path. This salience was also reflected in our findings, as comics produced by authors with satellite-framed languages used more paths overall, especially routes. This distinction cut across cross-cultural differences, and suggested the potential of an influence of the spoken language structure on that of the visual languages.

A second possible finding of permeability was suggested by the analysis of framing complexity in Chapter 6. Overall, panels from Asian comics exhibited a distinct pattern that used lower framing complexity (fewer macros, more monos, micros, and amorphics) than American and European comics, which used greater framing complexity (more macros). Although this primarily appeared to be a cross-cultural difference, I also posited there may be a permeable influence, as the European languages all maintained an obligatory subject in their sentences, while the Asian languages allowed for subjects and objects to remain unexpressed (Haspelmath et al. 2001, Huang 1984). When subjects or objects remain unexpressed, a comprehender must infer the missing information, and this inference would be similar to what occurs with lower framing complexity: a comprehender would need to infer what is not framed by the panels. Nevertheless, here this typological distinction in languages was conflated with that of culture, making it hard to fully attribute to a permeable effect, and such influence may be one of many motivating the contrast in framing complexity, if at all.

Finally, a third domain of analysis of permeability in Chapter 7 looked at the tradeoff between complexity of units (panels) and sequencing (narrative). As this tradeoff in structures resembled the relationship between morphology and syntax in the structure of spoken languages (Ehret 2018, Koplenig et al. 2017), I asked whether there might be a permeable relationship between the unit-sequence tradeoff in spoken languages and visual languages. Again, a correlation suggested this was the case.

To close this discussion, I should point out that in most of these domains where analyses did suggest evidence of permeability, I have also proposed alternative interpretations and possibilities for the results. We should be cautious of over-interpreting the influence of one linguistic structure on another, and further replication of these findings should provide additional evidence. It is also worth emphasizing that visual languages should not necessarily be expected to bear any such influence of spoken languages at all, and they could merely exist as expressive systems with their own independent patterns completely detached from the structures of other modalities. Nevertheless, with the conception of communicative modalities sharing a broader architecture, conceptual permeability can be thought of as an abiding potential, as we've seen in other relationships between speech and graphics (Cohn 2016a, Wilkins 2016, Green 2014) and speech and gesture (e.g., Gu et al. 2017, Haviland 1993, Núñez and Sweetser 2006).

11.4 Comprehension

An important correlate of this work on the typologies of visual languages is for their implications on how people comprehend and produce them. This follows a growing trend within the cognitive and language sciences for

TOWARDS A VISUAL LANGUAGE TYPOLOGY

uniting observations from linguistic typology with those from psychology (Kemmerer 2014, Christiansen and Chater 2016). In the case of visual language, recent models have posited general cognitive principles and mechanisms for how we process visual sequences (Cohn 2020b, a, Loschky et al. 2020). But, the diversity in structures shown here implies that comprehenders of these different visual languages engage such processes in different ways.

First off, it is important to recognize that the consistency within and between visual languages implies that they are encoded within the minds of creators. Patterns do not float around in the cultural ether, but rather reflect information that is stored in the long-term memories of the people who create (and comprehend) these works. This basic observation contrasts views that the comprehension of the various levels of structure within comics are all dynamically construed with no stored constraints (e.g., Bateman and Wildfeuer 2014a). Although readers certainly do make some interpretations and inferences dynamically in the comprehension process, the presence of such systematicity across works means that patterns are encoded in the minds of the users of these visual languages.

Secondly, based on these patterns, readers may engage different comprehension processes while processing a sequence of images. In a more "subjective" system of storytelling that uses fewer complex units and more complex sequencing, as observed in more Asian systems, there will be less demand on the "front-end" processing of engaging the contents of the images. However, they will require more complex "back-end" processing to connect those units. This would demand more complex narrative sequencing structures, and additional inferencing to relate the contents of panels. In contrast, more "objective" storytelling using more complex units and simpler sequencing, such as those in European and many American comics, will reverse these demands. Here, the attentional system will need to work harder to navigate the potential complexities of the units, but there will be less demand of back-end costs to link those images together.

This is to say that comprehending comics varies based on the structural properties of their visual languages, and which strategies are used by a comprehender depends on familiarity with those structures (Cohn 2020a). If a person reads Japanese manga more often than European comics, they will be habituated to certain comprehension processes that may make European comics more daunting (and vice versa). Similarly, given that visual languages might change over time, readers familiar with patterns from one time period may respond differently to patterns from another time period. Note again that these differences are all relative: there is no idealized process and deviations from it, but rather different engagement of the same posited principles.

As described above, work studying the comprehension of visual narratives has often taken a stance generalizing into universalist processes. But, the diversity shown here implies additional nuance should be devoted to both being specific about the origins of particular constructs under investigation, and for detailing how structural variation and individuals' background expertise might factor into those comprehension processes. Thus, work on how people comprehend visual languages (not to mention in theories about their structure in the first place) must be sensitive to the diversity persisting between visual languages, rather than just thinking of their structure in the abstract.

11.5 Towards a visual language typology

This investigation of the properties of diversity, universality, and permeability sought an empirical study of visual languages in line with studies of corpus linguistics and linguistic typology. Although this work provides an initial attempt, such analyses provide only a starting point for asking questions about the diversity and typology of visual languages broadly, and those used within comics.

The interpretations reported here are constrained solely by the data that is included in the VLRC, and as discussed, it is limited in a variety of ways. First, it only includes analysis of comics from a dozen countries. Although the consistency across comics from these sample countries suggests systematic trends, the VLRC lacks data from many of the comics around the world. Indeed, there are many rich comic traditions across the globe that are worth studying (Mazur and Danner 2014). Expanding the inclusivity and diversity of our analysis is necessary to both have a better understanding of visual languages, as well as to fairly represent the structures that are present across systems in communities across the world.

This diversity can extend beyond comics of various cultures, including comparisons of visual languages used in comic books with those of other formats and media, such as comic strips, picture books, or non-fiction works of graphic medicine or science communication. It also could compare the visual languages used in entertainment comics to those in other contexts, such as instruction manuals or expository works of graphic non-fiction (science comics, health comics, etc.). Although the works analyzed here do well to confirm the idea of cross-cultural diversity of structures, the inclusion of more diverse sources is especially necessary to fully have an assessment of the possibility of universality or permeability of structures.

Second, within our corpus we have some limits in the consistency of publication dates from different cultures. Although we analyzed comics from the United States, the Netherlands, and Flemish Belgium since the 1940s, other countries only extend back to the 1980s, leaving questions about the development over time for structures in other types of comics. Most glaringly, how does the development of JVL and/or visual language(s) used in Asia progress over time since the early part of the twentieth century compared to those in America or Europe?

Finally, the analyses within the VLRC are heterogeneously analyzed across comics. Because different comics were originally used in targeted studies, not all analyses were applied to all works in the corpus. This meant that I was unable to compare the complete corpus of comics in all the analyses throughout, and thus some of the conclusions remain focused to an even smaller sample. In addition, many additional constructs could of course be analyzed beyond those annotated here, both from VLT and other theoretical frameworks.

Some work ongoing at the time of writing is already working to address these limitations. My own research group has been working on the *TINTIN Project* funded by the European Research Council to build a corpus of comics from all around the world. This project is underway from 2020 to 2025, and as of this writing we are annotating the properties of comics from roughly 100 countries, and with revised and expanded annotation schemes. Our aim is to provide a broader and more inclusive and diverse sample than the VLRC.

We have also used a different method of gathering data. Rather than simply looking at comics and recording their properties in spreadsheets, we designed annotation software that allows us to select visual regions within a comic (panels, characters, parts of characters, etc.) and then annotate those regions with any number of constructs (Cardoso and Cohn 2022). We are also able to make connections between annotations to create dependencies or hierarchic structures. Because of this visual methodology, we're not only able to ask about the frequency of elements in the corpus, but also spatial dimensions, such as: Does panel size have a relationship to the number of characters per panel? What is the relative sizing of panels and their layout in a page? With the resulting TINTIN Corpus, we hope to replicate, expand on, and/or correct the results reported in this book.

The analyses of the VLRC looked also at particular structures of VLT. Although we provided coverage of a range of primary structures of visual languages (morphology, external compositional structure, situational coherence, framing, narrative structure), many other dimensions both within and outside of these structures could also be analyzed. For example, the basic aspects of graphic "style" involve basic building blocks that are measurable (Cohn 2013c, Gauthier 1976, Kloepfer 1977, Kim 2018), and no doubt interact with these more abstract properties in multiple ways. Such work has been a primary focus of approaches to comic research in computer vision (Augereau, Iwata, and Kise 2018, Nguyen et al. 2021, Rigaud and Burie 2018). However, this work has largely used corpora to train and assess computational models, rather than using these techniques to analyze the corpora themselves.

In addition, this work has yet to broach many aspects of the visual lexicon aside from a selection of closed-class morphology, whether in the VLRC or in other previous corpus work (Forceville 2011b, Forceville, Veale, and Feyaerts 2010b, Tasić and Stamenković 2018). But, theoretical work has already posited many other patterns that would be ripe to investigate with corpus analyses, including metaphors evoked by morphology (Forceville 2016, Shinohara and Matsunaka 2009), templates of panels (Schilperoord and Cohn 2021, Cohn 2013c, Arts and Schilperoord 2016), constructions of narrative inference (Cohn 2019a), or specific layout constructions for full pages (Bateman et al. 2016b, Gavaler 2017). Other such patterns may arise as encoded constructions cutting across multiple structures at once (Klomberg and Cohn forthcoming, Schilperoord and Cohn 2022).

These empirical analyses allow us to address many questions about visual languages that otherwise remain in the domain of speculation. Such questions include, but are not limited to:

- How many visual languages are used in different comics of the world?

- What is the range of different varieties within visual languages, and what motivates them?

- What are the "family trees" of visual languages used in comics, and what are their relationships to other contemporary and historical visual languages?

- How did and do visual languages develop over time?

- What determines the variation observed within and between visual languages from different places and contexts?

- How are visual languages influenced or constrained by their ecological contexts?

- How are visual languages influenced or constrained by their formats and materiality?

- Are the structures of authors' visual languages used in comic strips different from comic books or graphic novels simply by the constraints of space?

- How does typological variation of visual languages affect their comprehension?

- How does typological variation of visual languages affect their learning and development?

- Are there cognitive universals that extend beyond modalities, and operate similarly in spoken, signed, and visual languages?

- To what extent is typological variation in visual languages influenced by the "permeable" structures of the spoken languages of their authors?

These types of questions can only be addressed through empirical analysis. Indeed, this extended analysis underscores that visual representations are built of systematic, conventionalized *patterns* that are quantifiable and measurable, just like those in any other modality of language. The potential for future analyses of the structures in visual languages is vast because visual languages themselves are complex and multifaceted systems. Understanding how they work requires acknowledging and detailing such complexity, extending beyond superficial inventories of the parts of a generic "comics medium" (e.g., panels, characters, gutters, bubbles, sound effects, etc.), and beyond the handwaving of abstract all-encompassing principles of comprehension (e.g., closure, braiding, etc.). Many patterns in visual languages are subtle and difficult to discern when fixating on the visual surface of pages or on theoretically-driven speculation about how meaning-making occurs.

Discovering patterns requires actually looking for them, and this involves transcending assumptions that visual representations lack such encoding or that the iconicity of graphics make them too heterogenous to be systematic. These latter notions are simply false, and are motivated by ideologies that make assumptions about what graphics are and how they work, not by any empirical observations. To truly understand how our graphic modality works—on its own, and in combination with other modalities—we need to recognize and inventory such patterns, and to explore what they mean for learning, comprehending, and producing visual languages, and for their implications about our broader cognition.

NOTES

Chapter 1

1 I should note that all the posited structures of VLT have been derived through analysis of and application to actual comics. Some people may have the wrong impression that VLT was formulated by seeing the structures that appear in linguistic theories, and then merely shoehorning them to fit visual depictions. Indeed, borrowing theory from another field and applying it without nuance to graphics is problematic. However, nothing could be further from the truth for how VLT was developed. VLT's structures arose from a cyclic process of observing phenomena in comics (and other graphics), deriving theoretical constructs to explain those phenomena, and then applying those constructs to other examples to see if they adequately explained what was occurring, which resulted in altering the theory when the constructs were inadequate. This creates an iterative process, and indeed many of the sub-theories within VLT have been progressively developing over decades (Cohn 2003, 2013d, 2015b, 2018b). When linguistic theories have been borrowed in VLT, they are for general, formal theoretical principles or properties, along with the empirical *methods* for making such analyses in the first place, such as diagnostic tests that are required to find linguistic structures (Cohn 2015a). That is, VLT has been created by following linguistic *methods* rather than attempting to fit visuals into linguistic theories. Theories with no such engagement with empirical observations, no such diagnostic methods, or no such justification of constructs run the risk of lacking evidence of validity.

Chapter 2

1 https://groups.uni-paderborn.de/graphic-literature/gncorpus/corpus.php

2 http://www.claremontrun.com, Twitter: @ClaremontRun

3 https://www.whatwerecomics.com

4 It is worth noting that several of the authors of books included in those from the United States are Canadians, such as Todd McFarlane and Bryan Lee O'Malley. Although we could refer to these broader works as North American, they were largely distributed by publishers in the United States and are associated with that industry. Across most analyses, this nuance would not make much of a difference.

5 http://www.visuallanguagelab.com/tintin

Chapter 3

1 Closed-class visual morphology have been described using many different terms in the literature. They have been called "emanata" in English within the comics community, although this term seems inconsistently applied to all visual morphology or sometimes to just select morpheme classes (Walker 1980, Abel and Madden 2008). Forceville et al. (2014) subdivided these elements into classes of "pictorial runes" for non-literal graphic elements, such as bloody noses or sleep bubbles (Forceville 2005, Kennedy 1982, Forceville, El Refaie, and Meesters 2014), "pictograms" for stylized depictions originating outside of the visual language of comics, such as hearts or dollar signs, and "balloons" for carriers of text. VLT does not necessarily distinguish these particular subdivisions of visual morphemes because comics are merely one place in which visual languages appear, and the lines between the visual vocabulary used in comics and general "visual culture" are often blurred (both synchronically and diachronically). For example, the morphemes used in many emoji first came from Japanese manga.

  Distinctions between these elements have also been made in Japanese-language manga scholarship. Visual morphemes are characterized within the broad class of kei yu ("metaphorical forms"), which breaks down into several subtypes (Natsume 1997, Takekuma 1995): Manpu ("manga specific signs") carry particular meanings, such as bloody noses and sleep bubbles, while koka ("impact") convey elements such as motion lines, zoom lines, and more general emotional and psychological states, including elements in an image's background (Takekuma 1995). VLT follows linguistics in categorizing visual morphemes in terms of their productive, combinatorial, and/or semiotic characteristics, discussed throughout the chapter.

2 A full listing of these morphemes with examples is available online at http://www.visuallanguagelab.com/jvl.

Chapter 4

1 Note that an alternative interpretation of this layout is possible. The first three panels all maintain similar features with tall vertical shapes and white borders. Along with their contiguous upper borders, if these similarities are enough to group together, then this layout simply has a single horizontal row with four panels, vertically arranged on top of the final panel: $[_{\text{Canvas: V}} [_{\text{H}} 1 - 2 - 3 \text{ -}4] - 5]$. In this case, both possible grouping structures yield the same reading order. This potential ambiguity underscores that assemblage structure is about the groupings made by a reader, rather than the physical features of layouts, which may cue those groupings.

Chapter 6

1 Portions of this chapter are reworked from Cohn, Hacımusaoğlu, and Klomberg (2022).

Chapter 7

1 Parts of this chapter are reworked from Cohn (2019b).

2 I omit some categories, such as Prolongations and Orienters here for simplicity, since I do not explore them further in the text related to the broader question here about narrative complexity (see Cohn 2013d). However, Orienters are implicated by analyses undertaken in Chapter 6. Orienters are panels that show superordinate spaces (i.e., exterior views of locations) followed by panels with the events that occur in that environment. The "scene shifts" observed in the analysis displayed in Figure 6.5 reflect this, with amorphic panels that use a full character and spatial location changes. The greater proportion of non-time shift examples of these cases used in European and American books rather than Asian books suggests that they use Orienters in slightly different ways. This further relates to the spatial location changes that align with page breaks shown in Chapter 5 (Figure 5.6). These collocations of amorphic panels with full character and spatial location changes occur at the first panel of a page in much higher proportion (54 percent) than in any other panel position (32 percent), again signaling their use as page starting Orienters. This proportion also differed across regions ($F = 3.6$, $p < .05$). These panels were used at the first panel position of a page more for American (.65) and European (.63) books than Asian books (.41), but at non-first panel positions these regions largely did not differ (America: .37, Europe: .31, Asia: .28). This again suggests that Asian comics do not use pages as segmental units in the same way as European or American comics, and this interacts with their narrative patterns of Orienters.

3 The final Release in this example is structurally ambiguous, and could attach either within the second constituent (as diagrammed) or to the upper-level constituent following the Peak. These varying options can serve as an illustration of how VNG analysis is carried out (Cohn 2015a). For evidence of its placement within the second constituent, a deletion diagnostic can be used: Omission of the whole first constituent renders a comprehensible sequence with or without the Peak included, although leaving out the Release entirely would render the sequence fairly abrupt regardless, which is characteristic of Releases in general (Cohn 2014c). To test its upper-level placement, a *paraphrase diagnostic* could be used that deletes all lower-level panels that are not Peaks. This would leave panel 2 as an Initial (since the Peak in its clause motivated this higher structure), panel 3 as a Peak (the Peak within the Peak), and the final panel Release. Since this sequence is also comprehensible, the Release can be concluded as having both placements possible.

4 This was previously called "Semantic field-Conjunction" or "S-Conjunction," but I've found that students were confused by the naming. We've subsequently been calling it Category-Conjunction, which seems to be a bit more intuitive.

5 This Action-Conjunction interpretation is motivated by the idea that the sequence emphasizes the defeat of each of the enemies successively. This interpretation can be confirmed using a paraphrase diagnostic, leaving a sequence only with panels 1, 3, 6, 10, and 11. Paraphrase tests take the primary components (Peaks) of each clause and drop out the rest. It is worth noting that another interpretation of panels 4 to 10 is possible, if the

confrontation with Jimmy is set as a primary action. In this case, Malcom's confrontation with Jimmy begins in panel 4 as a higher-level Initial, and the defeat of the fiery girlfriend sets up the actions in panels 7 to 8, again leading to the main climax in panel 10 of Malcom punching Jimmy. This sequence would be paraphrased by panels 4 (Initial), 10 (Peak), and could remain in an Action-Conjunction of a Peak connecting to panel 11 (Release).

Chapter 8

1 These terms have changed since the original publication that reported the results of our analysis of superhero comics across time (Cohn, Taylor, and Pederson 2017). Symmetrical interactions were previously called "assertive," asymmetrical interactions were "dominant," and unimodal expressions were "autonomous." That previous approach also considered aspects of semantic weight under different terms. Balanced semantic weight was given the prefix "Co," while imbalanced weight was assigned to either "visual" or "verbal." Our new terms better reflect our expanded framework for multimodality and grammatical interactions (see Cohn and Schilperoord 2022b).

2 A similar trend to the word count has been reported in conference presentations by Bart Beaty, Nick Sousanis, and Benjamin Woo as part of their analysis of American comics over a similar span of time in their *What Were Comics?* project.

3 As noted in Chapter 2, Todd McFarlane is actually Canadian, but has lived in the United States and worked in the American comic industry for most of his life. Given that the comic itself belongs to the American comic industry, this classification seems appropriate.

Chapter 10

1 In general, I have tried to not select types of trendlines for graphs, but it is noteworthy that in the correlations in Figures 10.7b and 10.7c I chose to use linear trendlines. This is because outliers otherwise warped trendlines in ways that would give an inappropriate interpretation of the data. For example, in Figure 10.7c, a U-shape trendline resulted from datapoints in the upper corners for Sunday strips. This would have given the misperception that very few words also led to greater complexity, but this would have been motivated by a single datapoint.

BIBLIOGRAPHY

Abbott, Michael, and Charles Forceville. 2011. "Visual representation of emotion in manga: Loss of control is Loss of hands in *Azumanga Daioh* Volume 4." *Language and Literature* 20 (2): 91–112. doi: 10.1177/0963947011402182.

Abel, Jessica, and Matt Madden. 2008. *Drawing Words and Writing Pictures*. New York, NY: First Second Books.

Allen, Kate, and John E. Ingulsrud. 2005. "Reading Manga: Patterns of Personal Literacies Among Adolescents." *Language and Education* 19 (4): 265–80. doi: 10.1080/09500780508668681.

Alonso, Rosa Alonso. 2022. "Thinking-for-translating in comics: a case-study of *Asterix*." *Perspectives*: 1–19. doi: 10.1080/0907676X.2022.2063062.

Altmann, Gabriel. 1980. "Prolegomena to Menzerath's law." *Glottometrika* 2 (2): 1–10.

Anderson, Stephen R. 1992. *A-Morphous Morphology*. Vol. 62. Cambridge: Cambridge University Press.

Arts, Anja, and Joost Schilperoord. 2016. "Visual Optimal Innovation." In *Multimodality and Performance*, edited by Carla Fernandes, 61–81. Newcastle-upon-Tyne, UK: Cambridge Scholars Publishing.

Augereau, Olivier, Motoi Iwata, and Koichi Kise. 2018. "A survey of comics research in computer science." *Journal of Imaging* 4 (87): 1–19.

Baerman, Matthew, and Greville G. Corbett. 2007. "Linguistic typology: Morphology." 11 (1): 115–17. doi: 10.1515/LINGTY.2007.010.

Baggio, Giosuè. 2018. *Meaning in the Brain*. Cambridge, MA: MIT Press.

Bálint, Katalin E., Janine Nadine Blessing, and Brendan Rooney. 2020. "Shot scale matters: The effect of close-up frequency on mental state attribution in film viewers." *Poetics* 83: 101480. doi: 10.1016/j.poetic.2020.101480.

Bálint, Katalin E., and Brendan Rooney. 2019. "Narrative Sequence Position of Close-Ups Influences Cognitive and Affective Processing and Facilitates Theory of Mind." *Art & Perception* 7 (1): 27–51. doi: 10.1163/22134913-20191095.

Barber, John. 2002. "The Phenomenon of Multiple Dialectics in Comics Layout." Masters Thesis, Typo/Graphic Studies, London College of Printing.

Barratt, Daniel, Anna Cabak Rédei, Åse Innes-Ker, and Joost van de Weijer. 2016. "Does the Kuleshov Effect Really Exist? Revisiting a Classic Film Experiment on Facial Expressions and Emotional Contexts." *Perception* 45 (8): 847–74. doi: 10.1177/0301006616638595.

Bateman, John A., and Karl-Heinrich Schmidt. 2012. *Multimodal Film Analysis: How Films Mmean*. New York: Routledge.

Bateman, John A., Francisco O. D. Veloso, and Yan Ling Lau. 2021. "On the track of visual style: a diachronic study of page composition in comics and its functional motivation." *Visual Communication* 20 (2): 209–47. doi: 10.1177/1470357219 839101.

Bateman, John A., Francisco O. D. Veloso, Janina Wildfeuer, Felix HiuLaam Cheung, and Nancy Songdan Guo. 2016b. "An Open Multilevel Classification Scheme for the Visual Layout of Comics and Graphic Novels: Motivation and Design." *Digital Scholarship in the Humanities* 32 (3): 476–510. doi: 10.1093/llc/fqw024.

Bateman, John A., and Janina Wildfeuer. 2014a. "Defining units of analysis for the systematic analysis of comics: A discourse-based approach." *Studies in Comics* 5 (2): 373–403. doi: 10.1386/stic.5.2.373_1.

Bateman, John A., and Janina Wildfeuer. 2014b. "A multimodal discourse theory of visual narrative." *Journal of Pragmatics* 74: 180–208. doi: 10.1016/j.pragma.2014.10.001.

Beaty, Bart, Nick Sousanis, and Benjamin Woo. 2018. "Two Per Cent of What? Constructing a Corpus of Typical American Comic Books." In *Empirical Comics Research*, 27–42. Routledge.

Bentz, Christian, Ximena Gutierrez-Vasques, Olga Sozinova, and Tanja Samardžić. 2022. "Complexity trade-offs and equi-complexity in natural languages: a meta-analysis." *Linguistics Vanguard*. doi: 10.1515/lingvan-2021-0054.

Booij, Geert. 2010. *Construction Morphology*. Oxford: Oxford University Press.

Bordwell, David, and Kristin Thompson. 1997. *Film Art: An Introduction*. 5th Edition ed. New York, NY: McGraw-Hill.

Borkent, Mike. 2017. "Mediated characters: Multimodal viewpoint construction in comics." *Cognitive Linguistics* 28 (3): 539. doi: 10.1515/cog-2016-0098.

Branigan, Edward. 2012. *Point of View in the Cinema: A Theory of Narration and Subjectivity in Classical Film*. New York: Mouton De Gruyter.

Brems, Elke. 2018. "Separated by the same language: Intralingual translation between Dutch and Dutch." *Perspectives* 26 (4): 509–25. doi: 10.1080/0907676X. 2017.1417455.

Brenner, R.E. 2007. *Understanding Manga and Anime*. Westport, CT: Libraries Unlimited.

Brienza, Casey. 2015. *Global Manga: "Japanese" Comics without Japan?* Surrey, UK: Ashgate Publishing, Ltd.

Brienza, Casey. 2016. *Manga in America: Transnational Book Publishing and the Domestication of Japanese Comics*. London: Bloomsbury Academic.

Brooks, Penelope H. 1977. "The Role of Action Lines in Children's Memory for Pictures." *Journal of Experimental Child Psychology* 23: 93–107.

Burr, David C. 2000. "Motion vision: Are 'speed lines' used in human visual motion?" *Current Biology* 10 (12): R440–R443. doi: 10.1016/s0960-9822(00)00545-5.

Calbi, Marta, Francesca Siri, Katrin Heimann, Daniel Barratt, Vittorio Gallese, Anna Kolesnikov, and Maria Alessandra Umiltà. 2019. "How context influences the interpretation of facial expressions: a source localization high-density EEG study on the 'Kuleshov effect'." *Scientific Reports* 9 (1): 2107. doi: 10.1038/s41598-018-37786-y.

Caldwell, Joshua. 2012. "Comic panel layout: A Peircean analysis." *Studies in Comics* 2 (2): 317–38. doi: 10.1386/stic.2.2.317_1.

Cao, Ying, Antoni B. Chan, and Rynson W. H. Lau. 2012. "Automatic stylistic manga layout." *ACM Transactions on Graphics* 31 (6): 1–10. doi: 10.1145/2366145.2366160.

Cardoso, Bruno, and Neil Cohn. 2022. "The Multimodal Annotation Software Tool (MAST)." In *Proceedings of the 13th Language Resources and Evaluation*

Conference (LREC 2022), 6,822–8. Marseille, France: European Language Resources Association.

Carroll, John M. 1980. *Toward a Structural Psychology of Cinema*. The Hague: Mouton

Chafe, Wallace. 1994. *Discourse, Consciousness, and Time: The Flow and Displacement of Conscious Experience in Speaking and Writing*. Chicago, IL: University of Chicago Press.

Chan, Ting Ting, and Benjamin Bergen. 2005. "Writing Direction Influences Spatial Cognition." In *Proceedings of the Twenty-Seventh Annual Conference of Cognitive Science Society*, 412–17. Stresa, Italy, July 21–23, 2005.

Chavanne, Renaud. 2010. *Composition de la bande dessinée ['The Composition of Comics']*. Montrouge, France: PLG.

Chen, Shukun, and Zenan Zhong. 2022. "Perceiving the poetic world: A corpus-assisted transitivity analysis of poetry comics." *Frontiers in Psychology* 13. doi: 10.3389/fpsyg.2022.1061169.

Chen, Yi-Chun, and Arnav Jhala. 2021. "A Computational Model of Comprehension in Manga Style Visual Narratives." *Proceedings of the Annual Meeting of the Cognitive Science Society* 43 (43).

Cherry, David, and David Brickler. 2016. "Analysis of Gaze on Comic Book Panel Structure." accessed 2/1/2016. https://pdfs.semanticscholar.org/5dd3/8f29c4df1a 2ec9fd3bd068d15ee954c10f77.pdf.

Chomsky, Noam. 1965. *Aspects of the Theory of Syntax*. Cambridge, MA: MIT Press.

Christiansen, Morten H., and Nick Chater. 2016. *Creating Language: Integrating Evolution, Acquisition, and Processing*. Cambridge, MA: MIT Press.

Cicci, Matthew. 2015. "Turning the page: Fandoms, Multimodality, And The Transformation Of The 'Comic Book' Superhero." Doctoral Dissertation, English, Wayne State University.

Clark, Herbert H. 1996. *Using Language*. Cambridge, UK: Cambridge University Press.

Coderre, Emily L., and Neil Cohn. Under review. "Individual differences in the neural dynamics of visual narrative comprehension."

Cohn, Neil. 2003. *Early Writings on Visual Language*. Carlsbad, CA: Emaki Productions.

Cohn, Neil. 2010a. "Japanese Visual Language: The structure of manga." In *Manga: An Anthology of Global and Cultural Perspectives*, edited by Toni Johnson-Woods, 187–203. New York: Continuum Books.

Cohn, Neil. 2010b. "The limits of time and transitions: Challenges to theories of sequential image comprehension." *Studies in Comics* 1 (1): 127–47. doi: 10.1386/stic.1.1.127/1.

Cohn, Neil. 2011. "A different kind of cultural frame: An analysis of panels in American comics and Japanese manga." *Image [&] Narrative* 12 (1): 120–34.

Cohn, Neil. 2012. "Explaining 'I Can't Draw': Parallels between the Structure and Development of Language and Drawing." *Human Development* 55 (4): 167–92. doi: 10.1159/000341842.

Cohn, Neil. 2013a. "Beyond speech balloons and thought bubbles: The integration of text and image." *Semiotica* 2013 (197): 35–63. doi: 10.1515/sem-2013-0079.

Cohn, Neil. 2013b. "Navigating comics: An empirical and theoretical approach to strategies of reading comic page layouts." *Frontiers in Psychology—Cognitive Science* 4: 1–15. doi: 10.3389/fpsyg.2013.00186.

Cohn, Neil. 2013c. *The visual language of comics: introduction to the structure and cognition of sequential images.* London, UK: Bloomsbury.

Cohn, Neil. 2013d. "Visual Narrative Structure." *Cognitive Science* 37 (3): 413–52. doi: 10.1111/cogs.12016.

Cohn, Neil. 2014a. "The architecture of visual narrative comprehension: the interaction of narrative structure and page layout in understanding comics." *Frontiers in Psychology* 5: 1–9. doi: 10.3389/fpsyg.2014.00680.

Cohn, Neil. 2014b. "Framing 'I can't draw': The influence of cultural frames on the development of drawing." *Culture & Psychology* 20 (1): 102–17. doi: 10.1177/1354067x13515936.

Cohn, Neil. 2014c. "You're a Good Structure, Charlie Brown: The Distribution of Narrative Categories in Comic Strips." *Cognitive Science* 38 (7): 1317–59. doi: 10.1111/cogs.12116.

Cohn, Neil. 2015a. "How to analyze visual narratives: A tutorial in Visual Narrative Grammar." www.visuallanguagelab.com/P/VNG_Tutorial.pdf.

Cohn, Neil. 2015b. "Narrative conjunction's junction function: The interface of narrative grammar and semantics in sequential images." *Journal of Pragmatics* 88: 105–32. doi: 10.1016/j.pragma.2015.09.001.

Cohn, Neil. 2016a. "Linguistic Relativity and Conceptual Permeability in Visual Narratives: New Distinctions in the Relationship between Language(s) and Thought." In *The Visual Narrative Reader*, edited by Neil Cohn, 315–40. London: Bloomsbury.

Cohn, Neil. 2016b. "A multimodal parallel architecture: A cognitive framework for multimodal interactions." *Cognition* 146: 304–23. doi: 10.1016/j.cognition.2015.10.007.

Cohn, Neil. 2018a. "Combinatorial morphology in visual languages." In *The Construction of Words: Advances in Construction Morphology*, edited by Geert Booij, 175–99. London: Springer.

Cohn, Neil. 2018b. "In defense of a 'grammar' in the visual language of comics." *Journal of Pragmatics* 127: 1–19. doi: 10.1016/j.pragma.2018.01.002.

Cohn, Neil. 2019a. "Being explicit about the implicit: inference generating techniques in visual narrative." *Language and Cognition* 11 (1): 66–97. doi: 10.1017/langcog.2019.6.

Cohn, Neil. 2019b. "Structural complexity in visual narratives: Theory, brains, and cross-cultural diversity." In *Narrative Complexity: Cognition, Embodiment, Evolution*, edited by Marina Grishakova and Maria Poulaki, 174–99. Lincoln: University of Nebraska Press.

Cohn, Neil. 2020a. *Who Understands Comics? Questioning the Universality of Visual Language Comprehension.* London: Bloomsbury.

Cohn, Neil. 2020b. "Your Brain on Comics: A Cognitive Model of Visual Narrative Comprehension." *Topics in Cognitive Science* 12 (1): 352–86. doi: 10.1111/tops.12421.

Cohn, Neil. 2022. "The Visual Language Research Corpus (VLRC) Project." doi: 10.34894/LWMZ7G.

Cohn, Neil, Jessika Axnér, Michaela Diercks, Rebecca Yeh, and Kaitlin Pederson. 2019. "The cultural pages of comics: cross-cultural variation in page layouts." *Journal of Graphic Novels and Comics* 10 (1): 67–86. doi: 10.1080/21504857.2017.1413667.

Cohn, Neil, and Hannah Campbell. 2015. "Navigating Comics II: Constraints on the Reading Order of Comic Page Layouts." *Applied Cognitive Psychology* 29 (2): 193–9. doi: 10.1002/acp.3086.

Cohn, Neil, and Sean Ehly. 2016. "The vocabulary of manga: Visual morphology in dialects of Japanese Visual Language." *Journal of Pragmatics* 92: 17–29. doi: 10.1016/j.pragma.2015.11.008.

Cohn, Neil, Jan Engelen, and Joost Schilperoord. 2019. "The grammar of emoji? Constraints on communicative pictorial sequencing." *Cognitive Research: Principles and Implications* 4 (1): 33. doi: 10.1186/s41235-019-0177-0.

Cohn, Neil, and Tom Foulsham. 2020. "Zooming in on the cognitive neuroscience of visual narrative." *Brain and Cognition* 146: 105634. doi: 10.1016/j.bandc.2020. 105634.

Cohn, Neil, and Tom Foulsham. 2022. "Meaning above (and in) the head: Combinatorial visual morphology from comics and emoji." *Memory & Cognition*. doi: 10.3758/s13421-022-01294-2.

Cohn, Neil, Irmak Hacımusaoğlu, and Bien Klomberg. 2023. "The framing of subjectivity: Point-of-view in a cross-cultural analysis of comics." Journal of Graphic Novels and Comics 14 (3): 336–350. doi: 10.1080/21504857.2022.2152067.

Cohn, Neil, and Marta Kutas. 2015. "Getting a cue before getting a clue: Event-related potentials to inference in visual narrative comprehension." *Neuropsychologia* 77: 267–78. doi: 10.1016/j.neuropsychologia.2015.08.026.

Cohn, Neil, and Marta Kutas. 2017. "What's your neural function, visual narrative conjunction? Grammar, meaning, and fluency in sequential image processing." *Cognitive Research: Principles and Implications* 2 (27): 1–13. doi: 10.1186/ s41235-017-0064-5.

Cohn, Neil, and Stephen Maher. 2015. "The notion of the motion: the neurocognition of motion lines in visual narratives." *Brain Research* 1601: 73–84. doi: 10.1016/j.brainres.2015.01.018.

Cohn, Neil, Beena Murthy, and Tom Foulsham. 2016. "Meaning above the head: combinatorial constraints on the visual vocabulary of comics." *Journal of Cognitive Psychology* 28 (5): 559–74. doi: 10.1080/20445911.2016.1179314.

Cohn, Neil, and Martin Paczynski. 2013. "Prediction, events, and the advantage of Agents: The processing of semantic roles in visual narrative." *Cognitive Psychology* 67 (3): 73–97. doi: 10.1016/j.cogpsych.2013.07.002.

Cohn, Neil, Martin Paczynski, and Marta Kutas. 2017. "Not so secret agents: Event-related potentials to semantic roles in visual event comprehension." *Brain and Cognition* 119: 1–9. doi: 10.1016/j.bandc.2017.09.001.

Cohn, Neil, and Joost Schilperoord. 2022a. "Reimagining Language." *Cognitive Science* 46 (7): e13164. doi: 10.1111/cogs.13174.

Cohn, Neil, and Joost Schilperoord. 2022b. "Remarks on Multimodality: Grammatical Interactions in the Parallel Architecture." *Frontiers in Artificial Intelligence* 4: 1–21. doi: 10.3389/frai.2021.778060.

Cohn, Neil, Ryan Taylor, and Kaitlin Pederson. 2017. "A Picture is Worth More Words Over Time: Multimodality and Narrative Structure across Eight Decades of American Superhero Comics." *Multimodal Communication* 6 (1): 19–37. doi: 10.1515/mc-2017-0003.

Cohn, Neil, Amaro Taylor-Weiner, and Suzanne Grossman. 2012. "Framing attention in Japanese and American comics: cross-cultural differences in attentional structure." *Frontiers in Psychology – Cultural Psychology* 3: 1–12. doi: 10.3389/fpsyg.2012.00349.

Cohn, Neil, Lincy van Middelaar, Tom Foulsham, and Joost Schilperoord. forthcoming. "Anaphoric distance dependencies in visual narrative structure and processing."

Cohn, Neil, Vivian Wong, Kaitlin Pederson, and Ryan Taylor. 2017. "Path salience in motion events from verbal and visual languages." In *Proceedings of the 39th Annual Meeting of the Cognitive Science Society*, edited by G. Gunzelmann, A. Howes, Thora Tenbrink, and E. J. Davelaar, 1,794–9. Austin, TX: Cognitive Science Society.

Coopmans, Cas W., and Neil Cohn. 2022. "An electrophysiological investigation of co-referential processes in visual narrative comprehension." *Neuropsychologia* 172: 108253. doi: 10.1016/j.neuropsychologia.2022.108253.

Croft, William. 2003. *Typology and Universals*. 2nd ed. Cambridge, UK: Cambridge University Press.

Culicover, Peter W., and Ray Jackendoff. 2005. *Simpler Syntax*. Oxford: Oxford University Press.

Cutting, James E. 2015. "The Framing of Characters in Popular Movies." *Art & Perception* 3 (2): 191–212. doi: 10.1163/22134913-00002031.

Cutting, James E., and Ayse Candan. 2013. "Movies, Evolution, and Mind: From Fragmentation to Continuity." *The Evolutionary Review* 4 (3): 25–35.

Cutting, James E., and Ayse Candan. 2015. "Shot Durations, Shot Classes, and the Increased Pace of Popular Movies." *Projections* 9 (2): 40–62. doi: 10.3167/proj.2015.090204.

Cutting, James E., and Catalina Iricinschi. 2015. "Re-presentations of SPACE in Hollywood movies: An event-indexing analysis." *Cognitive Science* 39 (2): 434–56. doi: 10.1111/cogs.12151.

Davies, Paul Fisher. 2019. *Comics as Communication: A Functional Approach*. Cham, Switzerland: Palgrave Macmillan.

Davies, Paul Fisher. 2022. "What We Do in the Gutters: Or, If Not Transitions, What?" *Inks: The Journal of the Comics Studies Society* 6 (3): 287–99.

Dean, Michael. 2000. "The Ninth Art: Traversing the Cultural Space of the American Comic Book." Doctoral Dissertation, University of Wisconsin-Milwaukee.

Díaz Vera, Javier E. 2013a. "Embodied emotions in Medieval English language and visual arts." In *Sensuous Cognition Explorations into Human Sentience: Imagination, (E)motion and Perception*, edited by Rosario Caballero and Javier E. Díaz Vera, 195–219. Berlin: de Gruyter.

Díaz Vera, Javier E. 2013b. "Woven emotions: Visual representations of emotions in medieval English textiles." *Review of Cognitive Linguistics* 11 (2): 269–84. doi: 10.1075/rcl.11.2.04dia.

Dierick, Mark. 2017. "Visual storytelling in Dutch and Flemish comic books: A corpus analysis across culture and time." Bachelors Thesis, Communication and Information Science, Tilburg University.

Dobel, Christian, Gil Diesendruck, and Jens Bölte. 2007. "How writing system and age influence spatial representations of actions." *Psychological Science* 18 (6): 487–91.

Drummond-Mathews, Angela. 2010. "What Boys Will Be: A Study of Shōnen Manga." In *Manga: An Anthology of Global and Cultural Perspectives*, edited by Toni Johnson-Woods, 62–76. New York: Continuum Books.

BIBLIOGRAPHY

Dryer, Matthew S. 2013. "Expression of Pronominal Subjects." In *The World Atlas of Language Structures Online*, edited by Matthew S. Dryer and Martin Haspelmath. Leipzig: Max Planck Institute for Evolutionary Anthropology.

Duncan, Randy, Matthew J. Smith, and Paul Levitz. 2015. *The Power of Comics*. 2nd ed. New York: Continuum Books.

Dunst, Alexander. 2021. "How We Read Comics Now: Literary Studies, Computational Criticism, and the Rise of the Graphic Novel." *MFS Modern Fiction Studies* 67 (4): 758–84.

Dunst, Alexander, Rita Hartel, and Jochen Laubrock. 2017. "The Graphic Narrative Corpus (GNC): Design, Annotation, and Analysis for the Digital Humanities." 2017 14th IAPR International Conference on Document Analysis and Recognition (ICDAR), 9–15 Nov. 2017.

Dupont, Patrick, GA Orban, B De Bruyn, Alfons Verbruggen, and Luc Mortelmans. 1994. "Many areas in the human brain respond to visual motion." *Journal of neurophysiology* 72 (3): 1,420–24.

Ehret, Katharina. 2018. "Kolmogorov complexity as a universal measure of language complexity." *Proceedings of the First Shared Task on Measuring Language Complexity*: 8–14.

Eisner, Will. 1985. *Comics & Sequential Art*. Florida: Poorhouse Press.

Engelhardt, Yuri. 2002. "The Language of Graphics." Doctoral Dissertation, FGw/FNWI: Institute for Logic, Language and Computation, University of Amsterdam.

Exner, Eike. 2021. *Comics and the Origins of Manga: A Revisionist History*. Rutgers, NJ: Rutgers University Press.

Forceville, Charles. 2005. "Visual representations of the idealized cognitive model of *anger* in the Asterix album La Zizanie." *Journal of Pragmatics* 37 (1): 69–88.

Forceville, Charles. 2011b. "Pictorial runes in *Tintin and the Picaros*." *Journal of Pragmatics* 43 (3): 875–90.

Forceville, Charles. 2013. "Creative visual duality in comics balloons." In *The Agile Mind*, edited by Tony Veale, Kurt Feyaerts, and Charles Forceville, 253–73. Mouton de Gruyter.

Forceville, Charles. 2016. "Conceptual Metaphor Theory, Blending Theory, and other Cognitivist Perspectives on Comics." In *The Visual Narrative Reader*, edited by Neil Cohn, 89–114. London: Bloomsbury.

Forceville, Charles. 2020. *Visual and Multimodal Communication: Applying the Relevance Principle*. Oxford UK: Oxford University Press.

Forceville, Charles, Elizabeth El Refaie, and Gert Meesters. 2014. "Stylistics and comics." In *The Routledge Handbook of Stylistics*, edited by Michael Burke, 485–99. London: Routledge.

Forceville, Charles, Tony Veale, and Kurt Feyaerts. 2010a. "Balloonics: The Visuals of Balloons in Comics." In *The Rise and Reason of Comics and Graphic Literature: Critical Essays on the Form*, edited by Joyce Goggin and Dan Hassler-Forest. Jefferson: McFarland & Company, Inc.

Forceville, Charles, Tony Veale, and Kurt Feyaerts. 2010b. "Balloonics: The Visuals of Balloons in Comics." In *The Rise and Reason of Comics and Graphic Literature: Critical Essays on the Form*, edited by Joyce Goggin and Dan Hassler-Forest, 56–73. Jefferson: McFarland & Company, Inc.

Foulsham, Tom, and Neil Cohn. 2021. "Zooming in on visual narrative comprehension." *Memory & Cognition* 49 (3): 451–66. doi: 10.3758/s13421-020-01101-w.

Foulsham, Tom, Dean Wybrow, and Neil Cohn. 2016. "Reading Without Words: Eye Movements in the Comprehension of Comic Strips." *Applied Cognitive Psychology* 30: 566–79. doi: 10.1002/acp.3229.

Fresnault-Deruelle, Pierre. 1976. "Du linéaire au tabulaire." *Communications* 24 (1): 7–23.

Friedman, Sarah L., and Marguerite B. Stevenson. 1975. "Developmental Changes in the Understanding of Implied Motion in Two-dimensional Pictures." *Child Development* 46: 773–8.

Gahman, Paul. 2021. "Where to draw the line when the lines are blurred: A computational and functional analysis of cohesion in superhero comics." *Discourse, Context & Media* 44: 100551. doi: 10.1016/j.dcm.2021.100551.

Gauthier, Guy. 1976. "Les Peanuts: un graphisme idiomatique." *Communications* 24: 108–39.

Gavaler, Chris. 2017. *Superhero Comics*. London: Bloomsbury.

Gavaler, Chris. 2018. "Undemocratic Layout: Eight Methods of Accenting Images." *The Comics Grid: Journal of Comics Scholarship* 8 (8). doi: 10.16995/cg.102.

Gavaler, Chris, and Leigh Ann Beavers. 2018. "Clarifying closure." *Journal of Graphic Novels and Comics* 11: 182–211. doi: 10.1080/21504857.2018.1540441.

Genette, Gérard. 1980. *Narrative Discourse*. Translated by J.E. Lewin. Ithaca: Cornell University Press. Original edition, 1972.

Gernsbacher, Morton Ann. 1990. *Language Comprehension As Structure Building*. Hillsdale, NJ: Lawrence Earlbaum.

Goldberg, Adele. 1995. *Constructions: A Construction Grammar Approach to Argument Structure*. Chicago, IL: University of Chicago Press.

Goldberg, Wendy. 2010. "The Manga Phenomenon in America." In *Manga: An Anthology of Global and Cultural Perspectives*, edited by Toni Johnson-Woods, 281–96. New York: Continuum Books.

Goldin-Meadow, Susan, Wing Chee So, Asli Ôzyûrek, and Carolyn Mylander. 2008. "The Natural Order of Events: How Speakers of Different Languages Represent Events Nonverbally." *Proceedings of the National Academy of Sciences* 105 (27): 9,163–68.

Goldsmith, Evelyn. 1984. *Research into Illustration: An Approach and a Review*. Cambridge: Cambridge University Press.

Gravett, Paul. 2004. *Manga: Sixty Years of Japanese Comics*. New York, NY: HarperCollins.

Green, Jennifer. 2014. *Drawn from the Ground: Sound, Sign and Inscription in Central Australian Sand Stories*. Cambridge, UK: Cambridge University Press.

Greenberg, Joseph H. 1966. "Some Universals of Grammar with Particular Reference to the Order of Meaningful Elements." In *Universals of Grammar*, edited by Joseph H. Greenberg, 73–113. Cambridge, MA: MIT Press.

Groensteen, Thierry. 2007. *The System of Comics*. Translated by Bart Beaty and Nick Nguyen. Jackson: University of Mississippi Press.

Gross, Dana, Nelson Soken, Karl S. Rosengren, Anne D. Pick, Bradford H. Pillow, and Patricia Melendez. 1991. "Children's Understanding of Action Lines and the Static Representation of Speed of Locomotion." *Child Development* 62: 1,124–41.

Gu, Yan, Lisette Mol, Marieke Hoetjes, and Marc Swerts. 2017. "Conceptual and lexical effects on gestures: the case of vertical spatial metaphors for time in

Chinese." *Language, Cognition and Neuroscience* 32 (8): 1,048–63. doi: 10.1080/23273798.2017.1283425.

Gubern, Román. 1972. *El lenguaje de los Comics*. Barcelona: Peninsula.

Hacımusaoğlu, Irmak, and Neil Cohn. 2022. "Linguistic typology of motion events in visual narratives." *Cognitive Semiotics*: 1–26. doi: 10.1515/cogsem- 2022-2013.

Hacımusaoğlu, Irmak, Bien Klomberg, and Neil Cohn. 2023. "Navigating meaning in the spatial layouts of comics: A cross-cultural corpus analysis." Visual Cognition 31:126-137. doi: 10.1080/13506285.2023.2198271.

Hagoort, Peter. 2003. "How the brain solves the binding problem for language: a neurocomputational model of syntactic processing." *NeuroImage* 20: S18–S29. doi: 10.1016/j.neuroimage.2003.09.013.

Hammarström, Harald. 2016. "Linguistic diversity and language evolution." *Journal of Language Evolution* 1 (1): 19–29. doi: 10.1093/jole/lzw002.

Haspelmath, Martin. 2018. "The last word on polysynthesis: A review article." *Linguistic Typology* 22 (2): 307–26.

Haspelmath, Martin, Ekkehard König, Wulf Oesterreicher, and Wolfgang Raible. 2001. *Language Typology and Language Universals: An International Handbook*. Vol. 2. Berlin: Walter de Gruyter.

Haviland, John. 1993. "Anchoring, Iconicity, and Orientation in Guugu Yimithirr Pointing Gestures." *Journal of Linguistic Anthropology* 3 (1): 3–45.

Hayashi, Hiromasa, Goh Matsuda, Yoshiyuki Tamamiya, and Kazuo Hiraki. 2013. "Visual Effect of 'Speed Lines' in Manga: An Experimental Study on Spatial Attention." *Cognitive Studies* 20 (1): 79–89. doi: 10.11225/jcss.20.79.

Horstkotte, Silke, and Nancy Pedri. 2011. "Focalization in Graphic Narrative." *Narrative* 19 (3): 330–57.

Huang, CT James. 1984. "On the typology of zero anaphora." *Language Research* 20 (2).

Hünig, Wolfgang K. 1974. *Strukturen des Comic Strip*. Hildensheim: Olms.

Hutson, John P., Joe Magliano, and Lester C. Loschky. 2018. "Understanding Moment-to-Moment Processing of Visual Narratives." *Cognitive Science* 42 (8): 2,999–3,033. doi: 10.1111/cogs.12699.

Inui, Toshio, and Kensaku Miyamoto. 1981. "The time needed to judge the order of a meaningful string of pictures." *Journal of Experimental Psychology: Human Learning and Memory* 7 (5): 393–6.

Ito, Hiroyuki, Takeharu Seno, and Miyuki Yamanaka. 2010. "Motion impressions enhanced by converging motion lines." *Perception* 39 (11): 1,555–61.

Iyyer, Mohit, Varun Manjunatha, Anupam Guha, Yogarshi Vyas, Jordan Boyd-Graber, Hal Daumé III, and Larry Davis. 2017. "The Amazing Mysteries of the Gutter: Drawing Inferences Between Panels in Comic Book Narratives." *CVPR*: 6,478–87.

Jackendoff, Ray. 1990. *Semantic Structures*. Cambridge, MA: MIT Press.

Jackendoff, Ray. 2002. *Foundations of Language: Brain, Meaning, Grammar, Evolution*. Oxford: Oxford University Press.

Jackendoff, Ray. 2010. *Meaning and the Lexicon: The Parallel Architecture 1975–2010*. Oxford: Oxford University Press.

Jackendoff, Ray, and Jenny Audring. 2016. "Morphological schemas." *The Mental Lexicon* 11 (3): 467–93. doi: 10.1075/ml.11.3.06jac.

Jackendoff, Ray, and Jenny Audring. 2020. *The Texture of the Lexicon: Relational Morphology and the Parallel Architecture*. Oxford, UK: Oxford University Press.

Jackendoff, Ray, and Eva Wittenberg. 2014. "What You Can Say Without Syntax: A Hierarchy of Grammatical Complexity." In *Measuring Linguistic Complexity*, edited by Frederick Newmeyer and L. Preston, 65–82. Oxford: Oxford University Press.

Jahn, Manfred. 2021. "A Guide to Narratological Film Analysis." In *Poems, Plays, and Prose: A Guide to the Theory of Literary Genres*. Cologne: English Department, University of Cologne. http://www.uni-koeln.de/~ame02/pppf.pdf.

Johnson, Mark. 1987. *The Body in the Mind: The Bodily Basis of Meaning, Imagination, and Reason*. Chicago: University of Chicago Press.

Juricevic, Igor. 2017a. "Aladdin Sane and Close-Up Eye Asymmetry: David Bowie's Contribution to Comic Book Visual Language." *The Comics Grid: Journal of Comics Scholarship* 7 (1): 4.

Juricevic, Igor. 2017b. "Analysis of pictorial metaphors in comicbook art: test of the LA-MOAD theory." *Journal of Graphic Novels and Comics*: 1–21. doi: 10.1080/21504857.2017.1313287.

Juricevic, Igor, and Alicia Horvath. 2016. "Analysis of Motions in Comic Book Cover Art: Using Pictorial Metaphors." *The Comics Grid: Journal of Comics Scholarship* 6.

Kacsuk, Zoltan. 2018. "Re-Examining the 'What is Manga' Problematic: The Tension and Interrelationship between the 'Style' Versus 'Made in Japan' Positions." *Arts* 7 (3): 1–18.

Kemmerer, David. 2014. "Word classes in the brain: Implications of linguistic typology for cognitive neuroscience." *Cortex* 58 (0): 27–51. doi: 10.1016/j.cortex.2014.05.004.

Kennedy, John M. 1982. "Metaphor in Pictures." *Perception* 11 (5): 589–605.

Kikuchi, T., F. Yoshida, and Y Yagi. 2005. "Effects of pattern and color of back lines on mood expression in Manga." In *Proceedings of Annual Conference of 69th Japanese Psychological Association*, 607.

Kim, Young-Min. 2018. "What Makes the Difference in Visual Styles of Comics: From Classification to Style Transfer." 2018 3rd International Conference on Computational Intelligence and Applications (ICCIA), July 28–30, 2018.

Kirtley, Clare, Christopher Murray, Phillip B. Vaughan, and Benjamin W. Tatler. 2022. "Navigating the narrative: An eye-tracking study of readers' strategies when Reading comic page layouts." *Applied Cognitive Psychology* n/a (n/a). doi: 10.1002/acp.4018.

Kloepfer, Rolf. 1977. "Komplentarität von Sprache und Bild – am Beispiel von Comic, Karikatur und Reklame." In *Zeichenprozesse. Semiotische Foxschung in den Einzelwissenschaften*, edited by Roland Zeichenprosesse Posner and Hans-Peter Reinecke, 129–45. Wiesbaden: Athenaion.

Klomberg, Bien, and Neil Cohn. 2022. "Picture perfect peaks: Comprehension of inferential techniques in visual narratives." *Language and Cognition* 14 (4): 596–621. doi: 10.1017/langcog.2022.19.

Klomberg, Bien, and Neil Cohn. forthcoming. "Give the floor to (dis)continuity: A model of coreference constructions in visual narrative sequencing."

Klomberg, Bien, Irmak Hacımusaoğlu, and Neil Cohn. 2022. "Running through the Who, Where, and When: A Cross-cultural Analysis of Situational Changes in Comics." *Discourse Processes* 59 (9): 669–84 doi: 10.1080/0163853X.2022.2106402.

BIBLIOGRAPHY

Klomberg, Bien, Irmak Hacımusaoğlu, Lenneke Lichtenberg, Joost Schilperoord, and Neil Cohn. Forthcoming. "Continuity, Co-reference, and Inference in Visual Sequencing."

Koch, Walter A. 1971. *Varia Semiotica*. Hildensheim: Olms.

Koelsch, Stefan, and Walter A. Siebel. 2005. "Towards a neural basis of music perception." *Trends in Cognitive Sciences* 9 (12): 578–84. doi: 10.1016/j.tics.2005.10.001.

Koplenig, Alexander, Peter Meyer, Sascha Wolfer, and Carolin Müller-Spitzer. 2017. "The statistical trade-off between word order and word structure – Large-scale evidence for the principle of least effort." *PLOS ONE* 12 (3): e0173614. doi: 10.1371/journal.pone.0173614.

Kourtzi, Zoe, and Nancy Kanwisher. 2000. "Activation in Human MT/MST by Static Images with Implied Motion." *Journal of Cognitive Neuroscience* 12 (1): 48–55. doi: 10.1162/08989290051137594.

Kuhnke, Philipp, Marie C. Beaupain, Johannes Arola, Markus Kiefer, and Gesa Hartwigsen. 2023. "Meta-analytic evidence for a novel hierarchical model of conceptual processing." *Neuroscience & Biobehavioral Reviews* 144: 104994. doi: 10.1016/j.neubiorev.2022.104994.

Kuleshov, Lev. 1974. *Kuleshov on Film: Writings of Lev Kuleshov*. Translated by Ronald Levaco. Berkeley: University of California Press.

Kunzle, David. 1973. *History of the Comic Strip*. Vol. 1. Berkeley: University of California Press.

Kutas, Marta, and Kara D. Federmeier. 2011. "Thirty years and counting: finding meaning in the N400 component of the event-related brain potential (ERP)." *Annual Review of Psychology* 62 (1): 621–47. doi: 10.1146/annurev.psych.093008.131123.

Lakoff, George. 1993. "The Contemporary Theory of Metaphor." In *Metaphor and Thought*, edited by Andrew Ortony. Cambridge, UK: Cambridge University Press.

Lakusta, Laura, and Barbara Landau. 2005. "Starting at the end: The importance of goals in spatial language." *Cognition* 96: 1–33.

Lambon Ralph, Matthew A., Elizabeth Jefferies, Karalyn Patterson, and Timothy T. Rogers. 2016. "The neural and computational bases of semantic cognition." *Nature Reviews Neuroscience* 18:42. doi: 10.1038/nrn.2016.150.

Laraudogoitia, Jon Pérez. 2008. "The comic as a binary language: An hypothesis on comic structure." *Journal of Quantitative Linguistics* 15 (2): 111–35.

Laraudogoitia, Jon Pérez. 2009. "The Composition and Structure of the Comic." *Journal of Quantitative Linguistics* 16 (4): 327–53.

Laubrock, Jochen, and David Dubray. 2019. "CNN-Based Classification of Illustrator Style in Graphic Novels: Which Features Contribute Most?" In *MultiMedia Modeling. MMM 2019. Lecture Notes in Computer Science*, edited by Ioannis Kompatsiaris, Benoit Huet, Vasileios Mezaris, Cathal Gurrin, Wen-Huang Cheng, and Stefanos Vrochidis, 684–95. Cham: Springer International Publishing.

Laubrock, Jochen, and Alexander Dunst. 2020. "Computational Approaches to Comics." *Topics in Cognitive Science* 12 (1): 274–310. doi: 10.1111/tops.12476.

Laubrock, Jochen, Sven Hohenstein, and Matthias Kümmerer. 2018. "Attention to Comics: Cognitive Processing During the Reading of Graphic Literature." In *Empirical Comics Research: Digital, Multimodal, and Cognitive Methods,* edited by Alexander Dunst, Jochen Laubrock, and Janina Wildfeuer, 239–63. New York: Routledge.

Lefèvre, Pascal. 2000. "The Importance of Being 'Published': A Comparative Study of Different Comics Formats." In *Comics and Culture: Analytical and Theoretical Approaches to Comics*, edited by Anne Magnussen and Hans-Christian Christiansen, 91–105. Copenhagen: Museum Tusculanum Press.

Lefèvre, Pascal. 2012. "The construction of national and foreign identities in French and Belgian postwar comics (1939–1970)." *Comicalités. Études de culture graphique*. doi: 10.4000/comicalites.875.

Lefèvre, Pascal. 2013. "Narration in the Flemish Dual Publication System: The Crossover Genre Humoristic Adventure." In *From Comic Strips to Graphic Novels: Contributions to the Theory and History of Graphic Narrative*, edited by Daniel Stein and Jan-Noël Thon, 255–69. Berlin: Walter de Gruyter.

Levin, Daniel T., and Daniel J. Simons. 2000. "Perceiving Stability in a Changing World: Combining Shots and Intergrating Views in Motion Pictures and the Real World." *Media Psychology* 2 (4): 357–80.

Levshina, Natalia. 2021. "Cross-Linguistic Trade-Offs and Causal Relationships Between Cues to Grammatical Subject and Object, and the Problem of Efficiency-Related Explanations." *Frontiers in Psychology* 12. doi: 10.3389/fpsyg.2021.648200.

Loschky, Lester C., Joseph Magliano, Adam M. Larson, and Tim J. Smith. 2020. "The Scene Perception & Event Comprehension Theory (SPECT) Applied to Visual Narratives." *Topics in Cognitive Science* 12 (1): 311–51. doi: 10.1111/tops.12455.

Maass, Anne, and Aurore Russo. 2003. "Directional Bias in the Mental Representation of Spatial Events." *Psychological Science* 14 (4): 296–301.

Magliano, Joseph P., Kristopher Kopp, Karyn Higgs, and David N. Rapp. 2016. "Filling in the Gaps: Memory Implications for Inferring Missing Content in Graphic Narratives." *Discourse Processes*: 0–0. doi: 10.1080/0163853X.2015.1136870.

Magliano, Joseph P., Adam M. Larson, Karyn Higgs, and Lester C. Loschky. 2015. "The relative roles of visuospatial and linguistic working memory systems in generating inferences during visual narrative comprehension." *Memory & Cognition*: 1–13. doi: 10.3758/s13421-015-0558-7.

Maier, Emar, and Sofia Bimpikou. 2019. "Shifting perspectives in pictorial narratives." In *Proceeding of Sinn und Bedeutung 23*, edited by Uli Sauerland and Stephanie Solt, 1–15. Barcelona: Leibniz-Centre General Linguistics (ZAS).

Maier, Emar, and Markus Steinbach. 2022. "Perspective Shift Across Modalities." *Annual Review of Linguistics* 8 (1): null. doi: 10.1146/annurev-linguistics-031120- 021042.

Mair, Victor H. 2019. *Painting and Performance: Chinese Picture Recitation and its Indian Genesis*. University of Hawaii Press.

Mandler, Jean M. 2010. "The spatial foundations of the conceptual system." *Language and Cognition* 2 (1): 21–44.

Mandler, Jean M., and Nancy S. Johnson. 1977. "Remembrance of things parsed: Story structure and recall." *Cognitive Psychology* 9: 111–51.

Martin, Cortney V., and Tonya L. Smith-Jackson. 2008. "Evaluation of pictorial assembly instructions for young children." *Human Factors: The Journal of the Human Factors and Ergonomics Society* 50 (4): 652–62. doi: 10.1518/001872008x 288592.

Masuda, Takahiko, and Richard Nisbett. 2006. "Culture and Change Blindness." *Cognitive Science* 30: 381–99.

Mazur, Dan, and Alexander Danner. 2014. *Comics: A Global History, 1968 to the Present*. London: Thames & Hudson.

McCloud, Scott. 1993. *Understanding Comics: The Invisible Art*. New York, NY: Harper Collins.

McCloud, Scott. 2006. *Making Comics*. New York, NY: Harper-Collins.

McDowd, Joan M. 2007. "An Overview of Attention: Behavior and Brain." *Journal of Neurologic Physical Therapy* 31 (3).

Meesters, Gert. 2012. "To and Fro Dutch Dutch: Diachronic Language Variation in Flemish Comics." In *Linguistics and the Study of Comics*, edited by Frank Bramlett, 163–82. New York: Palgrave MacMillan.

Menzerath, Paul. 1928. "Über einige phonetische Probleme." Actes du premier Congres international de linguistes.

Mikkonen, Kai. 2012. "Focalization in Comics: From the Specificities of the Medium to Conceptual Reformulation." *Scandinavian Journal of Comic Art* 1 (1): 70–95.

Mikkonen, Kai. 2017. *The Narratology of Comic Art*. Vol. 3. New York: Routledge.

Moisich, Oliver. In prep. "Towards an Experimental Narratology for Graphic Narrative." Doctoral Dissertation, Department of English and American Studies, University of Paderborn.

Molés-Cases, Teresa. 2020a. "Manner salience and translation: A case study based on a multilingual corpus of graphic novels." *Lebende Sprachen* 49 (5): 346. doi: 10.1515/les-2020-0020.

Molés-Cases, Teresa. 2020b. "On the translation of Manner-of-motion in comics: Evidence from an inter- and intratypological corpus-based study." *Languages in Contrast* 20 (1): 141–65. doi: 10.1075/lic.19007.mol.

Molotiu, Andrei. 2012. "Abstract Form: Sequential Dynamism and Iconostasis in Abstract Comics and in Steve Ditko's *Amazing Spider-Man*." In *Critical approaches to comics: theories and methods*, edited by Matthew J. Smith and Randy Duncan, 84–100. New York: Routledge.

Murata, N. 1994. "The effects of expertization reading manga notations." *The Science of Reading* 38: 48–57.

Naidu, Viswanatha, Jordan Zlatev, Vasanta Duggirala, Joost van de Weijer, Simon Devylder, and Johan Blomberg. 2018. "Holistic spatial semantics and post-Talmian motion event typology: A case study of Thai and Telugu." *Cognitive Semiotics* 11 (2). doi: 10.1515/cogsem-2018-2002.

Nakazawa, Jun. 1998. "Development of manga notation understanding." In *Proceedings of the 9th Annual Conference of Japan Society of Developmental Psychology*, 182.

Nakazawa, Jun. 2005a. "Development of manga (comic book) literacy in children." In *Applied Developmental Psychology: Theory, Practice, and Research from Japan*, edited by David W. Shwalb, Jun Nakazawa, and Barbara J. Shwalb, 23–42. Greenwich, CT: Information Age Publishing.

Nakazawa, Jun. 2005b. "The development of manga panel reading literacy." *Manga Studies* 7: 6–21.

Natsume, Fusanosuke. 1997. *Manga wa naze omoshiroi no ka: Sono hyōgen to bunpō [Why are Manga Fascinating?: Their expressions and grammar]*. Tokyo, Japan: NHK Library.

Neff, William Albert. 1977. "The Pictorial and Linguistic Features of Comic Book Formulas." Doctoral Dissertation, University of Denver.

Newton, Douglas P. 1985. "Children's Perception of Pictorial Metaphor." *Educational Psychology* 5 (2): 179–85. doi: 10.1080/0144341850050207.

Nguyen, Nhu-Van, Christophe Rigaud, Arnaud Revel, and Jean-Christophe Burie. 2021. "Manga-MMTL: Multimodal Multitask Transfer Learning for Manga Character Analysis." Document Analysis and Recognition – ICDAR 2021, Cham, 2021.

Nisbett, Richard. 2003. *The Geography of Thought: How Asians and Westerners Think Differently . . . and Why*. New York: Nicholas Brealy Publishing Ltd.

Nisbett, Richard, and Takahiko Masuda. 2003. "Culture and point of view." *Proceedings of the National Academy of Sciences* 100 (19): 11,163–70.

Nöth, Winfried. 1990. "Comics." In *Handbook of Semiotics*, 472–5. Indianapolis, IN: University of Indiana Press.

Núñez, Rafael, and Eve Sweetser 2006. "With the Future Behind Them: Convergent Evidence From Aymara Language and Gesture in the Crosslinguistic Comparison of Spatial Construals of Time." *Cognitive Science* 30: 1–49.

Omori, Takahide, Taku Ishii, and Keiko Kurata. 2004. "Eye catchers in comics: Controlling eye movements in reading pictorial and textual media." 28th International Congress of Psychology, Beijing, China.

Packard, Stephan. 2016. "The Drawn-Out Gaze of the Cartoon: A Psychosemiotic Look at Subjectivity in Comic Book Storytelling." In *Subjectivity across Media*, edited by Maike Sarah Reinerth and Jan-Noël Thon, 121–34. London: Routledge.

Padakannaya, Prakash, M.L. Devi, B. Zaveria, S.K. Chengappa, and Jyotsna Vaid. 2002. *Directional scanning effect and strength of reading habit in picture naming and recall*. Amsterdam: Elsevier.

Paivio, A. 1986. *Mental Representations: A dual coding approach*. New York: Oxford University Press.

Patel, Aniruddh D. 2003. "Language, music, syntax and the brain." *Nature Neuroscience* 6 (7): 674–81. doi: 10.1038/nn1082.

Pederson, Kaitlin, and Neil Cohn. 2016. "The changing pages of comics: Page layouts across eight decades of American superhero comics." *Studies in Comics* 7 (1): 7–28. doi: 10.1386/stic.7.1.7_1.

Peeters, Benoît. 1998 [1991]. *Case, Planche, Récit: Lire la Bande Dessinée*. Paris: Casterman.

Peirce, Charles Sanders. 1931. "Division of Signs." In *Collected Papers of Charles Sanders Peirce: Vol. 2: Elements of Logic.*, edited by Charles Hartshorne and Paul Weiss, 134–73. Cambridge, MA: Harvard University Press.

Petersen, Robert S. 2011. *Comics, Manga, and Graphic Novels: A History of Graphic Narratives*. Santa Barbara, CA: ABC-CLIO.

Piantadosi, Steven T. 2014. "Zipf's word frequency law in natural language: A critical review and future directions." *Psychonomic Bulletin & Review* 21 (5): 1,112–30. doi: 10.3758/s13423-014-0585-6.

Poharec, Lauranne. 2018. "Focalized split panels: Bridging the borders in comics form." *Studies in Comics* 9 (2): 315–31. doi: 10.1386/stic.9.2.315_1.

Postema, Barbara. 2013. *Narrative Structure in Comics: Making Sense of Fragments*. Rochester, NY: RIT Press.

Pratha, Nimish K., Natalie Avunjian, and Neil Cohn. 2016. "Pow, Punch, Pika, and Chu: The Structure of Sound Effects in Genres of American Comics and Japanese Manga." *Multimodal Communication* 5 (2): 93–109.

Prough, Jennifer. 2010. "Shojo Manga in Japan and Abroad." In *Manga: An Anthology of Global and Cultural Perspectives*, edited by Toni Johnson-Woods, 93–106. New York: Continuum.

Regier, T. 1996. *The human semantic potential: Spatial language and constrained connectionism*. Cambridge, MA: MIT Press.

Regier, T. 1997. "Constraints on the learning of spatial terms: A computational investigation." In *Psychology of learning and motivation: Mechanisms of perceptual learning*, edited by R. Goldstone, P. Schyns and D. Medin, 171–217. San Diego, CA: Academic Press.

Rigaud, Christophe, and Jean-Christophe Burie. 2018. "Computer Vision Applied to Comic Book Images." In *Empirical Comics Research: Digital, Multimodal, and Cognitive Methods*, edited by Alexander Dunst, Jochen Laubrock, and Janina Wildfeuer, 104–24. New York: Routledge.

Round, Julia. 2007. "Visual Perspective and Narrative Voice in Comics: Redefining Literary Terminology." *International Journal of Comic Art* 9 (2): 316–29.

Sadock, Jerrold M. 1991. *Autolexical Syntax: A Theory of Parallel Grammatical Representations*. Chicago, IL: University of Chicago Press.

Sakurai, Sho, Takuji Narumi, Tomohiro Tanikawa, and Michitaka Hirose. 2011. "Augmented emotion by superimposing depiction in comics." Proceedings of the 8th International Conference on Advances in Computer Entertainment Technology, Lisbon, Portugal.

Salt, Barry. 2016. "The exact remake: a statistical style analysis of six Hollywood films." *New Review of Film and Television Studies* 14 (4): 467–86. doi: 10.1080/17400309.2016.1198635.

Saraceni, Mario. 2016. "Relatedness: Aspects of textual connectivity in comics." In *The Visual Narrative Reader*, edited by Neil Cohn, 115–29. London: Bloomsbury.

Schilperoord, Joost, and Neil Cohn. 2021. "Let there be . . . visual optimal innovations: making visual meaning through Michelangelo's *The Creation of Adam*." *Visual Communication*: 14703572211004994. doi: 10.1177/1470357221 1004994.

Schilperoord, Joost, and Neil Cohn. 2022. "Before: Unimodal Linguistics, After: Multimodal Linguistics: An Expoloration of the *Before-After* Construction." *Cognitive Semantics* 8 (1): 109–140. doi: 10.1163/23526416-bja10025.

Schipper, Dieuwertje. 2018. "Visual storytelling in *Calvin and Hobbes*." Bachelor's Thesis, Communication and Cognition, Tilburg University.

Schodt, Frederik L. 1983. *Manga! Manga! The World of Japanese Comics*. New York: Kodansha America Inc.

Schodt, Frederik L. 1996. *Dreamland Japan: Writings on Modern Manga*. Berkeley: Stonebridge Press.

Senior, C., J. Barnes, V. Giampietroc, A. Simmons, E. T. Bullmore, M. Brammer, and A. S. David. 2000. "The functional neuroanatomy of implicit-motion perception or 'representational momentum'." *Current Biology* 10 (1): 16–22. doi: 10.1016/S0960-9822(99)00259-6.

Shamoon, Deborah. 2011. "Films on Paper: Cinematic Narrative in Gekiga." In *Mangatopia: Essays on Manga and Anime in the Modern World*, edited by Timothy Perper and Martha Cornog, 21–36. Westport, CT: Libraries Unlimited.

Shinohara, Kazuko, and Yoshihiro Matsunaka. 2009. "Pictorial metaphors of emotion in Japanese comics." In *Multimodal Metaphor*, edited by Charles Forceville and Eduardo Urios-Aparisi, 265–93. New York: Mouton De Gruyter.

Shipp, Stewart. 2004. "The brain circuitry of attention." *Trends in Cognitive Sciences* 8 (5): 223–30. doi: 10.1016/j.tics.2004.03.004.

Slobin, Dan I. 1996. "From 'thought and language' to 'thinking for speaking'." *Rethinking linguistic relativity* 17: 70–96.

Slobin, Dan I. 2000. "Verbalized events: A dynamic approach to linguistic relativity and determinism." In *Evidence for linguistic relativity*, edited by Susanne Niemeier and René Dirven, 107–38. Amsterdam: John Benjamins.

Smolderen, Thierry. 2014. *The Origins of Comics: from William Hogarth to Winsor McCay*. Translated by Bart Beaty and Nick Nguyen. Jackson: University of Mississippi Press.

Stainbrook, Eric J. 2016. "A Little Cohesion between Friends; Or, We're Just Exploring Our Textuality: Reconciling Cohesion in Written Language and Visual Language." In *The Visual Narrative Reader*, edited by Neil Cohn, 129–54. London: Bloomsbury.

Stump, Gregory T. 2001. *Inflectional Morphology: A Theory of Paradigm Structure*. Vol. 93: Cambridge University Press.

Takahashi, Mizuki. 2008. "Opening the Closed World of Shōjo Manga." In *Japanese Visual Culture: Explorations in the World of Manga and Anime*, edited by Mark W. MacWilliams, 114–37. London: Routledge.

Takekuma, Kentaro. 1995. "Hito me de wakaru 'keiyu' zukan" [Pictorial guide of 'keiyu' understandable at a glance]." In *Manga no yomikata [How to read manga]* 78–105. Tokyo: Takarajimasha EX.

Takeuchi, Kaori. 2012. "ASL Manga: Visual representation in storytelling." *Deaf Studies Digital Journal* 3.

Talmy, Leonard. 1985. "Lexicalisation patterns: semantic structure in lexical forms." In *Language Typology and Syntactic Description: Vol. 3. Grammatical categories and the lexicon*, edited by T. Shopen, 36–149. Cambridge: Cambridge University Press.

Talmy, Leonard. 2000. *Toward a Cognitive Semantics*. Vol. 1. Cambridge, MA: MIT Press.

Tanaka, Takamasa, Kenji Shoji, Fubito Toyama, and Juichi Miyamichi. 2007. "Layout analysis of tree-structured scene frames in comic images." International Joint Conference on Artificial Intelligence, Hyderabad, India, January 6–12, 2007.

Tasić, Miloš, and Dušan Stamenković. 2018. "Exploring pictorial runes in Luca Enoch's comic book series *Gea*." *Facta Universitatis, Series: Linguistics and Literature* 15 (2): 123–41.

Thon, Jan-Noël. 2016. *Transmedial Narratology and Contemporary Media Culture*. Lincoln: University of Nebraska Press.

Tsai, Yi-Shan. 2018. "Close-ups: an emotive language in manga." *Journal of Graphic Novels and Comics* 9 (5): 473–89. doi: 10.1080/21504857.2018.1480502.

Tseng, Chiao-I, and John A Bateman. 2018. "Cohesion in Comics and Graphic Novels: An Empirical Comparative Approach to Transmedia Adaptation in City of Glass." *Adaptation* 11 (2): 122–43. doi: 10.1093/adaptation/apx027.

BIBLIOGRAPHY

Tseng, Chiao-I, Jochen Laubrock, and Jana Pflaeging. 2018. "Character Developments in Comics and Graphic Novels: A Systematic Analytical Scheme." In *Empirical comics research: Digital, multimodal, and cognitive methods*, edited by Alexander Dunst, Jochen Laubrock, and Janina Wildfeuer, 154–75. Routledge.

Tversky, Barbara, and Tracy Chow. 2017. "Language and Culture in Visual Narratives." *Cognitive Semiotics* 10 (2): 77–89. doi: 10.1515/cogsem-2017-0008.

Tversky, Barbara, Sol Kugelmass, and Atalia Winter. 1991. "Cross-cultural and developmental trends in graphic productions." *Cognitive Psychology* 23 (4): 515–57.

van Dijk, Teun, and Walter Kintsch. 1983. *Strategies of Discourse Comprehension*. New York: Academic Press.

van Middelaar, Lincy. 2017. "It ain't much, if it ain't Dutch: Visual morphology across eight decades of Dutch and Flemish comics." Bachelors Thesis, Communication and Information Science, Tilburg University.

van Nierop, Jeroen. 2018. "Scientific Progress Goes 'Boink': A systematic study in page layout of *Calvin and Hobbes*." Bachelors Thesis, Cognition and Communication, Tilburg University.

Vries, Rudolf Willem de. 2012. "Comics and co-evolutions: a study of the dynamics in the niche of comics publishers in the Low Countries." Doctoral Dissertation, SOM research school, Economics and Business Administration, University of Groningen.

Walker, Mort. 1980. *The Lexicon of Comicana*. Port Chester, NY: Comicana, Inc.

Watterson, Bill. 1995. *The Calvin and Hobbes Tenth Anniversary Book*. Kansas City, Missouri: Andrews McMeel Publishing.

Werning, Daniel A. 2018. "The Representation of Space, Time, and Event Sequence in an Ancient Egyptian Netherworld Comic." In *Time and Space at Issue in Ancient Egypt*, edited by Gaëlle Chantrain and Jean Winand. Hamburg: Widmaier.

Whorf, Benjamin Lee. 1956. "The Relation of Habitual Thought and Behavior to Language." In *Language, Thought, and Reality: Selected Writings of Benjamin Lee Whorf*, edited by John B. Carroll, 134–59. Cambridge, MA: MIT Press. Original edition, 1956.

Wichmann, Søren, and Jesper Nielsen. 2016. "Sequential Text-Image Pairing among the Classic Maya." In *The Visual Narrative Reader*, edited by Neil Cohn, 282–313. London: Bloomsbury.

Wildfeuer, Janina, Ielka van der Sluis, Gisela Redeker, and Nina van der Velden. 2022. "No laughing matter!? Analyzing the Page Layout of Instruction Comics." *Journal of Graphic Novels and Comics*: 1–22. doi: 10.1080/21504857. 2022.2053559.

Wilkins, David P. 2016. "Alternative Representations of Space: Arrernte Narratives in Sand." In *The Visual Narrative Reader*, edited by Neil Cohn, 252–81. London: Bloomsbury. Original edition, 1997. Proceedings of the CLS Opening Academic Year '97 '98, edited by M. Biemans and J. van de Weijer, 133–64. Nijmegen: Nijmegen/Tilburg Center for Language Studies.

Willats, John. 1997. *Art and representation: New principles in the analysis of pictures*. Princeton: Princeton University Press.

Willats, John. 2005. *Making Sense of Children's Drawings*. Mahwah, NJ: Lawrence Erlbaum.

Wilson, Brent. 1988. "The Artistic Tower of Babel: Inextricable Links Between Culture and Graphic Development." In *Discerning Art: Concepts and Issues*, edited by George W. Hardiman and Theodore Zernich, 488–506. Champaign, IL: Stipes Publishing Company.

Witek, Joseph. 2009. "The arrow and the grid." In *A Comic Studies Reader*, edited by Jeet Heer and Kent Worcester, 149–56. Jackson: University Press of Mississippi.

Woo, Benjamin. 2019. "What Kind of Studies Is Comics Studies?" In *The Oxford Handbook of Comic Book Studies*, 3–15. Oxford Handbooks Online, Oxford University Press New York.

Zipf, George K. 1935. *The psycho-biology of language*. Oxford, England: Houghton-Mifflin.

Zlatev, Jordan, Johan Blomberg, Simon Devylder, Viswanatha Naidu, and Joost van de Weijer. 2021. "Motion event descriptions in Swedish, French, Thai and Telugu: a study in post-Talmian motion event typology." *Acta Linguistica Hafniensia* 53 (1): 58–90. doi: 10.1080/03740463.2020.1865692.

Zwaan, Rolf A. 2004. "The Immersed Experiencer: Toward an Embodied Theory of Language Comprehension." In *The psychology of learning and motivation*, edited by B.H. Ross, 35–62. New York: Academic Press.

Zwaan, Rolf A., and Gabriel A. Radvansky. 1998. "Situation models in language comprehension and memory." *Psychological Bulletin* 123 (2): 162–85.

INDEX

Comics discussed

Amazing Spider-Man, The 99, 100, 137, 194–6, 237

Boxers 79, 80

Calvin and Hobbes 27, 29, 34–6, 215–31, 233, 237, 239
Captain Marvel Adventures 194–6
Captain Midnight 137
City of Glass 138

Far Arden 5–18, 37, 63, 96–8

Green Lantern Corps 192

Heck 136–7
Het Grote Kabouter Wesley Boek 81

Katzenjammer Kids, The 236
Kocchi Muite! Miiko 201

Lady Luck 181

Nick Fury Agent of S.H.I.E.L.D. 192

Otto 62

Punisher, The 186

Rosario+Vampire II 56

Savage Dragon, The 161–4
Set to Sea 81, 82

Twilight X 62

Vagabond 159–62
Venom: Funeral Pyre 79–80

Wonder Woman 62, 186

Yellow Kid, The 236

Comics creators discussed

Binder, Jack 137

Colan, Gene 62, 186
Cannon, Kevin 5–18, 37, 63, 96–8
Cannon, Zander 136–7

De Decker, Frodo 62
Dirks, Rudolph 236

Edmunson, Nathan 187

Garney, Ron 100
Geirnaert, Jonas 81
Gerads, Mitch 187
Gleason, Patrick 192

Karasik, Paul 138
Kirby, Jack 22, 194–6

Larsen, Erik 161–4
Lyle, Tom 79–80

McFarlane, Todd 194–6, 237, 247, 250
Mazzuchelli, David 138
Michelinie, David 194–6

Nordling, Klaus 181

Ono, Eriko 201
Outcault, Richard F. 236

Potts, Carl 79–80

Simon, Joe 194–6
Steranko, Jim 192
Straczynski, J. Michael 100, 137

Takehiko Inoue 159–62
Thomas, Roy 62, 186
Tomasi, Peter 192

Watterson, Bill 29, 34–6, 215–31, 237
Weing, Drew 81, 82
Wight, Joseph 62

Yang, Gene 79, 80

General index

access (state of processing) 98, 99,
        210–13
activity constraint 13
affixation 45–8, 61
affixes, visual 10, 14, 45–8, 60, 61, 66,
        118, 120
alignment of panels (layout) 7, 8, 75,
        77–80, 81, 89, 112, 119
Alternation 153–6, 158, 161, 162–4,
        179
amorphic panels 118–23, 125, 126,
        128–31, 133–42, 164, 176–7,
        188, 192, 200, 211, 223–4,
        238, 240, 249
American comics 1, 2, 21, 22, 32, 33,
        35, 36, 43, 53, 62, 68, 71–3,
        77, 80–8, 91, 94, 95, 104–8,
        111–13, 119–25, 128–34,
        138–40, 158–62, 166,
        169–98, 200–3, 206–7, 209,
        213, 221–30, 233–7, 240–1,
        249, 250
American Visual Language (AVL)
        21–2, 25, 28–9, 37, 53,
        191–6, 206–8, 230

arrangement of panels 8, 28, 75–9,
        82–91, 94, 170–3, 192, 195,
        219–20
assemblage structure 8–9, 28, 76,
        79–81, 91–3, 110–12, 172–4,
        248
asymmetrical (grammatical symmetry)
        184–6, 189, 192, 194, 227–9,
        250
attention 19, 33, 98, 115, 119, 125–7,
        142, 155, 211–13, 241
    units 115
attentional
    selection 98
    framing structure 115–43, 164–6,
        175–8, 195, 224, 238
Australian sand narratives 21, 26, 236

back-end processes 97, 98, 115, 116,
        142, 210–14, 241
balanced semantic weight 180–3,
        187–9, 192–4, 196, 197,
        226–8, 250
bande desinée 90, 138
    see also French comics
base paneling 118–19, 134, 140
Basic Narrative Progression (BNP)
        155–8, 160–2, 179–80, 192–4
Bateman, John xiv, 15, 32, 33, 75, 76,
        81, 96, 99, 106, 109, 154,
        170, 214, 241, 244
Belgium 35, 36, 38, 52, 57, 62, 81,
        169, 208–9, 242
    see also Flanders
bleeding panels 78, 218–19
blockage (layout) 8, 77–9, 81, 84–6,
        88, 89, 91, 94, 170–2, 192,
        220
borderless panels 78, 79, 84, 218–20
bottom-up cues 149, 212
bound morphemes 45–8
    see also affixes

canonical narrative schema 147–50,
        153, 161–2
center-embedded clause 145–6
character change across panels 13–14,
        28, 32, 95–113, 125–31, 134,
        141–2, 145, 147, 174–5, 180,

INDEX 271

192–4, 196, 197, 200, 202, 205, 207, 209, 201, 222–3, 238, 249
see also situational coherence
China 34, 36, 69–70, 72, 82–5, 87–9, 91–3, 102, 121, 132, 137, 159, 201
Chinese manhua 34, 36, 62, 65, 68–72, 82–94, 102, 121, 132, 137–8, 158–9, 166, 172, 200–1, 234
cluster analyses 29, 39, 56, 59, 164, 191–4, 196, 199–210, 234, 235, 239
cognition xii, xiii, 1, 19, 20, 22, 25, 26, 45, 97, 225, 230, 237, 239, 245
cognitive universals 25, 27, 167, 238–9, 244
coherence relationships, *see* situational coherence
complexity 11, 15, 24, 28, 44, 73, 125, 184–8, 245, 250
framing 28, 124, 164–6, 176–7, 188, 192–4, 196–7, 200–11, 224–5, 230, 238–40
layout 90–1, 109–10, 171–2, 192–4
narrative 150, 155–67, 179–80, 187–9, 192–4, 196–7, 200–10, 224–5, 230, 238–40, 249
comprehension 33, 67, 75, 97–9, 115–17, 142–3, 210–14, 240–2, 244, 245
conceptual
permeability 25–7, 68, 72, 127, 166, 239–40, 242
structure 4, 5, 7, 13, 15, 16, 25, 27, 67, 147, 150
conjunction schema 148, 150–63, 179–80, 192, 196, 249, 250
constructions 20, 26, 44, 68, 131, 148, 151, 153, 155, 160–4, 179, 212, 239, 244
continuity constraint 13
corpus
linguistics xii, 23, 31, 242
research xii–xiv, 22–3, 24, 27, 31–41, 95, 119, 139, 164, 178, 236, 243, 244

cross-cultural diversity xii, xiii, 1, 2, 20–3, 32, 34, 50, 69–71, 81, 83, 94, 108, 109, 112–14, 119–28, 139, 166, 197, 199–214, 215, 233, 238–40, 242
cross-cutting, *see* Alternation
cross-linguistic
diversity 19–24, 27, 29, 40, 233, 238
equivalence hypothesis 20–3
Cutting, James 131, 133, 138, 139, 178

Daily strip (*Calvin and Hobbes*) 36, 216–29
dialects, *see* varieties
direction, *see* panel direction
Dirksian visual language 236–7
discontinuity 101, 105–8, 110, 113, 130, 192–4, 201–2, 206–9, 222, 223, 238
divisional paneling 119, 134–40
domain-specific, *see* modality-specific
dominant paneling 77, 79, 119, 134
see also inset paneling
Dunst, Alexander xiv, 32, 33
Dutch comics 28, 34–6, 38, 50–2, 57–60, 65, 73, 174, 209

Environmental-Conjunction 151–4, 156–63, 179–80, 192, 196
Establisher 148–50, 154, 160–1
event structure 5, 13, 65–72, 145, 147, 148, 162
eye
movements 31, 33, 75, 80, 115–17, 210–13
tracking 27
eye-umlaut 49
European comics 32, 40, 51, 57, 62, 71, 72, 77, 81–3, 86, 87–90, 93, 94, 95, 103, 105–8, 111–13, 121–5, 128–34, 140–2, 158–9, 165, 169, 170, 175–80, 189–91, 197, 201–3, 207, 209–13, 223, 225, 234, 240, 241, 249

European Visual Language 199,
208–10, 236, 237
external compositional structure (ECS)
7, 76–80, 83–91, 170–2, 243
see also layout

film 115, 118, 133, 136, 138, 139, 145,
148, 154, 178
filmic shot scale, *see* shot scale
fixation (eye fixation) 115, 125
Flanders 35, 36, 57, 62, 208–9
Flemish comics 28, 34–6, 38, 50–2,
57–60, 62, 65, 73, 81, 138,
169, 174, 208–9, 242
Fluency 3, 14, 143, 213, 214
focal framing 117, 124–6, 136, 138,
140–3, 238
Forceville, Charles xiv, 20, 32, 45, 46,
50, 51, 63, 65, 67, 214, 233,
243, 244, 248
framing complexity 28, 124, 164–6,
176–7, 188, 192–4, 196–7,
200–11, 224–5, 230, 238–40
France 1, 34, 36, 62, 69–72, 81–5,
86–8, 90–3, 102, 121, 137,
158–9, 200–1, 208–9
French comics 26, 57, 71, 84, 87, 90,
112, 138, 139, 208
front-end processes 97, 115, 142,
211–14, 241

German comics 36, 62, 65, 68, 71, 81,
82, 166
Germany 34, 36, 62, 69, 71, 139, 208
gesture 18, 26, 187, 240
grammar 4, 5, 11, 14, 15, 24, 25, 27,
50, 147–67, 169, 184–9, 206,
201, 233, 238
linear 11–12, 15–18, 184, 236
narrative 12, 15–18, 147–67, 227,
206–7
grammatical interactions 184–9,
227–9
Graphic Novel Corpus (GNC) 33
graphic structure 5–8
Greenberg, Joseph 24–5, 238
grid (layout) 7–9, 75, 77–90, 92–4,
110, 170–2, 192, 194–6,
216–20, 236

gutter 7, 8, 77, 89–91, 111–13, 119,
170, 172, 219–20, 245

historical linguistics 169, 244
horizontal staggering, *see* staggering

independent (indie) US comics 35–6,
86, 91, 94, 119, 122, 139,
158, 204–8, 234
inference 11, 12, 14, 34, 76, 95, 119,
124, 136, 149, 151, 152,
202–3, 211–14, 240, 241,
244
information extraction 97–9, 116, 142,
211
Initial 148–54, 161–4, 249, 250
inset paneling 77, 79, 91, 119, 134,
140, 192, 220

Jackendoff, Ray xiii, 4, 11, 16, 43, 44,
50, 67, 148–9, 153
Japan 1, 22, 32–6, 43, 50–7, 69, 79,
83, 95, 105, 119–24, 158–9,
197, 199, 210, 234, 237
Japanese manga 1, 21, 22, 32–6, 38,
43, 50–7, 59, 62, 64, 71, 73,
79, 80, 83–94, 95, 105,
119–24, 130, 138–9, 158–9,
166, 172, 175, 178–80, 183,
196, 197, 200, 201, 203–8,
234–5, 242, 248
Japanese Visual Language (JVL) 21,
22, 25, 26, 28, 29, 35, 46–9,
52–57, 73, 204–6, 234–5,
242

k-means clustering 56, 192, 200
Kirbyan American Visual Language
(Kirbyan AVL) 22, 28, 35, 53,
191, 192, 194
Korea 34, 36, 62, 69, 71, 139, 158,
200, 234
Korean manhwa 62, 71, 158, 234

language
definition of 4
family 235–6, 244
spoken xii, 2–5, 12, 13, 15–18, 20,
24–6, 28, 29, 43–6, 50, 52–4,

57, 65, 68, 69, 71–3, 124,
165, 166, 214, 225, 233,
237, 239, 240, 244
signed xii, 2, 4, 15, 20, 25, 29, 43,
45, 54, 214, 244
layout 1, 3, 5, 7–9, 28, 33, 34, 75–94,
106, 109–13, 119, 161,
169–74, 191–6, 214, 215–22,
225, 226, 230, 234–9, 243,
244, 248
see also external compositional
structure
linear grammar 11–12, 15–18, 184,
236
linguistic
relativity 26
typology, *see* typology
universals 24–5, 27, 167, 238–9
Loschky, Les 16, 96, 97, 98, 115, 116,
210, 211, 212, 241

McCloud, Scott xiii, 14, 20, 32–3, 67,
95, 96, 99, 105, 122, 125,
130, 140, 172, 210, 214,
236
macro panels 118–42, 150, 155, 162,
164, 176, 187, 188, 192–4,
200, 202, 204, 223–5, 230,
238, 240
macro-mono panel trade-off 120–1,
224–5, 230
Magliano, Joseph 98, 116, 149
mainstream US comics 1, 22, 28, 35,
36, 86, 91, 94, 119, 122, 123,
139, 158, 170, 172, 180,
182–7, 193–6, 204, 206–8,
226, 227–8, 229, 230, 234,
235
manga 1, 2, 21, 22, 26, 28, 29, 32–8,
43, 47–59, 62–4, 71–3, 79,
86–8, 91–95, 105, 119,
122–6, 130, 138, 139,
158–61, 172, 175–8, 180,
183, 196, 197, 201–8, 234–5,
241, 248
see also Japanese manga; US Manga
manga demographics 22, 28, 35, 36,
52, 57, 91, 122, 123, 158,
199, 204–6, 234

josei 22, 35, 36, 52, 86, 87, 91, 122,
123, 139, 203–5, 234
seinen 22, 35, 36, 52, 86, 87, 91,
122, 123, 139, 203–5, 234
shonen 22, 28, 35, 36, 50, 52–6, 73,
86–8, 119, 122, 123, 139,
203–6, 234
shojo 22, 28, 35, 36, 50, 52–6, 73,
86–8, 122, 123, 139, 158,
201, 203–5, 234
manga, influence on US comics 29, 35,
123, 158, 172, 175–6, 178,
180, 196, 197, 199, 203, 206,
208, 234–5
meaning, *see* semantics
mental model, *see* situation model
micro panels 118–42, 150, 155, 161,
164, 176, 187, 188, 192, 196,
211, 223, 238, 240
modality 4, 5, 6–8, 15, 16, 18–20,
24–7, 34, 43, 44, 68, 69, 166,
180, 184, 226, 227, 238, 239,
245
modality-general universals 25
see also cognitive universals
modality-specific universals 24
mono panels 118–42, 150, 161, 164,
176, 187, 188, 192, 223–5,
230, 238, 240
morphology 9, 21, 24, 28, 32, 34,
43–73, 115, 139, 164–6,
189–91, 204, 206, 208, 210,
234, 239, 240, 243, 244, 248
morphological cues 13, 65–72, 136,
147–9
motion
cues 13, 65–72
events 13, 26, 28, 59, 65–73, 239
lines 1, 10, 13, 26, 28, 45–8, 51, 53,
58, 59, 65–71, 126, 248
Multimodal Annotation Software Tool
(MAST) 38, 243
Multimodality 5, 14–20, 24–8, 31, 32,
34, 62, 169, 180–91, 193–6,
222, 226–30, 236, 250

N-path (layout) 8, 78, 79, 87
narrative
categories 44, 147–55, 162–4, 249

complexity 150, 155–67, 179–80, 187–9, 192–4, 196–7, 200–10, 224–5, 230, 238–40, 249
grammar 12, 16, 147–67, 184, 227
schema 147–55, 157, 161–2, 164
structure 5, 11–13, 15, 16, 145–67, 174–5, 178, 179, 180, 184, 185, 189, 192–7, 205, 212, 225–7, 230, 234, 239, 243
navigational structure 76–80, 171
see also assemblage structure
Netherlands 34, 36, 38, 52, 57, 62, 81, 138, 169, 208, 242
newspaper comics 197, 216–20, 235–6
no gutter 8, 77, 89–91, 111, 220
non-sentient carriers 63–5, 191
normal gutter 77, 89–91, 112, 220

ordered linear grammar 12
Original English Language (OEL) manga, *see* US manga
overlap (layout) 78–81, 89–91

page layout, *see* layout
panel
    direction 81, 86–92, 125, 170–3, 192, 195, 218–20
    framing, *see also* attentional framing structure 10–12, 28, 34, 115–43, 155, 160–6, 169, 174–8, 188, 192–7, 200–11, 222–6, 230, 234, 238–40, 243
    shape 32, 78, 83–4, 90, 91, 94, 116, 172, 218–19, 248
    transitions, *see also* semantic coherence 14, 32–3, 95–6, 99, 101, 105, 122, 130
panels
    per page 38–9, 81–3, 94, 106, 124, 169–71, 174, 176, 197
    per row 87–8, 173–4
paneling structure 117–20, 133–5
parallel architecture 4, 5, 16–20, 24–7
parallel-cutting, *see* Alternation
Peak 148–54, 161–4, 249
permeability, *see* conceptual permeability
polymorphic morphology 68

Principle of Equivalence 19–20, 25, 27
private carriers 63–5, 189–91
Prolongation 249
proximity of panels 7, 75, 77, 89–91, 220
    see also gutter
public carriers 63–5, 189–91
pure grid 8, 77, 79, 83, 84, 89, 90, 93–4, 170–1, 194–6, 219–21

recursion 150
Refiners 151, 153–7, 160–2
Refiner Displacement 154–7, 161–4
Release 12, 148–62, 249, 250
row-based layout 84–94, 170, 194, 196, 220

S-path (layout) 77, 79–80
sand narratives, *see* Australian sand narratives
satellite carriers 63–5, 189–91
satellite-framed language 68–72, 190, 191, 239
semantic
    features 63
    coherence, *see* situational coherence
    memory 4, 98
    processing 98–9
    weight 15, 180–9, 192–6, 226–9, 250
separation (layout) 77, 81, 89, 91, 112
shot scale 120, 131–3, 135, 138, 177–8, 193–5, 200–9
sign language xii, 2, 4, 15, 20, 25, 29, 43, 45, 54, 214, 244
situation model 97–9, 211–12
situational
    coherence 95–113, 127–30, 134–5, 169, 174–6, 195, 197, 200–5, 222–3, 226, 234, 238, 239, 243
    discontinuity 101, 105–8, 110, 113, 130, 192–4, 201–2, 206–9, 222, 223, 238
spatial location change across panels 13–14, 28, 95–113, 127–30, 145–7, 174–5, 192, 197, 200, 202, 205, 207, 209, 222–3, 238, 249
    see also situational coherence

INDEX

speech balloons 10, 14, 28, 45, 46, 51, 60–5, 118, 184, 189, 236
staggering (layout) 8, 77, 79, 84–6, 89–94, 170–1, 192, 194, 219, 220
storyboards 139
style 2, 3, 20–3, 33, 43, 48, 52–6, 127, 131, 143, 172, 192, 203, 206, 207, 231, 234–7, 243
Sunday strips (*Calvin and Hobbes*) 36, 216–29, 250
superhero comics 2, 21, 22, 32, 34, 35, 43, 53, 161, 169, 250
Sweden 34, 36, 83, 86, 91, 92, 138, 208
Swedish comics 34, 36, 83–7, 90–2, 138–9, 208
symmetry, grammatical 15, 184–9, 192–193, 226–8
symmetrical complex (grammatical symmetry) 184–9, 192–3, 226–9, 250

Talmy, Len 67, 68, 239
thought bubbles 10, 28, 45, 51, 60, 62, 63, 65, 78, 189
time change across panels 13–14, 28, 95–113, 127–31, 134, 142, 145–7, 174–5, 192, 194, 197, 200–9, 222–3, 238, 249
see also situational coherence
TINTIN Project 38, 243, 247
top-down knowledge 29, 40, 76, 149, 199, 200
tradeoff 24, 25, 94, 108–9, 113, 120, 127, 156, 164–7, 201–2, 224–5, 230, 239–40
 frequency and length 25, 94, 108–9, 113, 239–40
 morphology and grammar 24, 164–7, 201–2, 224–5, 230, 239–40
typology xiii, 24, 29, 68, 69, 72, 94, 233–45
typological universals 24, 238

United States of America 1, 2, 21, 27, 28, 29, 32, 33, 35, 43, 61, 62, 64, 69, 79, 81–95, 102–6,

109, 112, 119–23, 133, 134, 139, 142, 158–9, 165, 167, 169–71, 180, 183, 187, 189–91, 194–6, 199–210, 214, 215, 223, 230, 233–6, 242, 247, 250
unimodal (grammatical symmetry) 17–18, 184–5, 188–9, 192, 194, 227, 229, 250
universality 19, 24, 94, 242
universals 24–5, 27, 92, 108, 109, 113, 120, 127, 165–7, 174, 225, 230, 233, 238–9, 241, 244
unordered linear grammar 12
updating processes 98–101, 155, 211–13
upfix 46, 47, 51, 54, 55, 59, 62
US comics, *see* American comics
US manga 35, 36, 62, 122, 123, 139, 158, 204, 206, 207, 234, 235

Varieties 22–3, 27–8, 52–9, 73, 196, 203, 204–6, 210, 233–4, 236–7, 244
verb-framed language 68–72, 239
verbal semantic weight 15, 180–3, 187–8, 192–5, 226–9, 250
vertical staggering, *see* staggering
visual features 63, 75
visual
 language
  definition of 2–27, 233–8
  cross-linguistic variation of, 20–3, 50–9, 199–210, 233–8
 lexicon 25, 32, 43, 44, 51, 54, 55, 59, 148, 233–4, 243
 list, *see* unordered linear grammar
 search 98, 115–16, 142, 211
 semantic weight 15, 180–4, 186–8, 192–5, 226–9, 250
 style 2, 20, 21–3, 43, 48, 52–4, 206, 231, 236–7, 243
Visual Language Research Corpus (VLRC) xiii, xiv, 27, 28, 31, 34–41, 169, 237, 242–3
Visual Language Theory (VLT) xiv, 2–4, 8, 15, 20, 22, 25, 27, 31, 34, 37, 44, 63, 76, 119, 214, 233, 237, 243, 247, 248

Visual Narrative Grammar (VNG) 147–67, 184, 227, 249

whole row (layout) 86–90, 94, 170, 171, 174, 192, 196

Wildfeuer, Janina xiv, 32, 33, 75, 96, 99, 109, 214, 236, 241

written language 3, 14, 16, 17, 18, 21, 31, 180, 189, 194

Z-path (layout) 8, 77–81, 84–93, 170, 172, 218–19

Zipf's law 25, 92, 109, 127, 173–4, 239